ENTANGLED ENGLISHES

Entangled Englishes offers an innovative approach to understanding the ongoing globalization of English by examining it in relation to its multiple, complex, and oftentimes unexpected entanglements.

The book explores entangled narratives of English that are imprinted and in circulation in various global contexts. The chapters examine the globalization of English as a phenomenon that is invariably entangled with and through various languages; cultural forms such as ideological commitments and social norms; or even (im)material objects such as food, signage, and attire. Offering a unique range of perspectives from leading scholars worldwide, this innovative volume presents exciting new research directions for anyone interested in the historical and contemporary complexities of language.

This text is key reading for students and researchers of World Englishes, sociolinguistics, multilingualism, and linguistic anthropology.

Jerry Won Lee is a professor of applied linguistics at the University of California, Irvine. His books include *Language as Hope*, co-authored with Daniel N. Silva (2024) and *Locating Translingualism* (2022), winner of the 2024 American Association for Applied Linguistics Book Award.

Sofia Rüdiger is postdoctoral researcher in English linguistics at the University of Bayreuth. She is author of *Morpho-Syntactic Patterns in Spoken Korean English* (2019) and editor of *Discourse Markers and World Englishes* (2021) and *Global and Local Perspectives on Language Contact* (2024).

ENTANGLED ENGLISHES

Edited by Jerry Won Lee and Sofia Rüdiger

LONDON AND NEW YORK

Designed cover image: Getty Images | diane555

First published 2025
by Routledge
4 Park Square, Milton Park, Abingdon, Oxon OX14 4RN

and by Routledge
605 Third Avenue, New York, NY 10158

Routledge is an imprint of the Taylor & Francis Group, an informa business

© 2025 selection and editorial matter, Jerry Won Lee and Sofia Rüdiger; individual chapters, the contributors

The right of Jerry Won Lee and Sofia Rüdiger to be identified as the authors of the editorial material, and of the authors for their individual chapters, has been asserted in accordance with sections 77 and 78 of the Copyright, Designs and Patents Act 1988.

All rights reserved. No part of this book may be reprinted or reproduced or utilised in any form or by any electronic, mechanical, or other means, now known or hereafter invented, including photocopying and recording, or in any information storage or retrieval system, without permission in writing from the publishers.

Trademark notice: Product or corporate names may be trademarks or registered trademarks, and are used only for identification and explanation without intent to infringe.

British Library Cataloguing-in-Publication Data
A catalogue record for this book is available from the British Library

ISBN: 978-1-032-57857-6 (hbk)
ISBN: 978-1-032-57853-8 (pbk)
ISBN: 978-1-003-44130-4 (ebk)

DOI: 10.4324/9781003441304

Typeset in Times New Roman
by Apex CoVantage, LLC

CONTENTS

Contributors	*viii*
Foreword	*xii*
Alastair Pennycook	
Introduction: entangled Englishes	1
Jerry Won Lee and Sofia Rüdiger	

PART I
Entanglements of sociopolitics · 15

1 Citizen sociolinguists on the entanglements between Pidgin
  and English in social media spaces · 17
  Christina Higgins and Kristen Urada

2 Rap in the local–global interface: social and political
  activism in South Asia · 32
  Shaila Sultana and Bal Krishna Sharma

3 Word-sound-power: entanglements of Global Patwa in India · 52
  Jaspal Naveel Singh

4 Entanglements within COVID-19 linguistic landscapes in
  Kyoto, Japan · 70
  Yumi Matsumoto and Ivan Jin

vi Contents

PART II
Entanglements of race

87

5 An entangled unease: intrusive Englishes and allyship in
Black feminism
Daniel N. Silva

89

6 "No English, no English": raciolinguistic
entanglements in Czechia
Stephanie Rudwick

105

7 Re-/imagining racialized entanglements of Englishes and
peoples: a call for a quantum ethos
Patriann Smith

118

PART III
Entanglements of practice

139

8 Entangled bodies, entangled ideologies: the case of Bikram
yoga practitioners
Kellie Gonçalves

141

9 Digital assemblages and their English entanglements:
digital design, voice assistant use and smartphone setting
choices of translingual speakers in Berlin
Didem Leblebici and Britta Schneider

158

10 English online/offline: disentangling material and
materialist perspectives of language
Ron Darvin

181

PART IV
Entanglements of education

199

11 Entangling English teaching with content teaching:
reflections of an English language educator in a content and
language integrated learning context
Keith S. T. Tong, Fay Chen, and Angel M. Y. Lin

201

Contents **vii**

12 Educators' reflections in Australian Aboriginal translingual
classrooms: entanglement of language, culture,
and emotionality 218
Ana Tankosić, Sender Dovchin, and Rhonda Oliver

Index *232*

CONTRIBUTORS

Fay Chen is an assistant professor in the Foreign Language Center at National Cheng Kung University, Taiwan. Her research interests include ESP, CLIL, and EMI. Her work has appeared in journals, including *English Teaching and Learning, Journal of Multilingual and Multicultural Development, English for Specific Purposes.*

Ron Darvin is an Assistant Professor in the Department of Language and Literacy Education of the University of British Columbia.. His research examines issues of identity, materiality, and inequality in online and offline spaces. He is the co-author of *Intercultural Communication and Identity* published by Cambridge University Press.

Sender Dovchin is Professor at the School of Education, Curtin University. Her research interests focus on critical applied linguistics including post-bi/multilingualism, translanguaging, linguistic diversity and discrimination from the southern perspectives. Her most recent book is *Translingual Practices: Playfulness and Precariousness*, co-edited with Rhonda Oliver and Li Wei, published by Cambridge University Press (2024).

Kellie Gonçalves is Senior Lecturer at the University of Bern, Switzerland. Her recent publications include *Language, Global Mobilities, Blue-collar Workers and Blue-collar Workplaces* (w. H. Kelly-Holmes (eds.), Routledge, 2021) and *Domestic Workers Talk* (w. A. Schluter, Multilingual Matters, 2024). Kellie is book review editor of the journal *Linguistic Landscape*.

Christina Higgins is a professor in the Department of Second Language Studies at the University of Hawai'i at Mānoa. Her research examines multilingualism from a discourse-based perspective, and she strives to engage the public through citizen sociolinguistics projects. Her most recent book is *Diversifying Family Language Policy*, co-edited with Lyn Wright (Bloomsbury, 2021).

Ivan Jin holds a M.S.Ed. degree in TESOL from the University of Pennsylvania and currently works as an ESL instructor in an international school in Shanghai. With a foundation in applied linguistics, he has contributed to research projects focused on multimodal conversation analysis, technology in language pedagogy, and linguistic landscape.

Didem Leblebici is a PhD candidate in sociolinguistics at the European University Viadrina Frankfurt (Oder), Germany. Her research focuses on the sociolinguistic implications of AI language technologies for language ideologies and multilingualism. Her paper on the role of English in voice assistant interactions was published in 2024 in *Multilingua.*

Jerry Won Lee is a professor of applied linguistics at the University of California, Irvine. His books include *Language as Hope*, co-authored with Daniel N. Silva (Cambridge University Press, 2024) and *Locating Translingualism* (Cambridge University Press, 2022), winner of the 2024 American Association for Applied Linguistics Book Award.

Angel Lin is Chair Professor of Language, Literacy and Social Semiotics at The Education University of Hong Kong. She has published extensively on Translanguaging, Trans-semiotizing, and Content and Language Integrated Learning (CLIL).

Yumi Matsumoto is an associate professor of applied linguistics at the University of Pennsylvania. Her research interests include English as a lingua franca, multilingual classroom discourse, multimodal conversation analysis, and linguistic landscape. Her work has appeared in journals, including *TESOL Quarterly, the Modern Language Journal,* and *Language Learning.*

Rhonda Oliver is Professor at the School of Education, Curtin University. She has researched extensively and is widely published in the areas of second language and dialect acquisition, and task-based language learning. Her more recent work includes studies within Australian Aboriginal education settings. Her extensive publication record includes her award-winning textbook *Indigenous Education in Australia Learning and Teaching for Deadly Futures.*

Alastair Pennycook is Professor Emeritus of Language, Society and Education at the University of Technology Sydney. He is known for his work on implications of the global spread of English, critical applied linguistics, the philosophical

x Contributors

foundations of language, and urban multilingualism. His most recent book is *Language Assemblages* (Cambridge University Press).

Sofia Rüdiger is postdoctoral researcher in English Linguistics at the University of Bayreuth. She is author of *Morpho-Syntactic Patterns in Spoken Korean English* (Benjamins, 2019) and editor of *Discourse Markers and World Englishes* (World Englishes special issue, 2021) and *Global and Local Perspectives on Language Contact* (Language Science Press, 2024).

Stephanie Rudwick is Associate Professor in African Studies at the University of Hradec Králové, Czech Republic. As a linguistic anthropologist, she combines ethnographic and sociolinguistic techniques in her studies and she recently published the monograph *The Ambiguity of English as a Lingua Franca: Politics of Language and Race in South Africa* (Routledge).

Britta Schneider is professor of language use and migration at European University Viadrina, Germany. She studies language ideologies, with a specific interest in the discursive and material construction of languages in transnational, multilingual settings and in digital culture. She is author of *Salsa, Language and Transnationalism* (2014, Multilingual Matters) and of *Liquid Languages: Constructing Language in Late Modern Cultures of Diffusion* (to appear, Cambridge University Press).

Bal Krishna Sharma is Associate Professor of Applied Linguistics at the University of Idaho, USA. His research interests include sociolinguistics, intercultural communication, and linguistic ethnography. His co-edited book with Shuang Gao *Language and Intercultural Communication in Tourism: Critical Perspectives* was published by Routledge in 2021.

Daniel N. Silva is a professor of applied linguistics at the Universidade Estadual de Campinas, Brazil. His books include *Language as Hope*, co-authored with Jerry Won Lee (Cambridge University Press, 2024) and *Pragmática da violência: O Nordeste na mídia brasileira* (7 Letras, 2012).

Jaspal Naveel Singh is a lecturer in applied linguistics and English language at the Open University in the United Kingdom. He is the author of the monograph *Transcultural Voices: Narrating Hip Hop in Complex Delhi* (Multilingual Matters, 2022) and he has co-edited several volumes, including *Global Hiphopography* (Palgrave Macmillan, 2023) with Quentin Williams.

Patriann Smith is a professor of literacy at the University of South Florida. She is the author of *Literacies of Migration: Translanguaging Imaginaries of Innocence* (Cambridge University Press, 2024) and *Black Immigrant Literacies:*

Intersections of Race, Language, and Culture in the Classroom (Teachers College Press, 2023).

Shaila Sultana is the Director and a professor of the BRAC Institute of Languages, BRAC University and a professor of the Institute of Modern Languages, University of Dhaka, Bangladesh. Her recent publications include co-edited books *Language in Society in Bangladesh and Beyond* (Routledge, 2024) and *Language and Sustainable Development in Bangladesh* (Routledge, 2024).

Ana Tankosić is a research fellow and sessional academic at Curtin University. Her research focuses on sociolinguistics of globalisation, transcultural identities, and migration discourses. She is a former Fulbright Visiting Student Researcher at Penn State University. Her volume, *Becoming a Linguist,* co-edited with Eldin Milak has recently been published with Routledge, while her collaborative monograph, *Linguistic Racism,* is currently in preparation.

Keith Tong is Visiting Chair Professor at National Pingtung University, Taiwan. He is interested in multilingualism, CLIL and translanguaging. He was Director of the Center for Language Education at the Hong Kong University of Science & Technology before retiring in 2020.

Kristen Urada is a PhD candidate in Second Language Studies at the University of Hawai'i at Mānoa. Her co-authored chapter with Lin Chen, Kathleen Griffin, Michaela Nuesser, and Christina Higgins on intercultural semiotics of commodified culture in tourism appeared in Bal Krishna Sharma and Shuang Gao's co-edited book (Routledge, 2021).

FOREWORD

Alastair Pennycook

To talk of entanglements is to suggest that linguistic complexities are to be found not so much in analysis of the inside of language – its structure, tenses, vocabulary and so on – but in its relations to the world around. This is to turn the tables on a linguistics that assumes the a priori existence of languages that can then be linked, after the fact, to a world beyond. This is to push back against the "extractionist-restrictivist-exclusionist program" of orthodox linguistics (Agha, 2007, p. 224) whereby the object of linguistics is extracted from language more broadly and restricted to that focus (a study of small elements of the wider phenomenon of language) to the exclusion of other possibilities. It avoids both the *extractivist* tendencies of linguistics to plunder languages of the Global South in the service of Northern theories of language and the *extractionist* propensities to take small aspects of language – grammar, for example – as somehow representative of a larger whole. An entanglement orientation starts instead with a world of people, things, places and events, and looks at the ways languages are assembled from a range of worldly resources. Complexity is to be found not in the analysis of the internal workings of reified languages but in the relations between language assemblages and the world around.

A focus on complexity has become a key aspect of new approaches to sociolinguistics. It was central to the work of the late Jan Blommaert, who insisted on the need to understand ethnographically how language works: sociolinguistics needs ethnography (rather than system, synchrony and variation, we need to see how linguistic resources are mobilised); discourse analysis needs ethnography (we cannot understand texts without investigating their use and users); literacy needs ethnography (literacy is a social and cultural practice that needs to be studied in the world); linguistic landscapes need ethnography (to have anything useful to say about signs in place we have to understand their location, history, authors and readers). This was not so much a methodological argument in favour of ethnography as it was an epistemological insistence that it was the relations among language, people and the world that mattered. The study of language in society, Blommaert (2017) noted, has to move away from "linear models towards complex models" (p. 47). This move to capture "adequate contextualization" entails a focus beyond linguistic signs in a narrower sense towards "semiotic, complex objects," a wider understanding of the total semiotic fact (p. 47). From this perspective, we have to account for the multiplicity of factors that come together around people and place: "These dense and complex objects are the 'stuff' of the study of language in society" (Blommaert, 2017, p. 59).

While it is evident that we can never arrive at a full account of the total linguistic or semiotic fact – once we search ethnographically for 'adequate contextualization,' there will always be things beyond our grasp – it is nonetheless useful to consider how we can move in the direction of a totality (Pennycook, 2023). To talk of entanglements, however, is also to push this search for adequate accounts of context or the total semiotic fact in new directions. A *new materialist* orientation recalibrates the relations between humans and the non-human world, questioning the boundaries between animate and inanimate (with implications for how we understand agency, for example), natural and cultural (undermining a distinction that has constrained thinking for several centuries) and humans and the material world (repositioning humans as part of their surrounds). These challenges to Euro-modernist thought question what is seen as inside and outside; where cognition or language resides; and what role a supposedly exterior world may play in thought, action and communication. The point is not to discount humans in the search for a more object-oriented ontology but to reconfigure where humans sit as *entangled* and *implicated* in other things. From this perspective, things, objects, artefacts are not separate from humans or each other but part of integrated wholes. Such *assemblages* address the ways that different things, people, objects and discourses come together in particular and often momentary constellations, as events that are greater than the sum of their parts (Tsing, 2015).

Assemblages and entanglements are closely connected, both seeking to show the relationality of the world. They differ, however, in terms of what they seek to describe. Assemblages focus on the often momentary coming-together of a diversity of elements. Languages can usefully be understood as assemblages, as the construction of seemingly stable entities from linguistic, semiotic or material resources (Pennycook, 2024). Understanding languages as assemblages overcomes the problem of viewing languages as autonomous, bounded systems in favour of an understanding of languages as "an ongoing project, with different bits added and others removed at different times" (Wee, 2021, p. 22). Entanglements, by contrast, point to the many connections between an assemblage and its material and discursive relations. Neither term has been constrained by attempts towards over-definition, though assemblage has a clearer intellectual lineage that is commonly traced to Deleuze and Guattari's (1987) notion of *agencement*. Such linear connections, however, may be at odds with an assemblage-oriented understanding of relationality. The idea of entanglements has less clear origins and remains a term with looser applications. Although used generally as a term to describe, for example, the complexity of personal relationships, the more specific use of entanglements comes from quantum mechanics and the philosophy of science.

A quantum entanglement (*Verschränkung* in Schrödinger's terms) is one of the defining differences between classical and quantum physics, describing the phenomenon whereby the quantum state of particles in a group cannot be described separately from each other. The idea gained wider recognition through Barad's (2007) interest in the entanglement of matter and meaning, an argument that things do not exist as individual elements but only in relation to their *mutual entanglements*. Looking at factory work from this perspective, "machines and humans differentially emerge and are iteratively reworked through specific entanglements of agencies that trouble the notion that there are determinate distinctions between humans and nonhumans" (Barad, 2007, p. 239). Workers, machines and managers are "entangled phenomena, relational beings," and to assume that only humans have agency in such settings is to miss the interconnected role of machines and thereby to overlook "possibilities for reworking unhealthy and unjust labor conditions" (ibid.). Entanglements, therefore, point to the ways things only exist in relation to each other and are inter-connected with a diversity of other matters.

To think in terms of entanglements can help us get beyond the *methodological nationalism* (Schneider, 2018) that has hindered World Englishes since its inception. Despite its laudable attempt to give greater status to English varieties outside the 'Inner Circle' and the related move to provincialize native speakers, World Englishes has tended to reproduce the linguistic frameworks it needs to supersede. While the World Englishes project has done a great deal to decentre English – insisting that English is the property of all, that ownership of English no longer rests in the hands of its so-called native speakers, that English is always locally inflected, no longer encumbered by conventional decrees – at the same time it "consistently classifies language use on grounds of the national context in which they appear" (Schneider, 2018, p. 8). This reinscribes Englishes along national lines (Singapore, Indian, Philippine English and so on), thus avoiding the very sociolinguistic challenges the global spread of English brings to the fore. Diverse uses of English around the world are better understood in terms of entanglements of English that can help us to move beyond the naming of new national varieties and to seek instead an understanding of how linguistic resources are connected to the world.

To talk of entanglements is also to move away from a constrictive insistence on language-as-object in relation to a single social process: Rather than assuming the existence of something called 'English' and seeking to map this against a social determinant such as imperialism or development, an entanglements perspective seeks a more varied account both of language and its connections. To talk of (English) linguistic imperialism, English as a pathway to development, English as a means to escape poverty and so on is to assume both the unproblematic ontological status of something called English (supposing in each case that 'English' refers to the same thing) and its easy correlation with a social, political or economic process. An entanglement perspective, by contrast, insists on the connections between language and worldly effects but does not do so by assuming such named languages can be mapped against social outcomes. When Tupas (2019) shows how "English has been entangled in the (re)making and preservation of the Philippine elites" (p. 531), the focus is on the ways English language use is embedded in colonial class structures across the country. A language entanglements focus draws attention to social language practices, the everyday making and unmaking of languages amid wider social forces.

Thinking in terms of entanglements is not a solution to language-political questions nor a program for political activism. It can help us see how humans and their supposed languages are not just connected to but part of the world. It can show how language is embedded, embodied and distributed in the world. The emphasis on complexity and relationality can nevertheless leave us with such a wide range of potential connections that the grounds for political activism are unclear (Giraud, 2019). We need to be cautious in our rush to flattened ontologies and interrelated politics lest we undermine the possibilities for political action. In my exploratory paper on entanglements of English (Pennycook, 2020), I sought to connect a sign for an English language school in Cebu (Philippines) to a range of social and political concerns. The original plan had been to sketch out connections between the sign and the wider world and then to move on to other topics, but as I wrote, more and more connections became apparent. Thinking in terms of entanglements can take us towards an ever more complex range of connections that may help or hinder a search for social change. I greatly welcome the attempt in this book to develop this project further and to put more flesh on the bones of the idea by working through the implications of entanglements and English in a variety of contexts. The editors and authors have done a great job in opening up these ideas to critical analysis and further development.

References

Agha, A. (2007). The object called "language" and the subject of linguistics. *Journal of English Linguistics, 35*(3), 217–235.

Barad, K. (2007). *Meeting the universe halfway: Quantum physics and the entanglement of matter and meaning*. Duke University Press.

Blommaert, J. (2017). Chronotopes, scales and complexity in the study of language in society. In K. Arnaut, M. S. Karrebaek, M. Spotti & J. Blommaert (Eds.), *Engaging superdiversity: Recombining spaces, times and language practices* (pp. 47–62). Multilingual Matters.

Deleuze, G., & Guattari, F. (1987). *A thousand plateaus: Capitalism and schizophrenia* (B. Massumi, Trans.). University of Minnesota Press.

Giraud, E. H. (2019). *What comes after entanglement? Activism, anthropocentrism, and an ethics of exclusion*. Duke University Press.

Pennycook, A. (2020). Translingual entanglements of English. *World Englishes, 39*(2), 222–235.

Pennycook, A. (2023). Toward the total semiotic fact. *Chinese Semiotic Studies, 19*(4), 595–613.

Pennycook, A. (2024). *Language assemblages*. Cambridge University Press.

Schneider, B. (2018). Methodological nationalism in linguistics. *Language Sciences*, *76*, 1–13.

Tsing, A. L. (2015). *The mushroom at the end of the world: On the possibility of life in capitalist ruins*. Princeton University Press.

Tupas, R. (2019). Entanglements of colonialism, social class, and *Unequal Englishes*. *Journal of Sociolinguistics*, *23*, 529–542.

Wee, L. (2021). *Posthumanist World Englishes*. Cambridge University Press.

INTRODUCTION

Entangled Englishes

Jerry Won Lee and Sofia Rüdiger

1. Octopus: monster of the sea?

The cover of O'Regan's 2021 book, *Global English and Political Economy*, features a terrifying image of a giant octopus-like creature attacking a large vessel out at sea, possibly in the midst of a storm. The image is titled *The Kraken, as Seen by the Eye of the Imagination*, an engraving that appeared in John Gibson's 1887 publication, *Monsters of the Sea: Legendary and Authentic*. It is not only visually striking but an especially apt depiction of the themes and perhaps even aspirations of O'Regan's book. O'Regan traces the global spread of English not to British colonialism alone (cf., Kachru, 1990; Phillipson, 1992; Saraceni, 2015) but more specifically to the emergence of a capitalist world-system. O'Regan historicizes the role played by British capital in its 'informal empire,' beyond those understood within conventional histories that trace the 'start' and 'end' of the British Empire to watershed moments, such as victory in the Battle of Plassey of 1757 – which facilitated the expansion of the East India Company (EIC) and thus British colonial influence – and the handover of Hong Kong to China in 1997.

It is perhaps no secret that the global proliferation of English is not the result of an automatic or even neutral process. The British Empire imposed English upon her territories in Asia, Africa, and the Middle East, oftentimes through force, with the stated goal of 'civilizing' its subjects, documented in countless places, including perhaps most notoriously in Thomas Babington Macaulay's 1835 *Minute on Indian Education*. When the US surfaced as the world's superpower following the conclusion of World War II, American cultural imperialism emerged as the next force that would ensure the globalization of English. Beyond the US's global militarization and 'diplomacy' efforts, phenomena such as media, including American popular music, facilitated the expansion of English. To this day, British and

DOI: 10.4324/9781003441304-1

2 Entangled Englishes

American varieties are considered the most 'prestigious' in many contexts, if not at the very least normative, unmarked, or 'neutral.'

O'Regan argues that the English language was not merely the beneficiary of colonial expansion, an account that perhaps few would deny. Instead, O'Regan (2021) posits that:

> the global spread of English and its ongoing dominance as a normative form needs to be understood in relation to the global spread of capital and capitalism, in which capital may be conceived in general terms as referring to the accumulation of trade relations and of commercial investments, including in the later twentieth century investments in financialized products.
>
> *(p. 5)*

From this perspective, English is presented as a "free rider" upon capital, a relationship O'Regan (2021) presents as a form of "parasitism": "English has given succour to the expansion and accumulation of capital, and capital has given succour to the expansion and accumulation of English" (p. 7). Not dissimilar to how a parasite might attach itself to a host, sometimes to the host's immediate destruction, the 'legendary' kraken in the engraving is attached to the vessel, also pursuing its immediate destruction. There are obviously no historically veritable accounts of a 'kraken' in real life, but that did not stop Walt Disney Pictures from co-producing, alongside Jerry Bruckheimer Films, a high-budget box office film franchise, *The Pirates of the Caribbean*, which would interweave the historically accurate EIC alongside the mythical kraken. In the films, the EIC are presented as the antagonists, though only in part because they represent the Empire – a construct that, following the combined efforts of postcolonial theory but arguably more like *Star Wars*, is bound to be vilified rather than valorized. They are also presented as antagonists by their very efforts to stifle the pirates, whom the films romanticize for their anti-establishmentarian ideals and efforts.

Coincidentally, as noted, the EIC is featured in O'Regan's account of not only the British empire formally speaking but the economy of British *informal* empire. The EIC, established in 1600, was a joint-stock trading company established to serve the political economic interests of the British Empire. With its goal being the extraction of varied resources from the East Indies and later other parts of Asia, it relied on the ruthless exploitation of the local natural and human (labor) resources in the region. By the early 1800s the EIC had established itself as the world's largest corporation. As the EIC grew in reach and influence, so did the British Empire. For at least a few centuries it was impossible to envision something that might rival this empire, except in 'the eye of the imagination,' where something like a kraken might dwell.

2. From World Englishes to entangled Englishes

A document familiar to many historians of the English language was published around this time: Macaulay's aforementioned *Minute*. The 1835 Minute reflected – in no subtle terms – the British Empire's sentiments toward its colonial subjects in India. According to the Minute, the goal of implementing an English language policy in education and society was to create "a class of interpreters between us and the millions whom we govern; a class of persons Indians in blood and colour, but English in taste, in opinion, in morals and in intellect" (Macaulay, 1835, p. 9). Nearly 200 years later, it is not difficult to see the denigrating assumptions guiding Macaulay's rhetoric: Indian taste, opinion, morals, and intellect were inferior, but learning English just might improve their taste, opinion, morals, and intellect to be on a par with those of the British. Rather than dwelling on a point that is hopefully self-evident, we would rather turn to an interesting detail that emerges from O'Regan's account: given that the primary motivation for the British Empire was economic, support for public service infrastructure was not considered an immediate priority. As O'Regan (2021) puts it, "the EIC persisted in giving preference to economic rapine over measures for national development" (p. 76). So while Macaulay's Minute has persisted as historical document exemplifying the harsh colonial imposition of English in the region (e.g., Bhabha, 1984), the materialist approach points instead not to the Minute itself but to underlying economic imperatives precipitating the conditions of its production alongside those that enabled it to be accepted as a logically sound and wholly unproblematic document in its time. In other words, what makes this account compelling is the way in which it looks not only to linguistic and language ideological issues related to the global spread of English but also its seemingly 'non-linguistic' – in O'Regan's case political and economic – *entanglements*.

Before discussing our understanding of entanglement for the purposes of this volume, we should describe our conceptualization of this volume around the theme of entangled *Englishes*. Our pluralized use of Englishes rather than 'English' reflects a recognition of the diversity of forms and functions of English worldwide. The idea of Englishes is oftentimes attributed to the pioneering work of Braj B. Kachru. He presented in the 1970s what was then a radical notion: Indians did not simply speak a substandard form of 'nonnative' English but instead a locally evolved and evolving variety of *Indian* English. Kachru (1976) proposed the following: "The strength of the English language is in presenting the Americanness in its American variety, and the Englishness in its British variety. Let us, therefore, appreciate and encourage the Third World varieties of English too" (p. 236).

Kachru would go on to develop a model for mapping and conceptualizing the worldwide spread of English in a series of publications (e.g., 1985, 1990, 2005). Known by some as the Kachruvian model or the Kachruvian circles, the model consists of three concentric circles reflective of the sociohistorical prevalence of English within a given nation:

Inner Circle: nations where English is used as a 'native' language and is an official if not *de facto* national language. Inner Circle nations include the UK, US, Australia, New Zealand, Canada, and South Africa.

Outer Circle: nations where English is used as a 'second' language. Representing mostly regions formerly colonized by Inner Circle nations, English is oftentimes an official language in Outer Circle nations, usually alongside other languages. Examples of Outer Circle nations include India, Nigeria, and the Philippines.

Expanding Circle: nations where English is used as a 'foreign' language. English typically does not have an official status and is not commonly used in intranational communicative contexts. Expanding Circle nations include Germany, South Korea, and Russia.

This framework has inspired countless researchers to systematically study discrete features of Englishes in numerous national contexts (e.g., unique lexical, pragmatic, and discursive features through corpus-based research), most prominently in journals such as *World Englishes* and *English Today*, among other venues.

In spite of the undeniable influence of the Kachruvian model, one can see why it might be subject to criticism by some. At the most obvious level, 'Inner Circle' might imply that such Englishes are privileged, exclusive, or otherwise exclusionary. 'Expanding' might also be seen as an endorsement of or complicity in the continued expansion of English in the interests of what Phillipson (1992) identifies as 'linguistic imperialism.' A range of other criticisms have been presented. The most influential include Parakrama's (1995) argument that depictions of World Englishes are based predominantly on "upper-class forms" of language use (p. 26). Canagarajah (1999) similarly notes that "legitimized periphery Englishes are themselves ideological constructs in valorizing the educated versions of local English" (p. 180). Saraceni (2010) warns that World Englishes is an "academic construct" that reifies the dominance of the political paradigm of the nation-state (p. 73), leading to what Schneider (2019) has called methodological nationalism. Bruthiaux's (2003) critique is among the most explicit: "the Three Circles model is a 20th century construct that has outlived its usefulness" (p. 161). Some scholars have even called for an abandonment of the construct 'World Englishes' altogether to dissociate from the concentric circle paradigm, preferring instead the expression 'Global Englishes' (e.g., Canagarajah, 2013; Jenkins, 2015; Pennycook, 2007).

What we are proposing in this volume is not an abandonment of World Englishes as such. We cannot dismiss the fact that World Englishes has been essential to shifting our collective view of English beyond a monolingual and monolithic norm in which only a small minority of the world's population partakes. Further, World Englishes is not merely about the diverse forms English takes and is taking worldwide but also the diverse functions through different Englishes. In other words, it is very much interested in the diversity of Englishes worldwide as reflective of everyday social realities. It goes without saying that the uncritical and dogmatic embrace of any epistemological paradigm – up to and including World Englishes – can turn out to be problematic. Certainly there are inherent conceptual limitations to the concentric circles, as noted, but they are not worth abandoning in their entirety just yet (indeed, some of the contributors to this volume invoke the concept in productive ways). Simultaneously, we do propose not so much an alternative to but a strategic expansion of the study of World Englishes, one that understands the globalization of English in relation to its multiple, complex, and oftentimes unexpected entanglements.

What would the study of World Englishes look like if it centered entanglement? In other words, what might World Englishes look like if we relied on entanglement as the *starting point* of inquiry rather than a mere contextual consideration? An increasingly large number of scholars in numerous fields – applied linguistics but of course also beyond – have made productive applications of entanglement as it is understood in the context of quantum mechanics. Entanglement, as originally described by physicist Erwin Schrödinger (1887–1961), refers to the phenomenon when two particles remain interdependent on one another even when separated by large distances, even when light years apart. Albert Einstein (1879–1955), meanwhile, derided entanglement in a letter to fellow physicist and longtime friend Max Born (1882–1970) as "*spukhafte Fernwirkung*," oftentimes translated as 'spooky action at a distance.' For Einstein, whose name remains today very much globally synonymous with – entangled with, we might say – intellectual aptitude (being a 'genius'), was apprehensive of that which could not be seen and, at least at the time, not empirically verified.

The popularization of entanglement within the broader domains of social scientific and humanistic inquiry is oftentimes attributed to the pioneering work of Karen Barad. Barad's academic trajectory is most unique and unusual: after earning a PhD in physics (Barad, 1984) and spending years researching and teaching in the same field, she transitioned to more humanistically oriented interdisciplinary research in feminist studies and philosophy. Barad's 2007 book, *Meeting the Universe Halfway: Quantum Physics and the Entanglement of Matter and Meaning*, leveraged entanglement theory to argue for a redistribution of political, epistemological, and ontological capital within and beyond varied categories otherwise treated as definitive, including the human and non-human. In this sense, Barad is simultaneously viewed as a critical progenitor of posthumanist thought. As Barad (2007) argues, posthumanism "doesn't presume the separateness of any 'thing,' let alone the alleged spatial, ontological, and epistemological distinction that sets humans apart" (p. 136). The very category of the human, in other words, should not be treated as a given but instead as an entanglement of ostensibly 'nonhuman' phenomena and objects.

Some of our sources of inspiration for prioritizing an entangled approach include Wee's (2021) work, which is among the first to draw explicit connection to posthumanist theory and World Englishes. A central premise to a posthumanist approach to World Englishes is the idea of agency as distributed: not located within humans alone but enabled by or otherwise entailments of materials, objects, or conditions outside of and beyond the human per se. If agency is distributed as such, what happens to other fundamental constructs such as the speech community or the variety of language? This question becomes challenging because we live in an era characterized by what Vertovec (2007) described as 'superdiversity,' a condition wherein social diversification exceeds the conceptual capacity and instruments of measuring diversity (e.g., census reports) in the first place. As the work of Arnaut et al. (2015) asks, what is an ethnolinguistic group in the context of such demographic shifts? Is it possible to conceptualize a homogeneous speech community using a given variety of English? To be fair, the realities of internal diversification were not missed on Kachru, even in his earlier instantiations of the World Englishes paradigm (e.g., 1985). However, Wee's treatment of Englishes – and language more broadly – as an assemblage wherein "signs (linguistic or otherwise) are both material and able to trigger other signs into self-organization" (2021, p. 17) is instructive for our purposes – without denying the sociolinguistic reality that there are indeed some varietal features that are simply unlikely to exist in one region or another. A posthumanist orientation to World Englishes cannot – at least for now – explain why a person born and raised in the US simply will not speak with a British accent unless through deliberate performances of what Rampton (1999) terms 'crossing.' Meanwhile, such assemblages are constituted by parts that are "always in the process of being assembled and reassembled" (Wee, 2021, p. 18). In other words, what kinds of global and/or local entanglements might drive one to use or try to use a given variety of English at a given moment in time and space, and how might such entanglements themselves be subject to disentanglement, unentanglement, and reentanglement?

Pennycook's (2020) essay, "Translingual Entanglements of English," relatedly argues for the value in exploring not only how English ends up in different global locations but also how it can be traced and made sense of in unexpected places (Pennycook, 2012). Such places include, for instance, a seemingly innocuous sign advertising English language lessons in the Philippines, which tells stories not only about the legacies of US colonial occupation but other entanglements that include racial hierarchies, domestic workers, Korean English frenzy, and, even more literally, tangled wires. The sign's placement near tangled wires is not insignificant, since "the state and precarity of municipal wiring is often a good indicator of economic development" (Pennycook, 2020, p. 3). However, that is just part of the story; as Pennycook (2020) argues:

> These tangled wires are more than just carriers of current, or lines indexical of economic development. Rather they are variously connected to forms of power. It is this way of looking at assemblages, and in this context the complex relations between a sign for an English school and its emplacement that is important for this paper: tangled wires are entangled wires.
>
> *(p. 4)*

Tangled wires are in fact an iconic feature of the favelas of Brazil, urban peripheralized communities built by their own residents, primarily freed slaves of African descent who were given no reparations or support to integrate into society. Featured on the cover image of Silva and Lee's (2024) *Language as Hope*, tangled wires in the favela are the result of the paralegal practice of wire tapping, representative of a demand for public services as a human right. Within such contexts, favela residents – known as *faveladas* and *favelados* – have adopted creative strategies of recalibrating linguistic and semiotic resources toward the facilitation of survival and hope. These include digital communication strategies such as *fogos virtual*, or virtual rockets, a way of signaling to other residents via social media warnings of dangerous activity (Silva & Lee, 2024), including unanticipated eruptions of violence, or the 'crossfire' (Menezes, 2015) between the State (police) and crime, including drug traffickers and *milicias* (police officers who extort residents).[1] In this multilayered and precaritized space, where "tangled wires are entangled wires" (Pennycook, 2020, p. 4) as well, English too is a communicative resource entangled with not only normative language ideologies but also the imperative and inherent right to survive (Silva, this volume).

The cover image of our present volume, an octopus, represents a different kind of tangling that also gestures to a range of entanglements surrounding World Englishes. Recall that earlier we spoke of the kraken on the cover of O'Regan's book on global English and political economy. What if Gibson's engraving, *The Kraken, as Seen by the Eye of the Imagination*, were seen not as a rendition of an unfortunate incident involving an unexpected attack on innocent human property and life? What if the kraken were simply an imaginary rendition of a real life cephalopod like the giant squid, acting as something akin to an indigenous steward, offering protection to her maritime territory against uninvited colonial imposition and extraction by the British Empire? We are reminded here of the *Vampyroteuthis infernalis*, the octopod featured in Flusser and Bec's (2012[1987]) extended treatise as having its own thought, culture, and even art. The treatise claims that the *Vampyroteuthis* can grow to exceed "twenty meters and their skull capacity exceeds our own" (Flusser & Bec, 2012[1987], p. 5). And while there is no historical record of such a large specimen, it does display significant human-like intelligence and capabilities, including language. The *Vampyroteuthis* communicates via chromatic secretions:

> It is known . . . that these displays of color give outward expression to the inner thoughts of the organism – that chromatic secretions serve to articulate its volatile immanence. These displays are coordinated to the extent that every chromatophore is singly controlled by the brain, and the individual glandular contractions can be synchronized. Their chromatic language is intraspecific. What remains unknown is whether the code has changed throughout history.
> *(Flusser & Bec, 2012[1987], p. 51)*

If *Vampyroteuthis infernalis* can be understood in this way, perhaps it could be argued that Gibson's kraken was simply acting in the calculated interest of sociolinguistic diversity, attempting to curtail the global spread of English through its free riding upon capital by destroying a vessel – literally – of the global hegemonization of English.

While we are still out at sea, let us consider another potential maritime entanglement with regard to the globalization of English. Earlier, we briefly referenced the significance of the 1757 Battle of Plassey in the expansion of the British Empire. Perhaps an arguably more significant moment was the defeat of the Spanish Armada in 1588. The fleet, known as the Invincible Armada, was the pride of Spain and symbolic of its unstoppable might, so its defeat by the British was a major blow to the Spanish collective psyche. It is widely known that the inclement weather in the English Channel was a major factor contributing to the armada's defeat, itself a kind of entanglement that is complicated further by the fact that the weather in that time of year was a historical aberration (Lamb, 1988). Of course, the defeat of the armada did not curtail Spanish colonial efforts in the Americas and other parts of the world. As a direct result of this, Spanish, as we know, is widely spoken across the Americas, including in the US. Unfortunately, today in the US, heritage speakers of Spanish face discrimination as a result of what Flores and Rosa (2015) term raciolinguistic ideologies. Meanwhile, it is easy to forget that Spanish was previously the dominant colonial language in the region, enregistered as racialized in the early years of the establishment of the state of California in 1850, closely following Mexico's defeat in the 1848 Mexican-American War (Fitzsimmons, 2021).

One cannot help but imagine what the status of Spanish would be today if history had played out differently. For instance, what if the US had lost that decisive war to Mexico? This is not insignificant because California today represents a GDP of nearly $4 trillion annually, which would rank it among the top five *nations* in the world by the same metric (alongside the US, China, Germany, Japan, and India). It therefore raises the question of how afterwards, having not been successful in obtaining California, the US would have turned out to be a much different political economic entity without the capital accumulation afforded by acquiring California. This in turn raises the question of whether the US have been positioned optimally as the obvious successor as global hegemon to the British Empire following WWII. In summary, would the US losing the 1845 Mexican-American war have facilitated a halt to the free riding upon capital for English by the mid-1900s? Or going back even further to 1588, what if the weather had been more cooperative and the armada emerged victorious as it was expected to? Perhaps we would not be focusing so much on World Englishes but instead World Spanishes. Perhaps this volume would be focused on Entangled Spanishes, or *Españoles entrelazados*.

To be clear, adopting an entangled approach to the study of World Englishes is not merely a theoretical thought experiment. Indeed, our approach to entangled Englishes also draws inspiration from the work of Tupas (2015, 2019, 2024) on *unequal* Englishes. For Tupas, study of the worldwide variations in form and function in Englishes can oftentimes inadvertently disregard the on-the-ground realities of inequality for users of different Englishes. Using the case of English in relation to postcolonial Philippine society, Tupas (2019) foregrounds the entanglements among class, language, and colonialism toward the reification and reinforcement of continued inequalities facing different Englishes and users of Englishes. As Tupas (2019) notes, "Unequal Englishes does not merely become a descriptive term to refer to any form of inequality within which varieties of English(es) are stratified but, more crucially, it is a critical term which highlights the coloniality of inequalities of Englishes" (p. 531). Meanwhile, through an entangled approach to the study of English in the Philippines, we are able to take stock of the privileging of class and the valorization of colonial logics in the sociolinguistic research tradition of Philippine English spanning nearly 50 years.

We hope that by now it is clear that in this volume we are adopting a deliberately capacious understanding of entanglement. Entanglement, in other words, can be reflective of a wide range of senses in relation to Englishes, whether entangled with languages other than English, with complex histories and sociopolitical forces, with conflicting language ideologies, or with material and spatial assemblages. Undoubtedly, scholars in applied linguistics and beyond will continue to make productive use of the originary understanding of entanglement. Meanwhile, we are hoping to adopt a much broader conceptualization that encompasses both dedicated and sustained treatments of entanglement from the quantum perspective but also a wider array of senses as well. It is no longer adequate to study the globalization of English merely as a language but instead as an entity or phenomenon that is invariably entangled with and through various languages, cultural forms (e.g., ideological commitments, social norms, teaching philosophies), or even (im)material objects (e.g., food, signage, attire). These entangled narratives of English are imprinted and in circulation in various global contexts, and the chapters in this volume are an attempt to showcase what kinds of paths of inquiry can be uncovered and explored.

3. Chapter overviews

This volume is divided into four sections: Entanglements of sociopolitics (Section I), Entanglements of race (Section II), Entanglements of practice (Section III), and Entanglements of education (Section IV). It is important to note that such categorization is not meant to be preemptive of an alternative taxonomy of the chapters. In fact, each of the chapters is multidimensional in its own right – perhaps expected given the theme of the volume – so we encourage readers to imagine other kinds of organizational frameworks in their reading experience based on what they deem to be the most significant takeaway from each chapter. We hope that at the very least our proposed schematic is something of a productive starting point.

Section I begins with Christina Higgins and Kristen Urada's 'Citizen sociolinguists on the entanglements between Pidgin and English in social media spaces.' Their chapter examines social media posts in which contributors discuss and debate the linguistic and cultural elements of Pidgin, the creole language of Hawai'i, in relation to English. These posts reveal an intrinsic interest in the relationship between these two languages that is entangled with the legacy of US imperialism and enduring social class divisions, yet which is also intertwined with local pride in Hawai'i's linguistic and cultural identity. As Higgins and Urada propose, a metapragmatic perspective is crucial to better understand the nature of multilingual practices in contexts like Hawai'i, where English and Pidgin intersect and flow in everyday people's linguistic repertoires while being entangled in ideologies of class, privilege, and socio-economic mobility.

The next chapter in this section is 'Rap in the local–global interface of South Asia: social and political activism in South Asia' by Shaila Sultana and Bal Krishna Sharma. This chapter looks to the case of South Asian hip-hop, where young artists use their music as a tool for organized social activism and civil resistance. It focuses on how artists in Bangladesh and Nepal use their art to connect with global hip-hop communities and address local issues, employing multilingual lyrics and profane expressions to highlight societal problems and resist corruption. Local languages and vernaculars are integrated alongside taboo expressions, swearing, and provocative body language to address societal issues, while English serves to connect these narratives with global audiences across different temporal and spatial contexts.

Jaspal Naveel Singh, in the next chapter, 'Word-sound-power: entanglements of global Patwa in India,' also considers the case of music, though through a decidedly different approach. Singh looks to the lyrics and visuals of an Indian reggae artist to show how language, music, materiality, technology, knowledge, and politics come to be entangled in ways that are both globally connected and locally rooted. The chapter shows how such semiotic entanglements enable reggae artists around the world to run their own systems of sound, language, and politics, amplifying their voices in collaboration with other activists to perform global decolonial solidarities.

In the final chapter of this section, 'Entanglements within COVID-19 linguistic landscapes in Kyoto, Japan,' Yumi Matsumoto and Ivan Jin examine how cultures, objects, embodiment, spaces, histories, ideologies, and languages – including Englishes – are intertwined in the linguistic landscape (LL; signage in public space). They focus on the case of the LL of Kyoto during the height of COVID-19 in 2020, analyzing how signage reveals complex meanings and diverse stances toward social changes unfolding as a result of the pandemic. The signs circulate new etiquette-related words and express varying stances on government regulations, reflecting local identities and efforts to contextualize COVID-19 within local histories and cultures.

The first chapter of Section II, Entanglements of race, is Daniel N. Silva's 'An entangled unease: intrusive Englishes and allyship in Black feminism.' While English is conventionally associated with – and therefore problematized on the basis of being associated with – global elitism, Silva shows how it can be appropriated by minoritized groups and repurposed beyond these frameworks of domination.

He focuses on the case of Black Brazilian feminists who recast trajectories of socialization into domains that are not normally imagined to include them, or are otherwise deliberately manufactured to systematically exclude them. Their usage of English is treated as *intrusive*, working toward a reimagination of semiotic domains beyond a devaluation of Black lives.

Afterwards, '"No English, no English:" raciolinguistic entanglements in Czechia' by Stephanie Rudwick looks to the racialization of Englishes in a different geographic context. This chapter explores race-related dynamics in Czech society, focusing on the experiences of long-term residents with African heritage and Afroczechs. Rudwick develops an account of specific language and socio-political dynamics in this central eastern European space where whiteness and the Czech language are hegemonic and blackness and English signifiers of 'Otherness.' Ultimately, the chapter points to generational changes in English language attitudes and competencies, reflective of how place and space are crucial determinants of the extent to which English is embraced or rejected, and how linguistic and racial Otherness plays out.

The final chapter of this section is Patriann Smith's 'Re-/imagining racialized entanglements of Englishes and peoples: a call for a quantum ethos.' Smith examines what she describes as *racialized entanglements of Englishes and peoples*. Alluding to a dynamic space, racialized entanglements of Englishes and peoples suggest complex relationships between racial identities and Englishes such that the racialized individual influences and is influenced by linguistic variation. It is asserted that this notion of *dynamic space* of racialized entanglements is necessary as a key unit of analysis if research is to affirm the linguistic repertoires of (trans)racialized communities while also imagining novel ecologies of quantum knowledges that further decolonize multilingual practice and research across multiple fields.

Section III, focusing on entanglements of practice, begins with 'Entangled bodies, entangled ideologies: the case of Bikram yoga practitioners' by Kellie Gonçalves. The chapter explores the discourses of work and leisure by taking account of the embodied and linguistic ideological entanglements of Bikram yoga practitioners in Oslo, Norway. Drawing on diverse data sets and theoretical frameworks of embodiment, ideologies, and assemblages, Gonçalves analyzes how individuals' language ideologies manifest in embodied practices alongside the complex relations of semiotic signs involved. The chapter attends to social relations, emotional and affective domains, multilingual practices, iterative activity, objects and assemblages, spatial repertoires, interactivity, and sensory relations.

In the next chapter, 'Digital assemblages and their English entanglements: digital design, voice assistant use and smartphone setting choices of translingual speakers in Berlin,' Didem Leblebici and Britta Schneider examine digital language technologies such as smartphones and voice assistants as socio-technical assemblages that are entangled with English due to the dominance of Anglophone technology industries. Examining translingual mobile users' experiences with digital devices, the chapter shows how English is constructed and reaffirmed as the unquestioned language of technology. The chapter argues for the need to move beyond methodologically nationalist and immaterial linguistic concepts toward a focus on the material and technological entanglements of language.

Section III concludes with Ron Darvin's chapter, 'English online/offline: disentangling material and materialist perspectives of language.' The chapter explores the interplay of English with other languages online, using a bifocal lens to distinguish material and materialist views of online discourse. It examines how users' linguistic choices on platforms like TikTok reflect shifting identities, power relations, and inequalities. Focusing on the case of a Filipino domestic worker in Hong Kong, the chapter highlights the impact of device materiality and platform design on language use and argues for a critical awareness of the inequalities and modes of exclusion that are rendered visible through such interactions.

The first chapter of Section IV, our final section, Entanglements of education, is 'Entangling English teaching with content teaching: reflections of an English language educator in a content and language integrated learning context' by Keith S. T. Tong, Fay Chen, and Angel M. Y. Lin. Focusing on the case of content and language integrated learning courses at a university in Taiwan, the chapter highlights the complexities and relational dynamics involved in implementing English medium instruction (EMI) in Taiwan, including challenges in teacher pedagogy, student agency, and self-efficacy. Proposing an entangled approach to education, the chapter underscores the necessity of moving beyond reductionist and dichotomous educational policies to embrace more holistic and inclusive frameworks.

The final chapter of this section and the volume is 'Educators' reflections in translingual classrooms: entanglement of language, culture, and emotionality in Australia' by Ana Tankosić, Sender Dovchin, and Rhonda Oliver. In this chapter, the authors discuss challenges involved in the teachers' emotional entanglement with racial, ethnic, cultural, and linguistic diversity in Australian Aboriginal translingual classrooms. The authors' narratives show the importance of empathy, familiarity, and intimacy and how supporting resilience, engaging in political discourse, addressing gaps in mental health support, and relatability are important factors that should be considered in such classrooms as ways to support culturally and linguistically diverse students.

4. Conclusion

The chapters collectively demonstrate and affirm that entanglement can be applied and explored from a variety of epistemological and methodological perspectives. As we hope will be evident, the sheer diversity of sites and approaches represented by the twelve chapters in this volume is a testament to the fact that there is no singular or optimal approach to the question of entanglement in relation to Englishes. And we must also acknowledge that there are countless regions, communities, and approaches that are not represented. Therefore, at the very least we hope that these chapters alongside the general framing around the question of entangled Englishes can inspire scholars working in the areas of World Englishes, the sociolinguistics of globalization, and applied linguistics and language studies more generally to seek out their own understandings of entanglement to be in conversation alongside our own.

Note

1 As Silva and Lee (2024) explain, *fogos virtual* is a non-standardized construction of Brazilian Portuguese: "Unlike standardized Portuguese, which marks number agreement through plural inflexion of all lexemes in the noun phrase (e.g., *fogo-s virtuai-s*), nonstandard Portuguese non-redundantly inflects only the first element with the plural morpheme/-s/(*fogo-s*) while omitting it in subsequent lexemes/-Ø/(*virtual*-ø)" (p. 117).

References

Arnaut, K., Blommaert, J., Rampton, B., & Spotti, M. (Eds.). (2015). *Language and superdiversity*. Routledge.
Barad, K. (1984). *Fermions in lattice gauge theories* [Doctoral dissertation, State University of New York at Stony Brook].
Barad, K. (2007). *Meeting the universe halfway: Quantum physics and the entanglement of matter and meaning*. Duke University Press.
Bhabha, H. (1984). Of mimicry and man: The ambivalence of colonial discourse. *Discipleship, 28*, 125–133.
Bruthiaux, P. (2003). Squaring the circles: Issues in modeling English worldwide. *International Journal of Applied Linguistics, 13*(2), 159–178.
Canagarajah, S. (1999). *Resisting linguistic imperialism in English teaching*. Oxford University Press.
Canagarajah, S. (2013). *Translingual practice: Global Englishes and cosmopolitan relations*. Routledge.
Fitzsimmons, M. (2021). *Raciolinguistic ideologies in the rhetoric of early California statehood* [Doctoral dissertation, University of California, Irvine].
Flores, N., & Rosa, J. (2015). Undoing appropriateness: Raciolinguistic ideologies and language diversity in education. *Harvard Educational Review, 85*(2), 149–171.
Flusser, V., & Bec, L. (2012[1987]). *Vampyroteuthis infernalis: A treatise* (V. Pakis, Trans.). University of Minnesota Press.
Jenkins, J. (2015). *Global Englishes: A resource book for students*. Routledge.
Kachru, B. (1976). Models of English for the Third World: White man's linguistic burden or language pragmatics? *TESOL Quarterly, 10*(2), 221–239.
Kachru, B. (1985). Standards, codification, and sociolinguistic realism: The English language in the Outer Circle. In R. Quirk & H. G. Widdowson (Eds.), *English in the world: Teaching and learning the language and literatures* (pp. 11–30). Cambridge University Press.
Kachru, B. (Ed.). (1990). *The other tongue: English across cultures*. University of Illinois Press.
Kachru, B. (2005). *Asian Englishes: Beyond the canon*. Hong Kong University Press.
Lamb, H. H. (1988). The weather of 1588 and the Spanish Armada. *Weather, 43*(11), 386–395.
Macaulay, T. B. (1835). *Minute on education*. Central Secretariat Library, Government of India.

Menezes, P. V. (2015). *Entre o "fogo cruzado" e o "campo minado": Uma etnografia do processo de "pacificação" de favelas cariocas* [Doctoral dissertation, Universidade do Estado do Rio de Janeiro].
O'Regan, J. (2021). *Global English and political economy*. Routledge.
Parakrama, A. (1995). *De-hegemonizing language standards: Learning from (post)colonial Englishes about "English."* Palgrave.
Pennycook, A. (2007). *Global Englishes and transcultural flows*. Routledge.
Pennycook, A. (2012). *Language and mobility: Unexpected places*. Multilingual Matters.
Pennycook, A. (2020). Translingual entanglements of English. *World Englishes, 39*(2), 222–235.
Phillipson, R. (1992). *Linguistic imperialism*. Oxford University Press.
Rampton, B. (1999). Crossing. *Journal of Linguistic Anthropology, 9*(1/2), 54–56.
Saraceni, M. (2010). *The relocation of English: Shifting paradigms in a global era*. Palgrave Macmillan.
Saraceni, M. (2015). *World Englishes: A critical introduction*. Bloomsbury.
Schneider, B. (2019). Methodological nationalism in linguistics. *Language Sciences, 76*, 101169.
Silva, D. N., & Lee, J. W. (2024). *Language as hope*. Cambridge University Press.
Tupas, R. (Ed.). (2015). *Unequal Englishes: The politics of Englishes today*. Palgrave Macmillan.
Tupas, R. (2019). Entanglements of colonialism, social class, and unequal Englishes. *Journal of Sociolinguistics, 23*(5), 529–542.
Tupas, R. (2024). Preface. In R. Tupas (Ed.), *Investigating unequal Englishes: Understanding, researching and analysing inequalities of the Englishes of the world* (pp. vii–viii). Routledge.
Vertovec, S. (2007). Super-diversity and its implications. *Ethnic and Racial Studies, 30*(6), 1024–1054.
Wee, L. (2021). *Posthumanist World Englishes*. Cambridge University Press.

PART I
Entanglements of sociopolitics

1
CITIZEN SOCIOLINGUISTS ON THE ENTANGLEMENTS BETWEEN PIDGIN AND ENGLISH IN SOCIAL MEDIA SPACES

Christina Higgins and Kristen Urada

1. Introduction

In this chapter, we examine social media posts in which contributors discuss the linguistic and cultural elements of Pidgin, the creole language of Hawai'i, (also referred to as Hawai'i Creole in academic contexts). Posts by everyday people reveal an intrinsic interest in the relationship between Pidgin and English that is entangled with the legacy of American imperialism and enduring social class divisions yet which is also intertwined with Local[1] pride in Hawai'i's linguistic and cultural uniqueness and a growing recognition of Pidgin as a legitimate language (Higgins et al., 2021; Saft, 2021). When Caucasian politicians overthrew the Hawaiian monarchy in 1893 and annexed Hawai'i as a U.S. territory, English proficiency became the linguistic marker of socio-economic mobility, and the Hawaiian language became endangered as Hawaiian families felt pressured to only speak English. At the same time, Pidgin, which developed on sugar plantations among laborers, became stigmatized as a language that would hold one back and interfere with the learning and use of English. Pidgin has long been known as 'broken English' even though it is a creole language and linguists do not categorize it as a variety of English. The term 'proper English' developed in reference to English that is devoid of Pidgin influence, and it is still presented as a worthy linguistic goal that is tied to good education and high levels of mobility, particularly in the job market.

Despite these rather negative takes on Pidgin, the language has been maintained, and English and Pidgin continue to intersect in everyday people's linguistic repertoires while remaining entangled in these complex discourses of the past and present. As Pennycook (2022) explains, "[t]he idea of entanglements of English aims to address the multiple ways that English is connected to all that surrounds it, from global political and economic forces to local relations of class, culture, and education, from the circulation of discourses and ideologies to the contextual dispositions of people, artefacts, and place" (p. 7). Pidgin and English are entangled in Hawaiʻi's past and present relationship with the continental U.S., politically, linguistically, and geographically. In this chapter, we consider how perspectives on the discreteness of these languages relates to the hegemony of American English and or pride in Pidgin and in the expression of Local identities.

Our approach follows what Rymes and Leone (2014) and Rymes (2020) conceptualize as *citizen sociolinguistics*, or how lay people talk about language. Rymes (2020) states, "[c]itizen sociolinguistics is the work people do to make sense of everyday communication and share their sense-making with others" (p. 57). Rymes takes pains to distinguish her view of citizen sociolinguistics (CSlx) from folk linguistics, which she describes as an approach that linguists use, rather than everyday people, for analyzing how speakers express their ideas about language in the form of cultural models. While folk linguistics is typically based on data gathered through interventions planned by and analyzed by linguists, CSlx emerges spontaneously among everyday people out of a shared interest in linguistic features and their analysis, independent from academic interference. CSlx thus provides a rich framework for understanding people's understandings and interests in their languages from a deeply metalinguistic perspective.

While linguists easily see differences that demarcate languages, it is less clear how people in Hawaiʻi interpret this multilingual flow and what social and historical entanglements are a part of their perspectives. Numerous studies have documented Pidgin and English mixing in a range of contexts, including classrooms (Lamb, 2015), public signage (Higgins, 2015), social media (Higgins et al., 2016), church sermons (Choy, 2010), advertising (Hiramoto, 2011), speeches by politicians, and public testimony (Saft, 2019, 2021). These studies show that language mixing is the norm, as speakers artfully exploit the linguistic distinctions between these languages to produce social meanings. However, Pidgin and English are regularly presented as separate and separable languages in public discourse, particularly from the perspective that keeping Pidgin separate from English is beneficial for being able to speak 'proper English' (Lockwood & Saft, 2016; Saft, 2019). Moreover, many people who identify proudly as Pidgin speakers will comment that it is important to be able to 'turn it on and turn it off,' thus purporting to maintain a monolectal linguistic competence in each language. Despite this avowed sentiment, research that has examined Pidgin in naturalistic discourse demonstrates just the opposite, as speakers use features of both Pidgin and English in the same social and discursive contexts, either as a hybrid mix or in the form of pragmatic codeswitching (Auer, 1999). The question we seek to shed light on is whether and how citizen sociolinguists differentiate these two languages from an emic perspective in CSlx discussions about language.

A CSlx perspective is needed in light of current research that explores speakers' metalinguistic perspectives on Pidgin and in which the language is often discussed by researchers and speakers alike as if it were used in monolectal ways, divorced from English. Interview studies such as Marlow and Giles (2008), for example, explore the ideologies that drive speakers' use of Pidgin or English at home, in schooling contexts, and at work. However, no discussion of mixing Pidgin and English arises, despite this frequent practice. Similarly, in an interview study with university faculty, Lockwood and Saft (2016) reveal that while there was increasing support for Pidgin in higher education, the comments about language were presented without discussion of how Pidgin and English intersect with one another in everyday practice. It is expected that CSlx perspectives, unfettered by researcher involvement, might offer more acknowledgment and also CSlx analysis of the entanglements of these two languages.

2. Pidgin in its socio-historical, multilingual context

Pidgin is a creole language that emerged on sugar plantations between 1880 and the turn of the 20th century, when indentured laborers chiefly from China, Portugal, Japan, and the Philippines toiled side by side. The name of this language is still 'Pidgin' (with a capital P), despite the fact that it is a creole language. The language emerged first as a pidginized form of Hawaiian (Roberts, 1998) and became increasingly relexified with English due to the decline of Hawaiian and the ascendency of English, which was the result of American political occupation. The language developed into a creole among children of plantation workers. Even though Pidgin was the norm on plantation camps, negative attitudes toward the language became widespread during the 1920s due to its associations with the working class and plantation life and its reputation as a deficient, 'broken' English (Saft, 2021). Over the decades, however, Pidgin has become a vehicle for expressing Local identity and solidarity, for it distinguishes the residents of Hawai'i from the many visitors and newcomers who populate the state. For many, it is the medium of communication in homes, churches, and at work, and it is a strong feature of personal expression in the form of slogans on t-shirts and bumper stickers and in written form in literature and advertising (Hiramoto, 2011; Saft, 2021). While the exact number of Pidgin speakers is not known, a 2016 report by the State of Hawai'i's Department of Business, Economic Development and Tourism on languages spoken at home indicated that there were 1,275 people in Hawai'i who self-identified as Pidgin speakers (State of Hawai'i Department of Business, Economic Development and Tourism, 2016), but this number is almost certainly a reflection of language ideologies rather than actual linguistic repertoires. There are Pidgin speakers who have moved to the U.S. mainland in recent years due to the high cost of living in Hawai'i pushing many Hawai'i residents to be 'priced out of paradise,' though the number of Pidgin speakers in the continental U.S. is not known. Previous studies have indicated that the use of Pidgin is limited depending on contextual factors (i.e., appropriate for casual conversations, but not professional settings) (Marlow & Giles, 2008) and regional factors (e.g., more spoken in areas with higher numbers of Native Hawaiians) (Drager & Grama, 2014).

In exploring the multilingual flow of Pidgin and English, it can be helpful to identify features of each language. Grammatically, there are numerous stark differences, including that Pidgin negation and past tense marking is preverbal (we *no* can go; we *wen* walk), while English negation and past tense marking is postverbal (we can*not* go; we walk*ed*). Moreover, Pidgin conventionally places adjectives first in predicate adjective structures without linking verbs (cute da baby), while they appear after the subject in English, with auxiliary verbs (the baby is cute). Other markers of Pidgin are the use of *stay* as a stative and locative marker (Where you stay?) and the use of *for* to mark infinitives (You ready for go?) (Sakoda & Siegel, 2003). Pidgin can also be considered distinct from English in its phonological system (e.g., /t/ and /d/ replace 'th' sounds) and its lexicon, though these are areas that are arguably more entangled with English in the flow of many people's linguistic repertoires.

3. Metapragmatics on social media

To explore how citizen sociolinguists make sense of linguistic boundary crossing, we turn to *metapragmatics,* which refers to how language use itself becomes an object of discourse (Silverstein, 1993). Rymes (2020) illustrates how social media is an ideal site for CSlx, since lay people regularly use it to engage one another in discussions of language. On one end of the spectrum are acts of 'citizens' arrests,' where people call out what they consider problematic linguistic practices, such as using the incorrect spelling for 'their' vs. 'there.' While the act of conducting a citizen sociolinguistics arrest might seem only negative and an opportunity to condemn people for their language practices, Rymes notes that social media provides the affordances for such acts to become "openings for deliberation, for everyday people to work things out on their own" (2020, p. 64). Higgins et al. (2016) examined the metapragmatics between Pidgin and English in a YouTube video in which a pair of Pidgin-speaking friends with the channel name 2Dudes1Car teach viewers 'Pidgin 101' by performing scenes in English and then again in Pidgin, thus suggesting that these languages can be used separately. The video centers on teaching 'da kine,' a placeholder word in Pidgin similar to 'whatchamacallit.' In contrast with 'whatchamacallit,' which can be a form of a word search, 'da kine' is used for a referent that both speakers are presumed to know, and there is no overt need to state the referent accordingly. 'Da kine' is an iconic feature of Pidgin and its semantic ambiguity yet shared understanding in interaction is the linguistic difference that the video underscores. In the following, we see the English version first, with one of the men asking about a restaurant. The scene fades to black, and Dude2 asks the same question, but in Pidgin:

Dude1: Have you eaten at that u:h new restaurant ↑yet?
((scene change))
Dude2: You wen sample ↑da ↓kine?

The video was produced to entertain Pidgin-knowing viewers rather than to teach Pidgin. The comments posted were only from Pidgin speakers and were often in Pidgin. The point seemed to be to collectively enjoy the linguistic differences and to recognize the preference for Pidgin in all cases.

This YouTube post differs from other uses of these languages that can be described as *translanguaging,* a term that has become widespread in discussions of multilingualism over the past decade. It has come to refer to a theoretical stance about the nature of bi/multilingualism with regard to the separability of languages. The 'strong' version of the theory treats bi/multilinguals as having a single linguistic repertoire rather than as speakers of more than one language or as speakers of languages that have undergone language contact (García & Lin, 2017). Scholarship in translanguaging frameworks generally avoids the term 'codeswitching' since it is suggestive of language boundaries and instead envisions bi/multilingualism as a borderless social practice whereby speakers select features from their unitary repertoire to engage in social meaning-making. A key concern of translanguaging scholarship with 'named languages' and the use of terms like 'codemixing' and 'codeswitching' is that these conceptualizations are etic categories that analysts impose on language data. Meanwhile, we suggest that CSlx offers an alternative approach to the question of language separability that foregrounds speakers' metalinguistic perspectives. We believe it is a promising framework for better understanding the nature of multilingual repertoires while honoring speakers' perspectives. Thus, turning to metapragmatic discussions about Pidgin and English on social media can illuminate how speakers are making sense of this entanglement themselves.

4. The case of 808Viral

We focus on social media posts about Pidgin and English so that we can identify what issues speakers, rather than scholars, discuss and debate in relation to Pidgin and English relationships. 808Viral is an online entertainment network specializing in Hawai'i content; 808 is the area code for the state and is a widely used reference for Hawai'i that demonstrates affection and pride. 808Viral was founded by Daniela Stolfi-Tow, who is a comedian, content creator, director, and digital marketing manager. 808Viral now posts on multiple platforms, including YouTube, Instagram, and Facebook, and its posts feature a number of locally well-known actors, influencers, and celebrities. 808Viral states that their network reached a billion impressions and garnered 2.5 million followers by 2018 (https://www.youtube.com/@808viral/about).

To further assess how entangled languages in Hawai'i are from a CSlx perspective, we examine four posts from 808Viral's Instagram and one post from an affiliated contributor to YouTube. In selecting data, we manually searched 808Viral's Instagram feed for all Pidgin-related posts, and we thematically analyzed all of the comments. The posts analyzed in the following were selected because they illustrate clear examples of recurring themes in citizen sociolinguists' discussions about the entanglement between Pidgin and English.

4.1. Solidarity through Local language

In 2021, 808Viral posted a photo of a "Hawai'i Light Switch" with labels 'open' and 'close,' which are widely used ways to indicate 'on' and 'off,' respectively, in Hawai'i (808Viral, 2021). The post invited responses by asking who else uses the phrases 'open' and 'close.' While the initial post by 808Viral does not label the language use one way or another, the comment thread offers some CSlx interpretations of these phrases as Pidgin, albeit indirectly:

(@User1) Try open da light . . . no can see . . . 🙈😂👏
(@User2) 😂😂 and den they look at you funny
(@User3) PAKA. "Try off da light." 👀😂
(@User4) My grandpa! I remember one time I thought he said, "Open da haole light!" What was that, grandpa? He meant "Turn on the hallway light!" 😂♡

Here, 'try' is a Pidgin grammatical marker that is used as an imperative to tell someone to turn the light on because they can't see well in the dark. This is followed by another comment where @User3 replaces 'close' with 'off' in a Pidgin framework, which is another Local way to express this action. The post frames the discussion as embedded in Pidgin, starting with the vocative 'PAKA' in all caps: "PAKA. 'Try off da light.' 👀😂." 'PAKA' here is a strategic misspelling of 'faka,' which is a vocative derived from English 'fucker,' but which is less vulgar, more akin to 'dummy.' The post serves as an illustration of a possible real-world voicing of this phrase in Pidgin, accompanied by this vocative, which portrays the presumed English-only speaking addressee as incompetent in following a simple request.

Other comments focus on other people's reactions to 'open' or 'close' the lights, illustrating linguistic confusion and irritation as a result. @User2 comments that "😂😂 and den they look at you funny." This is echoed by @User4, who shares a small story about their grandpa who uses these expressions. The response demonstrates a lack of comprehension, presumably due to linguistic difference, followed by the laughing/crying emoji. The following are some other responses:

(@User5) Ikr so local!
(@User6) Yes!! My husYes!! My husband gives me sh*t when I say open the light . . . he trys to find a way to open it 🤦 so irrahz . . . he grew up in hawaii to!!band gives me sh*t when I say open the light . . . he trys to find a way to open it 🤦 so irrahz . . . he grew up in hawaii to!!

@User5 assesses this language as "so local," which is not a clear claim on identifying these forms as English or Pidgin, but as nonetheless marked by place. Another post notes how some Local people can also question this form, which illustrates a knowing, metalinguistic act of rejecting Local English/Pidgin in order to (perhaps playfully) mock Local linguistic practices. The reaction of irritation from @User6 demonstrates a normalized use of this expression for speakers in Hawai'i and a rejection of the imposition of English-only norms.

Other posts draw attention to the CSlx recognition that expressions such as these might be cases of regional Englishes:

(@User7) What about "ice box" instead of refrigerator 😂 😂 😂
(@User8) Speaking of which I call a shopping cart a "wagon". Is this a Hawaii thing?
(@User9) Who says rubbish? 🙋

Citizen sociolinguists consider other lexical items that are widely used in Hawai'i but are less commonly used in Mainstream U.S. English, or MUSE, (Lippi-Green, 1997), including 'ice box' for refrigerator, 'wagon' for shopping cart, and 'rubbish' for trash. While these vocabulary items are also used in other regional Englishes, they are presented in the comment thread as unique to Hawai'i and on a par with the light switch example.

Other parts of the comment thread reveal how people develop an awareness of these forms as local to Hawai'i upon interacting with people from the continental U.S.:

(@User10) Yes always "open" the light. I went to the mainland and someone told me to "cut" the light on. I was like what?!?
(@User11) I remember when I was in the Army, Ft. Lewis, WA. I told a guy "Close the lights when you leave" he was like "What!?" "You can close a door, you can close a window but you can't close a light!" Then I was like "Ok! Turn it off then!" 😂

For people who grew up using 'open' and 'close' the light, they may think they are speaking English rather than Pidgin. However, when these phrases are used outside of Hawai'i, people then realize that these forms might be regional English. @User11 posted their experience of using 'open' and 'close' the light in Washington state, where they were corrected.

In this CSlx discussion of 'open and close the light,' citizen sociolinguists do not spend time labeling languages. Instead, they express a newfound awareness of linguistic difference, imposed on them through exposure to other contexts and norms. They also debate the linguistic origins of these collocations and express solidarity with one another about their accepted use in Hawai'i.

4.2. The resilience of Local language over time

In 2022, 808Viral asked, "What's a Pidgin word or phrase you don't hear as much?" and initiated a discussion by providing "Cho Cho Lips" as an example, which is a term for full lips (808Viral, 2022a).[2] The post, which features this comment alongside an image of puckered lips, is accompanied by the caption, "I feel like there's been a mayjah explosion of #chocholips in the last 4 years, and we don't hear it used enough" (@808viral). While full lips have recently become sought after, they were less desirable several decades ago. 808Viral observes that despite this trend, the Pidgin phrase 'cho cho lips' has not returned.

The initial post is in English (aside from a Pidgin spelling of 'mayjah' in the first post/caption on the right-hand side), but it invites followers to report their observations of whether certain forms of Pidgin are fading away. The post presupposes that Pidgin has either changed over time or that it has been reduced in people's linguistic repertoires. In the comments, Instagram users respond by offering their favorite words and phrases, many of which are still in use in Pidgin. Nonetheless, the comments indicate a loss of some forms of Pidgin across time by making reference to older generations' language use or to other timebound reference points:

(@User12) "Bumbai" never hear anyone under 25 or 30 say that, if I do it's rare. It's crazy how language changes every generation pretty much. And it's different form island to island to.
(@User13) My grandparents used to always say "Chicken Waiwai" instead of "chicken sh*t".

@User12 notes how the Pidgin word "bumbai" ('later, otherwise') is not heard among the younger generation, and he notes how much Pidgin changes across time and geography. This leads @User13 to comment on their grandparents' use of "Chicken Waiwai" (in Pidgin, 'waiwai' is 'excrement' but in Hawaiian 'wealth'). The comparison with "chicken sh*t" shows a move towards English lexical items among the younger generation.

Some comments on the thread resulted in brief exchanges that analyze the concept of language change, as seen in the following example that was initiated by @User14, who contributed "shoots baloots" as a Pidgin phrase they hardly hear:

(@User14) shoots baloots
(@808viral) is this a Kauai thing?
(@User14) @808viral it could have been an eighties thing but I don't hear it anymore along with "ka-rang your alas"
(@User15) @User14 I still say om cuz I always see om on my feed. Right @User16 You da reason we still use that term. I think it's more of an 80's thing.

'Shoots baloots' is used as an interjection akin to 'certainly!' While 'baloots' likely comes from the Tagalog word 'balut' ('fertilized duck egg'), it is being used here with 'shoots' as a rhyming expression to mean 'definitely.' The author of the original post follows up asking whether 'shoots baloots' is specific to Kaua'i. @User14 suggests it is more of a generationally marked Pidgin phrase, and @User15 confirms it is something that was said in the 1980s. However, the comment by @User15 also points to the use of social media that helps maintain some of these disappearing Pidgin phrases.

Other posts on the thread indicate that Pidgin is not always seen as having been lost over time. One commenter notes that her own use of 'kakaroach' (Pidgin, 'to steal,' but also a reference to the insect, cockroach) is used by her son. What the post reveals, however, is that the son has a lack of clarity about whether 'kakaroach' is English or Pidgin:

(@User17) I grew up saying kakaroach. When my son went to type in kakaroach online he could not find it. Hahahaha . . . telling me mom all these years you taught me wrong. I said no, its correct the rest of the world is off! Hahahaha

This post raises the question of what "the rest of the world" refers to in terms of language. The discussion about Pidgin words that are not heard as often prompts @User17 to divulge that her own understanding of Pidgin was deeply entangled with English and that she grew up understanding 'kakaroach' as English rather than Pidgin. Such posts reveal how 'kakaroach' has an ambiguous language identity as Pidgin and English. In this post, we see the mother describing 'kakaroach' as being correct, which is true enough in terms of regular use in Hawai'i. Even after her son identifies it as incorrect based on his internet search, she resists the idea that the word she has been using all her life is wrong. This post demonstrates the extent to which Pidgin is entangled with English in that people who grew up with Pidgin do not realize that they are using Pidgin forms rather than English, and illustrates the ability to assert linguistic confidence in Local ways of using language ("no, its correct the rest of the world is off!").

4.3.   Untangling Pidgin from English through humor

Another example from Instagram is a post about 'scraps,' or 'fights' in Hawai'i (808Viral, 2022b):

Why do people in Hawai'i ask if you want to fight? They say "Like scrap?"
What if someone says no? Is that an option?
It's nice they ask tho. That's Aloha.

The question 'Like scrap' ('Do you want to fight?') is typically used as a rhetorical question to try to end a conflict, though it can also start a physical altercation. In this post, the author poses the non-serious question "Why do people in Hawai'i ask if you want to fight? They say 'Like scrap?'," which knowingly

26 Entangled Englishes

exploits the English meaning of 'like' as 'desire to' rather than the Pidgin meaning of 'like' as 'want.' The post also comically puts forth the idea that perhaps there may be an option to decline, in the English framing of the question. The post goes on to further comment that "It's nice that they ask tho," thereby creating a humorous take. Ending the post with "That's Aloha" underscores this humor, as the tone of 'like scrap' is anything but aloha, or love and kindness for one's fellow human.

While the post is tongue-in-cheek, the responses allow multivocal meanings from English and Pidgin to emerge in the CSlx discussion. Entanglement is seen at the lexical level, in which many users wrote comments using a play on words:

(@User18) That's actually very polite of them to ask. I don't like scrap and also no, I don't like beef. Aloha

(@User19) Right? Like, what if they was asking if you "like" scrap as in are you a fan of scrapping? Not necessarily saying would you like to fight me right now . . . like asking if you like spam musubi but with an intense vibe. "WHAT, YOU LIKE SPAM MUSUBI?"

In English, 'scrap(s)' refers to extra pieces of something (e.g., food, metal), and 'beef' refers to the meat from cows; however, 'beef' is a Pidgin term for 'fight.' @User18's comment signals their linguistic knowledge of both languages by using the double meanings these Pidgin words have with their English equivalents. @User19 adds to this framing by reflecting on the Pidgin and English meanings of 'like' and considering the importance of intonation in speech. Their post illustrates the ludicrous scenario of imposing the stance and intonation of Pidgin 'like scrap?' on a mundane offering of a spam musubi (a rice, spam, and seaweed snack).

These playful engagements with the initial post reveal that citizen sociolinguists are deeply aware of their multivalent language practices. Here we also see a sophisticated awareness of the role of prosody in multiple levels of linguistic structures in meaning-making alongside other linguistic structures.

4.4. Entanglement of Pidgin and English in constructing Local identities

In addition to discussion-generating posts on Instagram about language use in Hawaiʻi, 808Viral's YouTube page features entertaining videos that are meant to engage their viewers in the enjoyment of Local culture, Pidgin, and Local stereotypes. One series that attracts a lot of discussion amongst the viewers is a series of videos about Local stereotypes, "You know you local when . . . ," which was first published on their YouTube channel in 2016. In each short video, the content creators present a stereotype of Local people in Hawaiʻi using the phrase "you know you local when . . ." For example, "you know you local when your whole pantry is filled with spam" (808Viral, 2016). Their second video in the series, "You know you are a Hawai'i local when . . . part 2," (https://www.youtube.com/watch?v=Qhqpo2YuzFs), also posted in 2016, has over 300 comments, with viewers sharing a Local stereotype or responding to the content in the video. In the video, @User20 discusses the following as an example: "You know someone's local when they turn everything into a question by adding *yeah* at the end, like this, 'the sky is blue, yeah?' 'It's raining, yeah?' 'Ho yeah, yeah?' Ho that's the extreme local action right there."

In taking part in identifying stereotypes and enjoying this shared knowledge, users unsurprisingly reference language in their responses:

(@User21) I had to teach myself to stop using, "yeah" when I left Oahu in 2000

Replies:

(@User22) User12 brah I live in Kansas fo 12 years now. And da slang still slippin 😄
(@User23) The slang has not left me yet. People in Wisconsin get so confused 😄
(@User24) Hard to do, YAH. Oooops! Sorry I did it
(@User25) I don't think I'd ever be able to, lol.
(@User26) I still say "talk story" or "under the lanai" here on the mainland otherwise it sounds weird to me aloha from Texas 😄 😄 👍
(@User27) Haha same here man. Shootz, and hoo are obvious. But "yea" is subtle. Can't catch myself saying it all the time lol

@User21 explains in their comment that they intentionally had to stop using 'yeah' at the end of the sentence after leaving Oʻahu. In response, others who have left Hawaiʻi shared similar experiences of being unsuccessful in no longer adding *yeah* to the ends of each utterance. @User27 replies that some words, such as 'shootz' (interjection meaning 'yes') and 'hoo' (a discourse marker similar to 'wow'), are obvious to recognize because of their distinct interjection and discourse functions, respectively. @User27 considers the sentence-ending tag 'yea' to be subtle because it is less salient as a linguistic difference to how *yeah* is used in English on the mainland.

The CSlx discussion also draws attention to the sociopragmatic norms of Hawaiʻi, drawing on Pidgin and English. Another example is provided by @User28:

(@User28) You know you local when, when you use insults as greetings and have no negativity behind it. Hey wassup mental. Sup you monkey. Sup panty how you doing? Eh hey you dummy, wassup? What up you fakas?
(@User29) Ho dis video is so relatable especially da one at 1:06 😄 I always call my cuzzos panty 😄 and I get one cuz name Junior and Tita 😄 Da slippah one (I get da local kine slippahs) and da coccokorach one. Basically all of em 😄

Reply:

(@User30) i call my friends mento and monkey all da time and when a new guy came my school from da mainland he go so mad dawg lmao

As @User28 mentions, these greetings have negative connotations elsewhere, but they may be used as unmarked and even friendly greetings in Hawaiʻi. For instance, *panty* is used to call out someone for lacking courage, but when addressing someone as a *panty*, it can be a form of an endearment. Viewers often align with this observation that Local people use these terms, as @User29 points out whom they use these greetings with. @User30 also normalizes these greetings by explaining that they use them all the time with their friends. However, they also note that when a new student arrived at their school, they were offended by these greetings. This example further demonstrates the place-based entanglement of the Local languages, Pidgin and Hawaiʻi English, with mainstream US English(es).

There were several comments that recognized Pidgin as being a part of the Local identity. This can be seen in @User31's comment about being temporarily stationed in Hawaiʻi and slowly picking up Pidgin:

(@User31) I was stationed in Hawaii from Jan 98 till Nov 2000. I loved the locals, but man that pigeon rubs off on you . . . lol

Replies:

(@User31) Pidgin
(@User32) chee cuz yeah you
. . .
(@User24) You know yu Local when you talk Pidgin.
 Wen you grab rubbah slippah wen get big cockroach.
 Wen you use one word sentence, "what?", got one dozen different meaning.
 Wen you fry da spam make um like crispy bacon, eat um wit rice.

@User24 also mentions that "You know yu Local when you talk Pidgin" as opposed to speaking Hawaiʻi English or American English. Another Local habit is using *what* as a homonym. As @User24 points out, it functions as its own sentence with multiple meanings, including as a request for repair in conversation and as a marker of a confrontational stance.

Ultimately, the absence of comments pinpointing an English word or phrase to Pidgin or English in the comment section may indicate that these two languages are entangled in such a way that they are considered 'Local' rather than Pidgin or English. These ways of speaking are entangled with distinctive pragmatics that are influenced by Pidgin and connected to Local practices such as mock-insulting friends to demonstrate rapport, using a rubber slipper to kill cockroaches, and eating spam.

5. Discussion

Our examination illustrates the potential of social media in providing a rich context for exploring metapragmatics and for investigating how speakers themselves make sense of linguistic boundaries, linguistic acceptability, language norms, and more. Our exploration of 808Viral posts has shown that citizen sociolinguists in Hawaiʻi are engaged in contemplating the sociohistorical factors related to language change, resisting the imposition of MUSE-like norms, and underscoring the close connections between language and place. These are topics that are also raised in sociolinguistics lessons in university classrooms, but the perspectives provided in those contexts are generally from the point of view of linguists or are based on data that linguists have collected through interviews, surveys, or experimental design. Exploring these topics without academic intervention arguably allows for a more unfiltered view of people's understandings and attitudes toward language.

A central goal of our chapter was to explore how citizen sociolinguists make sense of linguistic boundaries involving Pidgin and English in light of the circulating discourse in academia around translanguaging that posits a lack of distinction between 'named' languages. One finding is that citizen sociolinguists do not dwell on labeling language boundaries themselves as they engage in discussing and debating whether certain words and phrases are still used and where. Instead, they explore the role of geography, generation, and the influence of the media on language in Hawaiʻi. While the social media posts 808Viral invited were framed with reference to the (also CSlx) categories of Local language, Pidgin, and being Local, the responses largely took up the issue of Localness via discussions that explored what aspects of language sound Local or how language is responded to by people not familiar with Hawaiʻi. Moreover, these discussions were conducted with a mix of Pidgin and English. It is possible to argue that their inattention to language boundaries and labels thus lends support to a CSlx translingual perspective on Pidgin and English in Hawaiʻi.

A second finding is that the posts reveal a prideful and positive stance toward Local language practices. This stands in contrast with many studies that have explored attitudes towards Pidgin (and Local English in Hawaiʻi; Lockwood & Saft, 2016; Marlow & Giles, 2010; Romaine, 1999), which involve some degree of intervention by a researcher. Studies that have used interviews, surveys, and focus groups have all demonstrated greater amounts of ambivalence and uncertainty about the legitimacy of Pidgin in particular. In contrast, the posts that we have examined here lean strongly toward wonderment, rather than citizens' arrests, as people express their interest in Local language practices. We suggest that studies which focus participants' attention on the social legitimacy of languages through these means likely heighten their linguistic anxiety and manifest deficit discourses in relation to marginalized languages like Pidgin. Our findings suggest that CSlx data might reveal a different and more favorable view that challenges the bulk of existing knowledge about language attitudes and ideologies. In future work, it will be important to consider what observations or interactional moves initiate CSlx engagement about language, as the starting points for these discussions surely shapes the direction they take. In the case of 808Viral, which celebrates all things Local in Hawai'i, it is no surprise that Local language is presented as an entity that is valued and appreciated, even if it is also an object of debate. Other social media discussions that depart from a different vantage point may well open the door for CSlx discourse of a more spurious and linguistically specific nature.

6. Conclusion

CSlx invites scholars in the field of language studies to reconsider how to establish linguistic expertise. In this chapter, we have examined how citizen sociolinguists express their expertise in reference to posts about Local language, Pidgin, and Local identity. In contrast with existing research that demonstrates ambivalent or negative attitudes towards Pidgin and Pidgin-influenced English, these perspectives are noticeably positive. Of course, the social media platform we selected celebrates the Local, and the CSlx posts in turn offer positive attitudes towards Local language practices. In this way, CSlx is more than a means of exploring citizens' expertise about language; citizen sociolinguists are doing the work of language advocacy as they push back against hegemonic discourses tied to 'proper' English and against ideologies that link language practices to negative social outcomes. For those who follow 808Viral and similar social media which celebrate the Local, new assemblages of sentiments are being constructed in these digital spaces that challenge deficit views of language and reframe the codemeshing between Pidgin and English as normalized sociolinguistic practice.

Notes

1 Local identity (with a capital L) in Hawai'i is broadly multicultural and contains many elements of Hawaiian culture, including placing importance on one's genealogy in terms of ethnicity, family, geography, and social network (Lum, 2008).
2 This word may come from a reduplication from the Japanese 'butterfly' (蝶).

References

808Viral. (2016, September 16). *You know you are a Hawaii local when . . . part 2*. https://www.youtube.com/watch?v=Qhqpo2YuzFs
808Viral. (2021, September 12). *Hawaii light switch*. https://www.instagram.com/p/CTuyFXivwoj/
808Viral. (2022a, August 13). *Cho Cho Lips*. https://www.instagram.com/p/ChN0kpkPeN2/
808Viral. (2022b, April 19). *Scrap*. https://www.instagram.com/p/Cci4PvfpT7-/
Auer, P. (1999). From codeswitching via language mixing to fused lects: Toward a dynamic typology of bilingual speech. *International Journal of Bilingualism*, 3(4), 309–332.
Choy, A. (2010). Eh, das jus like da kine, ah?: Researching the role of pidgin in church. *SLS Papers*. University of Hawai'i at Mānoa. http://hdl.handle.net/10125/40708

Drager, K., & Grama, J. (2014). "De tawk dakain ova dea": Mapping language ideologies on Oʻahu. *Dialectologia*, *12*, 23–51.

García, O., & Lin, A. M. (2017). Translanguaging in bilingual education. In O. García, A. M. Y. Lin & S. May (Eds.), *Bilingual and multilingual education* (pp. 117–130). Springer.

Higgins, C. (2015). Earning capital in Hawaiʻi's linguistic landscape. In R. Tupas (Ed.), *Unequal Englishes across multilingual spaces* (pp. 145–162). Palgrave Macmillan.

Higgins, C., Furukawa, G., & Lee, H. (2016). Resemiotizing the metapragmatics of Konglish and Pidgin on YouTube. In S. Leppänen, S. Kytölä, H. Jousmäki, S. Peuronen & E. Westinen (Eds.), *Discourse and identification: Diversity and heterogeneity in social media practices* (pp. 310–334). Routledge.

Higgins, C., Schwartz, B., Lamb, G., & Urada, K. (2021). *Towards a public sociolinguistics for social justice: Promoting Pidgin language rights in Hawaiʻi*. Paper presentation at the American Association of Applied Linguistics, March 2021.

Hiramoto, M. (2011). Consuming the consumers: Semiotics of Hawaiʻi Creole in advertisements. *Journal of Pidgin and Creole Languages*, *26*(2), 247–275.

Lamb, G. (2015). "Mista, are you in a good mood?": Stylization to negotiate interaction in an urban Hawaiʻi classroom. *Multilingua*, *34*(2), 159–185.

Lippi-Green, R. (1997). *English with an accent: Language, ideology, and discrimination in the United States*. Routledge.

Lockwood, H. M., & Saft, S. L. (2016). Shifting language ideologies and the perceptions of Hawaiʻi Creole among educators at the university level in Hawaiʻi. *Linguistics and Education*, *33*, 1–13.

Lum, D. H. (2008). What school you went? Local culture, local identity, and local language: Stories of schooling in Hawaiʻi. *Educational Perspectives*, *41*, 6–16.

Marlow, M. L., & Giles, H. (2008). Who you tink you, talkin propah? Hawaiian Pidgin demarginalised. *Journal of Multicultural Discourses*, *3*(1), 53–68.

Marlow, M. L., & Giles, H. (2010). "We won't get ahead speaking like that!" Expressing and managing language criticism in Hawaiʻi. *Journal of Multilingual and Multicultural Development*, *31*, 237–251.

Pennycook, A. (2022). Entanglements and assemblages of English. *Crossings: A Journal of English Studies*, *1*, 7–21.

Roberts, S. J. (1998). The role of diffusion in the genesis of Hawaiian Creole. *Language*, *74*(1), 1–39.

Romaine, S. (1999). Changing attitudes to Hawaiʻi Creole English. In J. Rickford & S. Romaine (Eds.), *Creole genesis, attitudes and discourse* (pp. 287–301). John Benjamins.

Rymes, B. (2020). *How we talk about language: Exploring citizen sociolinguistics*. Cambridge University Press.

Rymes, B., & Leone, A. R. (2014). Citizen sociolinguistics: A new media methodology for understanding language and social life. *Working Papers in Educational Linguistics*, *29*(2), 25–43.

Saft, S. (2019). *Exploring multilingual Hawaiʻi: Language use and language ideologies in a diverse society*. Rowman & Littlefield.

Saft, S. (2021). *Language and social justice in context*. Springer International Publishing.

Sakoda, K., & Siegel, J. (2003). *Pidgin grammar: An introduction to the Creole English of Hawaiʻi*. Bess Press.

Silverstein, M. (1993). Metapragmatic discourse and metapragmatic function. In J. Lucy (Ed.), *Reflexive language: Reported speech and metapragmatics* (pp. 33–58). Cambridge University Press.

State of Hawaiʻi Department of Business, Economic Development and Tourism. (2016, March). *Detailed languages spoken at home in the state of Hawaiʻi*. https://files.hawaii.gov/dbedt/census/acs/Report/Detailed_Language_March2016.pdf

2
RAP IN THE LOCAL–GLOBAL INTERFACE

Social and political activism in South Asia

Shaila Sultana and Bal Krishna Sharma

1. Introduction

Previous research on rap presents two main perspectives on its societal impact. One view emphasizes negative influences, such as promoting sexism and violence. Studies draw parallels between rappers' experiences and life in society and highlight rap's authenticity (Alim et al., 2010). These studies show that although rap serves as a discursive space for contesting societal ideologies including racism and sexism, they simultaneously reproduce dominant norms like glorifying violence and sexualizing women (Herd, 2009; Weitzer & Kubrin, 2009; Forchu, 2019). The second perspective highlights rap's potential for social transformation by promoting political awareness and critiquing societal structures like sexism and corruption. This perspective celebrates rap as a medium for youth to engage in critical discourse on social identities and ideologies (Chettri, 2024; Hasan & Kundu, 2022). Historically music has played a significant role as a liberatory force and has also been a vehicle of social and political activism. Hip-hop, reggae, or rap, for example, have raised awareness about racism, ethnicism, colorism, or genderism across the world. While we acknowledge the existence of both views on rap, the perspective we advance in this chapter is rap's potential for social and political activism. In this chapter, we want to see the liberatory forces generated by rap songs, when we are keenly aware of its function of reinforcing genderism, sexism, or racism.

In recent times, the music industries in South Asia seem to be a fertile ground for hip-hop music and dance. Younger generations of music artists create opportunities to participate in organized social actions and civil resistance through the music genre, challenging national, religious, political, and other forms of ideologies (Lipenga, 2023). Hip-hop or rap has also been, on many occasions, critiqued for its 'alien' languages and culture in South Asia (Lundqvist, 2021). Hence, vernacular

DOI: 10.4324/9781003441304-4

voices need to be listened to seriously. Research has been done beyond the United States of America and nations like France, the United Kingdom, Germany, Italy, and Japan (Williams, 2017). Consequently, there is a growing body of research focusing on South Asian contexts, with studies emerging from countries such as Bangladesh (e.g., Hasan & Kundu, 2022), India (e.g., Singh, 2022), and Nepal (Sharma, 2023). This work has covered various aspects of societal, cultural, and linguistic dynamics unique to each country, including hip-hop activism (Hasan & Kundu, 2022); its political roles in promoting political visions and divisions (Lundqvist, 2021); participatory popular culture and the negotiation of collective identity, aspirational individuality, and spatial collectivity (Chettri, 2024; Cardozo, 2023; Dattatreyan & Singh, 2020; Singh, 2021; Sharma, 2023); and its decolonial efforts (Singh, 2023).

There is much more to explore regarding the potentiality of rap music as a means of political activism, specifically in the South Asian context, where corruption and political violence are rampant. For example, Bangladesh has been on the list of the most corrupt countries in the world and has drawn the attention of international audiences for the patriarchal control of autocratic political parties. For the general population, alternative platforms, among them music, seem to become spaces for resistance and raising awareness (Sultana, 2022). Our chapter examines the less-researched rap music in Bangladesh and Nepal to understand how the specific genre of music becomes the voice of rebelliousness and sustains varied forms of activism. Specific attention is paid to English, as the language is widely associated with colonialism, internationalism, and neoliberalism in South Asia. This is also the language of protest in rap and hip-hop culture and a pan-South Asian lingua franca. The chapter, thus, on the one hand, sheds light on the use of English, other multilingual and multimodal resources, and their functions in rap in the South Asian region. On the other hand, it explores how these resources are entangled with alternative discourses for giving voices to socially, culturally, and politically marginalized segments of society. In summary, the chapter unravels how 'entangled Englishes' allow younger musicians to create a niche within the local and global interface to make their voices audible and themselves visible, breaking the boundaries of time and space.

2. Music, entangled Englishes, and enmeshed identities

We draw on Pennycook's (2022) conceptualization of entangled Englishes to take into account how the English language intertwines with local languages, cultures, and contexts to create hybrid forms that reflect diverse linguistic and cultural influences. Global rap exemplifies this concept by blending English with local languages and cultural references so that the language becomes relevant to various regional audiences. Rappers often switch between English and their native languages and incorporate local issues and traditions into their lyrics, which allows English to serve as a medium for expressing unique cultural identities and sociopolitical concerns. This linguistic and cultural fusion enriches English with new meanings and perspectives. The rap songs we analyze in this chapter exemplify the entangled nature of English in two South Asian countries by demonstrating the language's fluidity, diversity, and hybridity on the one hand and its nexus with the ideologies of social activism and political resistance, on the other.

English is a popular medium in rap/hip-hop music in diverse cultural contexts. English in rap songs has its own linguistic features that seem relevant to youths across the world, even though African American English (AAE) has a fundamental influence on the genre of rap music. That is why Alim (2009) calls it the 'global hip-hop nation language.' Youths may feel disassociated with Standard English and the countries associated with it, but they may use global hip-hop nation language to break linguistic and cultural barriers bestowed on people for their races, ethnicities, nationalities, and classes. The global hip-hop nation language, thus, is a means to express a liberatory spirit and protest against varied forms of discrimination and marginalization. The global hip-hop nation language is unique for its linguistic features, lexical meaning potentiality, and other multimodal resources that contribute to its meaning-making processes. Amongst all the linguistic features, English slang seems to be an important dynamic of rap songs, so much so that rap songs are considered vulgar by some. However, slang in rap songs is also appreciated for its uniqueness. Evadewi and Jufrizal (2018), for instance, showed that the slang used in the rap songs of Eminem is creative, flippant, and fresh.

With Creolizing practices, the use of linguistic features from different local and global resources, English, and antilanguages, rappers seem to negotiate varied facets of their identities as young urbanites. As Androutsopoulos and Scholz (2002) put it

> [r]ap lyrics in several European societies are saturated with English elements which fulfil both referential and aesthetic/socio-symbolic functions. . . . Rappers explicitly claim for themselves a fused national-cultural identity, thereby foregrounding the language of rapping to support their claim.
>
> *(p. 27)*

Pennycook (2010) gives examples from a range of lyrics from French rap which has elements from a variety of languages influenced by its diasporic flow. French rappers seem to avoid association with Standard French language and culture as they disregard France for its colonial history and exploitation of the colonized. They liberally use neologisms, 'relexified French,' and *verlan* – the popular form of French slang. They also use "a streetspeak version of French that includes African, Arab, gipsy and American roots" (Huq, 2001, qtd. in Pennycook, 2010, p. 595). In addition, they maintain distance from the values of their traditional society and supposedly the dominant Western society. Lexical items from the Holy Quran are borrowed and localized in rap songs of the Arab world and countries in Asia (Pennycook, 2010). The plurality of identities (African, Mediterranean, Muslim,

Indonesian, or Urbanite) entirely lies in their vocation. Thus, musicians show their agency in what mixed *métissée* identity they want to negotiate.

Hip-hop and rap are used by global youths to reconstruct their identities. Nigerian hip-hop, for instance, draws from Yoruba, English, and Pidgin with Igbo borrowings (Weird MC); English, Pidgin, and Yoruba (D'Banj); or Pidgin and Igbo (2-Shotz) (Bramwell & Butterworth, 2019). With a blend of different languages and vernacular/non-standard English and gestures, rappers become trans-local while remaining rooted in highly local subjectivities (Bramwell & Butterworth, 2019). For instance, White rappers have started incorporating a variety of linguistic features from AAE into their rap songs. Fascina (2017) attributed the increasing popularity of hip-hop music among White youth to two reasons: first, mainstream White American society considers AAE as ungrammatical and inferior, and second, hip-hop and rap genres traditionally and historically treat White Americans as an oppositional force. Hence, Fascina (2017) proposed that rap has the linguistic and cultural elasticity to reimagine racial divisions. The White youths reinvent their racialized selves in AAE. In other words, linguistic diversity in hip-hop and rap adds diversity to rappers' linguistic, ethnic, or racial identity attributes.

The mixture of linguistic and semiotic resources from varied contexts, however, does not make these resources foreign to these artists. Historically, hip-hop epitomizes diversity inherited from the rich languages and cultures of Africa. Even at present, hip-hop is claimed as an African art form by hip-hop singers and rappers from different countries in the world. One of the participants in Pennycook's (2010) extensive research on popular culture stated that "[b]orn in Africa, brought up in America, hip hop has come full circle" (p. 597).

3. Hip-hop, rap, socio-political activism, and resistance

The history of rap as an opposing force against political corruption and injustice has been long. Rap artists consciously put words in rap music so that they may address history, oppression instigated by state institutions, and resistance through solidarity. In West Africa, rap artists are compared with *griots*. Griots are West African storytellers, singers, poets, musicians, historians, and most importantly, "sages and repositories of knowledge:"

> Rappers, like griots, are to their communities valuable human instruments who are entrusted to carry and preserve society's history and culture. They build on the rich and complex hip-hop tradition and respect the tradition through historically grounded and contextualized critical insights.
>
> *(Monroe, 2020, n.p.)*

That is why, historically, rap artists are named 'conscious' or 'political' rappers (Monroe, 2020). Even today, provocative and compelling issues such as access to education, voting rights and registration, or criminal justice reformation are addressed extensively in hip-hop. Politicians also see immense potential in hip-hop media to engage with young voters and show their concerns about racial equity and relevant legislation and reformation (Shawel, 2023). Senegalese rap artists such as Xuman sing for the emancipation of the marginalized and silenced ones in society by engaging the community and motivating them to change. They have continued invoking the tradition of resistance formed within the historical, political, and cultural traditions. Thus, hip-hop culture and rap artists are entangled with the resistance tradition of black communities. They have a rich history of fighting against colonialism, imperialism, and capitalism (Monroe, 2020). Concerning *Zouglow*, *Samba*, and *reggae*, Akindes (2002) found that youths in the Ivory Coast raise questions about social inequality and injustice via their relocalization of reggae, other diasporic music forms such as *Zoul*, hip-hop, rap, and Afro-Cuban sounds; local rhythms and dances; and mixing of Nouchi, local languages, and French. They thus carve out "new ways of being and struggle, and of making history" (Akindes, 2002, p. 86; cf. Browning, 1995).

Rap and hip-hop, with a combination and blend of poems and music, develop strong emotion and resistance to oppressive hegemony and regimes. They help nurture a collective identity among youths with a keen awareness of their selves and their culture (Ogbar, 2007). Al-Jezawi et al. (2024) concluded that "[r]ap and hip-hop serve as peaceful tools of resistance and function as a therapeutic outlet for managing anger, contrary to claims by some critical theorists that they stimulate violence in society" (p. 57). Thus, rap has the potential to be integrated into various settings from prisons to nightclubs to schools to create dialogues amongst people struggling with maintaining mental health. Even though rap has the potential to reproduce misogynistic ideologies against women and queer people, rap has also demonstrated its function as a social and political activity going beyond its confinement of popular culture. In the Haitian refugee crisis, the Million Man March, the Million Youth March, the east coast/west coast conflict, social programs, and foundations – hip-hop music has demonstrated its power of transformation (Kitwana, 2004). Musicians use the multimodal features of reggae and hip-hop music to question the over-representation of Africans as unskilled street vendors, low-paid workers, beggars, sex workers, the unemployed and homeless, criminals, or prisoners. Hip-hop activism combines progressive youth politics, community organizing, and hip-hop culture to address such issues as the prison industrial complex, emerging democracy and globalization, and education.

Here it should be mentioned that the purpose of the chapter is not to paint a romanticized picture of rap and hip-hop or demonstrate them as a panacea for all ills in the world. Nor does the chapter want to demonstrate the purely transformative power of rap and hip-hop. As we have shown previously, mainstream rap in the U.S. and Europe may sustain, nurture, and promote ideologies disfavoring women and queer people. In addition, the obscenity observable in rap and hip-hop, which are considered anti-establishment forces by many, can be the reason for their incrimination by law enforcement agencies. Law enforcement agencies may prosecute marginalized youths using drill music as evidence in court (Quinn, 2024). Keeping in consideration of these issues, the chapter wants to see in what ways the rappers use English and other linguistic and semiotic resources to engage with political and social issues in Bangladesh and Nepal. The research questions we engage with in this chapter are:

- In what ways do English and other linguistic and semiotic resources in rap songs in Bangladesh and Nepal demonstrate rappers' engagement with local and global social and political issues?
- How does English, entangled with other linguistic and semiotic resources in rap songs in Bangladesh and Nepal, reflect rappers' performances of identities and social and political activism?

4. Multimodal discourse analysis of rap

The rap performances under analysis in this chapter are inherently multimodal, encompassing lyrics, music, body language, emotions, attire, and cultural elements tightly interwoven. This integrated cultural production challenges our understanding of language, culture, and modality. Therefore, for us, a comprehensive analysis of rap necessitates an examination of both lyrics and the content presented in the video performances. Positioning this study within the digital landscape presents opportunities for widespread participation among individuals, emphasizing that meaning is not solely contained within the text but rather emerges through the interplay of the socio-political environment, consumption context, and the text itself (Way, 2021). This holistic approach emphasizes that language or text must be understood as one among many other forms of semiosis. Pennycook's observations (2007) on transmodality in rap highlight that meaning transcends traditional channels, making it essential to explore how meaning is reconfigured across these modalities. In our analysis of rap performances, we therefore draw on multimodal discourse analysis tools (Kress, 2010). Adopting a three-fold approach, we include the analysis of (1) lexical choices, examining metaphors and rap jargon to understand how individuals, actions, and events are portrayed; (2) visual elements in digital music videos, including textual, material, and design features that represent people, actions, and events; and (3) auditory aspects, encompassing music, voice, and sound, to assess their role in meaning-making alongside lyrics and visual elements (Kress, 2010; Pennycook, 2007; Way, 2021). To conduct our analysis, we chose recent, representative videos from both Bangladesh (two) and Nepal (one), using three specific criteria: (1) the video should have a substantial online viewership, (2) it should effectively illustrate the entangled nature of the English language with other linguistic and semiotic resources, and (3) it should address themes related to social or political activism.

5. Political and social issues in South Asia

Political corruption is a pervasive issue in South Asian countries and occurs at the policy and political levels (Khatri et al., 2013). This form of corruption often remains hidden from plain view (Baniamin & Jamil, 2018). The most recent rankings published by Transparency International (2023) categorize all South Asian nations in the red zone, designating South Asia as one of the most corrupt regions worldwide. Bangladesh is ranked as the second most corrupt country in South Asia and the twelfth most corrupt country in the world according to the Global Corruption Perception Index (Azran, 2024). It is also a poverty-stricken country overburdened with poor education, high disease, uneven resources, and inadequate infrastructure and funds. The country is ideologically divided based on language, politics, religion, and demographic locations, and usually, the country is run authoritatively in a top-down fashion in which decisions exclude people at grassroots levels. The Digital Security Act 2018 in Bangladesh initiated by the government reflected an enactment of the mono-political biases and ideologies of the political elite, creating insecurities and anxieties among Bangladeshis (Sultana, 2019). The general nonchalance of the government and opposition parties about the well-being of Bangladeshis, unhealthy political competitions, political patronage, undemocratic practices, and the ludicrousness of Bangladeshi politics are known across the country. The harassment and jailing, torture to death in police custody, extrajudicial killing, and abuses of human rights have made people in Bangladesh more cautious about political commentary in public spaces (Zafarullah & Rahman, 2002). The vicious circle of hostility and bitterness between the ruling and opposition parties has also created public distrust about the competence and capacity of both (Moniruzzaman, 2009).

Nepal, like other South Asian neighbors, grapples with a severe corruption problem (Shah, 2018), as evidenced by its ranking of 110 out of 180 nations in the Corruption Perceptions Index. Likewise, an alarming 84% of Nepal's population perceives government corruption as a significant issue (Transparency International, 2023). Bhatta (2020) notes that Nepali youth have started losing trust in politicians due to rising corruption, a slow economy, poor accountability, nepotism, false promises, and lack of development. The older generation in particular has faced criticism for holding onto power without delivering on promises to improve lives or advance the country. This has caused political instability, with 15 different governments in 17 years, and has slowed economic growth. Frustrated youth have started becoming more vocal, demanding fresh leadership for positive change. The younger population, making up 49% of Nepal's populace, now seek leaders to tackle these challenges. The youth's frustration with the current situation in the country led to the 'no not again' campaign on social media during the general election in 2022. The campaign urged voters to reject long-standing leaders and advocate for young leadership for a more inclusive, transparent, and progressive political system (Gurubacharya, 2022). These issues seem to be strong motivations underlying the gradual emergence of young rappers and hip-hoppers in South Asia who predominantly deal with societal issues in their lyrics and performances.

5.1. Case study 1: Bangladesh

Rap songs in Bangladesh have recently received immense attention among the younger generations. Rap activism nowadays addresses issues that affect the marginalized communities of society, including concerns about freedom of speech, religious intolerance, or lack of democracy. For example, Bangladeshi rapper Nizam Rabby reflected on the murder and arrest of journalists, police brutality, violence against women, lack of freedom of expression, the culture of fear and apathy, lack of human rights, disregard for politicians, and other issues in the bilingual (Hindi and Bangla) song *Brasht* (meaning 'wrong'), which was released in 2020. The title of our first case study rap song is a combination of the Bangla word *Rajdhani* ('capital city') and the English word *street* – together they form the compound "Rajdhani Street," meaning the capital city street. In the rap song by Critical ft. Crown E and Lazy Panda, the singers express their frustrations about the recent developments in street culture not palatable to their tastes (see Extract 1).

Extract 1: "Rajdhani Street" by Critical ft. Crown E and Lazy Panda

Available at https://www.youtube.com/watch?v=ERm0QINSUJc

Language guide: Translation from Bangla to English: Underlined

	Lyrics	Translation
1	Bengali brown hot brigga	Bengali brown hot brigga (brother)
2	Flex with the লুঙ্গি, gold sneaker	Flex with the <u>lungi</u>,[1] gold sneaker
3	I got my brother OGs	I got my brother OGs
4	Sipping লাল চা with strong ginger (uh)	Sipping <u>red tea</u> with strong ginger (uh)
5	I'ma crack cocaine, flow methamphetamine	I'ma crack cocaine, flow methamphetamine
6	Straight রাজধানী street present ঢাকা scene	Straight <u>capital city</u> street present <u>Dhaka</u> scene

The lyrics show the influence of specific English vocabulary associated with Black American rap. However, the rappers replace some lexical items with more racially appropriate substitutes. For example, the phrase, "Bengali brown hot brigga" (line 1) phonetically resembles the commonly used 'yo brother n***a' in rap. The creativity and critical consciousness of the locality lie in the deracialization of the heavily racialized term 'n***a' with 'brigga.' It is not an established term in Bangladesh but seems to be used in rap songs. For substitution, the hip-hop spelling seems to be followed here instead of the Standard American spelling of 'n****r.'

The official lyrics (https://www.jiosaavn.com/lyrics/rajdhani-street-lyrics/FCYp Sy1Xe0Y) show that the word 'brigga' refers to 'brother.' The 'brigga' refers to the role played by the 'big brother' (*boro bhai*) in Bangladeshi street culture. In line 5, we find a case of a-suffixation ("I'ma"), which in this instance stands for 'I am going to' (Escoto & Torrens, 2012, p. 58), a common AAE form. However, it is difficult to identify from which sources these expressions are localized exactly. Rappers in South Asia are influenced by UK rappers, German DJs, Korean b-boys, and Japanese producers.

Shortening of words is commonly observed in rap songs to ensure their fitting in with the rhythm and beat (Escoto & Torrens, 2012) and this can be found in Extract 1 in the word *OGs* (line 3) as the acronym for 'original gangstars'/'gangsta.' OGs, an established lexical item in hip-hop and rap culture, are the senior esteemed rappers from the golden time of rapping. They are respected and admired because of their seniority in the industry and are given special status by the younger generations, who sometimes consider it their responsibility to carry on the ethos of the OGs (Nzinga, 2022). At other times, they are critiqued for their misogynistic lyrics and dead-end careers in the past, specifically because rappers nowadays want their music to be commercially successful (Lee, 2009). Here, however, the OGs seem to have a localized meaning with little reference to the historical and political role they play in the hip-hop industry in North America.

The Bangla 'lungi' (line 2), a long piece of traditional cloth worn by men in South Asia, and 'gold sneaker' symbolize the Bangladeshi and American rap cultures side by side. Famous rap artists such as Jay-Z, Rick Rose, Kanye West, Eminem, KRS-One, Nas, Rakim, or Foxy Brown frequently refer to famous brands like Adidas, Lottos, Reebok, Nike, Gucci, Timberlands, and ASICS in their rap songs (BJoseph, 2013). The brand endorsement is demonstrated when rappers wear them in official music videos (BJoseph, 2013). The 'brigga' in Extract 1 wears a lungi and golden sneakers to show his affiliation with the street culture represented in American and South Asian hip-hop. The Bengali 'brown hot brigga' also sips 'raw tea' with strong ginger – a popular kind of tea in South Asian countries (line 4). These references to the brown brother in a lungi, golden sneakers, and sipping raw tea with ginger indicate the localization of the rap culture in Bangladesh.

The entire official video is recorded in the streets of Dhaka, the capital of Bangladesh. It shows shoe stores, streets, and train stations in the city. The rappers are covered in their full-body framing together (a camera shot capturing their bodies from the heads to feet), creating a sense of unity (Figure 2.1). They stand in groups in a way observable in music videos of different rap groups across the world.

The rappers, in addition, demonstrate hip-hop hand gestures that symbolize their association with global rap culture (see Figure 2.1). Hand gestures are quintessential to rap music and are used to show rappers' confidence in their performance and ownership of the performance (Dodds, 2016). They emphasize words, phrases and key points that make the performance engaging and dynamic. Rappers also accentuate and enhance the rhyme and beat of the music with their hand gestures and create a visual appeal while taking command of their performance on the stage.

Rap in the local–global interface 41

FIGURE 2.1 Rappers from Case Study 1 standing in unity

FIGURE 2.2 Rappers from Case Study 1 showing hip-hop hand gestures

FIGURE 2.3 Rappers wearing chunky jewelry and a bandana

Rappers are also known for showing off their chunky jewelry. Accessories such as oversized baggy clothes, bold and bright figures and prints, Kangol hats, flashy big golden jewelry, sneakers, fat-laced tennis shoes, or sweatshirts show the imagination and color of hip-hop fashion (Hunter, 2011). Here it should be mentioned that wearing jewelry is not common for men in Bangladesh. By wearing specific kinds of jewelry, the rappers of Extract 1 thus show their allegiance to rappers across the world and connect the local with the global music. In addition, in Figure 2.3, the rapper is wearing a bandana, whereas in Figure 2.2, the rapper is making a gangster rapper westside bandana hand sign. Even though the bandana is originally from South Asia (used for covering the mouth and nose from dust or ensuring anonymity), it is also a widely used emblem for hip-hop aesthetics and has been worn by rappers since the 1980s. In Figure 2.3, the rapper wears his bandana on his head, possibly imitating the style of legendary rapper, artist, actor, and activist Tupac. Taken together, these multimodal resources indicate the localization of global rap and hip-hop culture in Bangladesh.

Our second extract stems from the song "Bust the Police" by the rap group D-Ruthless, which illustrates a strong use of profanity.

Extract 2: "Bust the Police" by D-Ruthless

Available at https://www.youtube.com/watch?app=desktop&v=dHLNNj3UT44

Language guide: Translation from Bangla to English: Underlined

	Lyrics	*Translation*
1	motherচোদ এর সাথে খেলতে হইলে	If you have to fight with the mother<u>fuckers</u>
2	হওয়া যায়না বাইনচোদ	<u>You can't be a sister-fucker</u>
3	হওয়া লাগে আরো বোরো motherচোদ	<u>You have to be a bigger</u> mother<u>fucker</u>
4	দেহি সব জাগায় justice এর sign board	A signboard <u>for</u> justice <u>is everywhere</u>
5	কিন্তু আইন তো অন্ধ	<u>But the law is blind</u>
6	পাই আমি রক্তের গন্ধ	<u>I smell blood</u>
7	এক মাত্র দেশ যেহানে media'র কাছে power নাই	<u>Only one country where</u> media <u>has no</u> power
8	জান এর ভয় মৃত্যু ছাড়া কিছু পাওয়ার নাই	<u>There is only one fear and that is to fear the death</u>
9	আমগো বোনদেরকে করোস rape	<u>You rape my sisters</u>
10	ছাত্র gang চোদার time নাই	<u>I have no</u> time <u>to fuck the student gang</u>[2]

The rappers here are vocal about political corruption, the destruction of democracy, weak institutions and governance, and the lack of transparency and efficacies observable in the activities of political parties. While people are fearful for their safety and security when they comment against the governmental forces of the country because of the Digital Security Act 2018 in Bangladesh (referred to in line 7), rap and hip-hop artists blatantly take a stand against the core political parties and actors who deviate from democratic norms. Many of them sing only in Bangla but are transcultural in ethos. We can find this instantiated in line 7, where the lyric given under the official music video (see the link given previously) shows the use of a possessive apostrophe, demonstrating the entangled nature of English and Bangla in rap songs. The use of impolite strategies, including sarcasm and curses (Delis, 2022), is prevalent in hip-hop songs (Tervo & Ridanpää, 2016) and can also be encountered in many of the rap songs in Bangladesh. The lyrics in Extract 2 contain items such as 'mother-fucker,' '<u>sister-fucker</u>,' and '<u>fuck the student</u> gang.'

Altogether, we have seen how rappers use their music to raise awareness about street life (Extract 1) or political corruption in Bangladesh (Extract 2). At the same time, they seem to reintroduce new forms of verbal violence and abuse against the marginalized and disempowered in society. For example, when they critique the political parties for raping young women, they use derogatory slang and sexist

Rap in the local–global interface 43

swear words which belittle women. Consequently, the question arises whether rappers produce themselves as misogynistic violent groups in the process.

5.2. Case study 2: Nepal

In recent years, there has been a noticeable intersection between rap and the dominant political culture in Nepal. Using rap as an aspirational tool, artists have started raising political issues and expressing their views and critiques of the existing political situation. They have highlighted issues like violence, corruption, inequality, and social injustice (Chettri, 2024; Sharma, 2023). Notable examples include "Mero Desh Birami" by Unik Poet, "Balidan" by Balen, and "Satta" by Prakash Neupane. Through this genre, the artists have been able to raise awareness, mobilize demand for change, and encourage active participation in shaping the country's future. Lundqvist (2021) highlights a recent trend of anti-politics being incorporated into Nepali rap, driven by a profound disillusionment with the corrupt political system and its perceived inability to enhance the daily lives of citizens. The video analyzed in the following is part of a broader wave of anti-government songs from Nepal that have proliferated on YouTube. It features a track titled "Hereko Herei" by the band SickJam, performed by the rap trio Easi 12, Dayjen, and Trix. The rap performance allows us to analyze diverse layers of linguistic, semiotic, and ideological entanglements. At the textual level, the lyrics contain irony with rich metaphors and idioms; the lines start with English and end with Nepali, transgressing the linguistic boundaries. Semiotically, the textual lines intersect with various multimodal images, musical beats and flows, and styles in the video. And, finally, the textual and semiotic elements are entangled with the notion of political critique via satirical humor to convey a message of political resistance and collective consciousness. This performance is an illuminating example of how multilingual rap is entangled with the "discourses and ideologies of change" (Pennycook, 2022, p. 16) on a global scale.

The video starts by showing the three artists who are sitting on a bench and waiting for their turn to play tennis (Figure 2.4). The image captures a compelling

FIGURE 2.4   The artists and the invitation

blend of emotions and aspirations prevalent among today's youth in Nepal. Way (2021) argues that a silent demeanor like this reflects the disempowered identity of those being represented. This is a powerful visual metaphor for the state of Nepali youth in the political space today. In the video, the three youths are continuously thwarted by two older adults dressed in traditional national attire who continue to monopolize the game and deny the youth their chance to participate. This visual representation symbolically signifies the entrenched power of the older generation of Nepali politicians who refuse to relinquish their hold on political leadership. Starting the rap, Easi-12 conveys frustration with society and the political system, as illustrated in Extract 3.

Extract 3: "Hereko Herai" by Sick Jam
Available at https://youtu.be/yucIIeOdT4M

1 Why would I die, for feeling the vibe
2 I'm feelin alive, I'm makin new waves
3 I'm making new faces, feeling contagious
4 People are raging
5 These demonstrations indicate hateful
6 Quickly get put behind bars if you say so
7 These politicians keep making decisions and
8 We are some sheep who keep playing the victims
9 हामी चैं हेरेको हेरेइ, हामी चैं हेरेको हेरेइ[3]

The starting lines constitute a blend of personal empowerment and social critique, exemplified by words such as 'vibe' (line 1) and 'alive' (line 2). The lines emphasize a sense of confidence and vitality and encourage self-expression and resilience. The phrase 'get put behind bars' (line 6), however, highlights the potential consequences of expressing dissenting views or speaking out against the political status quo and indicates a climate of repression or authoritarianism. When the artist uses the metaphor of 'sheep' (line 8) in the context of social commentary to imply a sense of conformity, passivity, and perhaps even perceived 'dumbness,' it implies a lack of individual agency, where individuals may blindly follow the decisions made by politicians, often without considering their own best interests. The use implies that people should be more assertive, informed, and proactive in speaking against social injustices. The last line 'हामी चैं हेरेको हेरेइ, हामी चैं हेरेको हेरेइ' (line 9), which serves as a hook[4] throughout the lyrics, carries a mocking tone suggesting a passive and disengaged attitude among Nepalis. Overall, this lyrical extract, which is delivered in a relatively fast flow with the help of an equally fast tempo and musical beats, signifies the energetic and upbeat vibe of the performance. It can be seen as a call to action, encouraging people to be more than passive spectators and to participate in effecting change or addressing the issues they are witnessing.

Rap in the local–global interface **45**

Maintaining the lyrical flow and using satire, Trix continues to deliver the lines in Nepali, as reproduced in Extract 4.

Extract 4: "Hereko Herei" by Sick Jam (continued)

	Lyrics	Translation
27	हेरेको हेर्यै के नै ख्यास्न	Just spectators, what the heck can we do?
28	सरकार झ्याप भाछ, rap चै rag छ	The government is drunk, rap is rag
29	दामी योजना, आन्दोलन र gang मा	Great plans in demonstrations and gangs
30	नेताको राज, राणाशासन झैं भाछ	Political leaders reign, feels like a Rana regime
31	सर्वसाधारण जोसेर ढुङ्गा हान्ने	The public throws rocks
32	पानीको छर्रा, तुङ्गनाको धुनमा फाल्ने	Water cannons blast, like a tungna's tune
33	मन्त्रिमण्डल, राजनीतिको सुरमा झरे	Cabinet ministers, serving their own political interests
34	वर्षौं भएसक्यो, गफकै गफमा टारे (Figure 2.4, right)	Years of idle chatter, the situation persists (Figure 2.4, right)
35	हजारौंको भिडमा लाउ नारा छरेर	Chanting slogans, in crowds of thousands
36	मन्त्रालय, गृह, अर्थ, संचार बसेर	Ministries of Home, Finance and Communications unite
37	कुर्सीको आडमा, भ्रष्टाचारको दारा	Backed up by power, corruption's teeth bite
38	राता रात जुलुस, काइदका कानून जाला मरेर	Overnight demonstrations, a law may crumble
39	चुनाव चिन्ह, भोट माग्दा दङ्ग पर्यो	Election signs, begging votes, they excite people
40	ढाका टोपी, पन्च काले राजा बन्न लाग्यो	In Dhaka hat, a pancha dude aspires to be the king
41	हामी नेपाली लाटो, समयसित चल्न गारो	We dumb Nepalis, struggle to move with time
42	हाम्रो देशमा मान्छे लोकतन्त्रले मर्न थाल्यो (Figure 2.5, left)	In our homeland, democracy brings death's tide (Figure 2.5, left)
43	हामी चैं हेरेको हेरेइ, हामी चैं हेरेको हेरेइ (Figure 2.5, right)	We're just spectators, we just keep watching (Figure 2.5, right)

Line 27 encapsulates the pervasive sense of powerlessness and inaction among the public. The symbolic use of the word 'drunk' in line 28 alludes to the government's incompetence and irresponsibility, while words like 'demonstrations' (line 29) highlight the ambition of protestors but also the challenges they face. Meanwhile, in these two lines, the English words 'rap,' 'rag,' and 'gang' are embedded in Nepali syntax in a way "that makes them hard to disentangle" (Pennycook, 2007,

p. 127) because of the blending of linguistic boundaries. The phrase 'Rana regime repeats' draws historical parallels by emphasizing a cyclical return to an oppressive regime. When the Rana oligarchy was in charge in Nepal between 1846 and 1950, the government was run by strict orders from the Ranas, who knew that if people got access to modern ideas or education, they might challenge their power (Hachhethu & Gellner, 2010). This expression here suggests authoritarianism and the suppression of people's voices. Likewise, the hyperbolic and metaphorical use of 'water cannons blast, like a tungna's tune' (line 32) portrays the brutality of authorities against the protestors. Line 34 highlights the 'गफ' (chatter) culture of Nepali political leadership and pokes fun at those who engage in empty rhetoric without taking substantive actions to advance the nation. When this line is delivered the video shows an image (Figure 2.4) on a board with the writing 'COME BACK HOME BROTHERS AND SISTERS.' The words invoke the increasing numbers of students who leave the country for work and study (Tamang & Shrestha, 2021). The drawings of a home and a flag in the background of the word metaphorically appear to indicate a welcoming message, rich with affective nuances of hospitality and patriotism. To reiterate Pennycook (2007), the image, the text, and the lyrical flow become so intertwined that meaning is dependent on the mixture of diverse codes and modes, and separating them becomes impossible. The text signifies a call for the younger generation to take charge, challenge the older generation of politicians, and actively participate in building the future of the country. The sign conveys hope and optimism and emphasizes the agency and responsibility of the youth in shaping Nepal's destiny. Line 37 underscores the intertwining of power and corruption, whereby the metaphorical use of 'corruption's teeth' implies that those in authority are often implicated in corrupt practices. Line 39 criticizes the manipulative nature of political campaigns in which empty promises can easily manipulate and excite the voting public. Last, line 40 indicates how a select number of individuals may seek positions of authority, often at the expense of the greater good. Furthermore, the use of the inclusive first-person pronoun in 'We dumb Nepalis' (line 41), appearing in a form of collective self-critique, serves as another instance of satire.

According to Kress (2010), in any social situation "meaning relations are established by the spatial arrangement of entities in a framed space" (p. 82). In the video, the lyrical lines are entangled with an image that contains several bilingual signs and a human body (Figure 2.5). The image with the artist lying on the road and facing the sky while holding a sign that says 'माया र ममता' ('love and compassion') alongside an Anjali mudra indexed by a namaste gesture embodies a profound message. His posture suggests vulnerability and a plea for unity and understanding. The call for 'love and compassion' highlights the importance of these values in fostering harmony. The surrounding handwritten placards that feature English and Nepali create a sense of inclusivity and global awareness. The placard reading 'THE POWER IS IN OUR HANDS' underscores the potential for collective action and change within society. It emphasizes the agency of Nepali youth to shape their future. The question

FIGURE 2.5   The placards with the message of hope and resistance

'हास्ने कि रुने?' ('laugh or cry?') on another placard represents the confusion that Nepali youth are facing today; it hints at a call for reflection and action in the face of challenges and injustices. The placard reading 'हामी नेपाली, देश हाम्रो नेपाल' ('We Nepalis, our nation Nepal') signifies a strong sense of national identity and unity, conveying a powerful message of collective responsibility for positive change.

Finally, the hook 'हामी चैं हेरेको हेरेइ, हामी चैं हेरेको हेरेइ' ('We just keep watching, we just keep watching,' line 43) that repeats eight times effectively and ironically reinforces the theme of public docility and frustration at being passive onlookers in one's own society's struggles. This line is entangled with a visual in the video of a human figure standing tall (Figure 2.5, right), adorned in a shirt made from a sack. The materiality of the sack itself is telling (Kress, 2010); it represents people with limited final resources who cannot afford regular clothes. Likewise, the phrase 'समय बदलियो, कथा उस्तै' ('time changed, the story remained the same') on the shirt conveys a hint of irony since it questions the perceived docility of the youth and their ability to adapt to evolving circumstances. Further, the sign 'शक्ति बढी, ऊर्जा कम।' ('More power, less energy') underscores the need for efficiency and effectiveness in driving change. The overtly visible vertical text on the shirt 'WHO AM I? I MATTER' signifies the importance of individual identity and worth, transcending borders and emphasizing the universality of the struggle for creating a just society. The text is entangled with slogans used in transnational activist movements, including Black Lives Matter. Likewise, the placard with the question 'IF NOT NOW, WHEN?' conveys a sense of urgency and responsibility. The video concludes with a message of hope, agency, and a compelling call for action, uniting local aspirations with global movements for social empowerment and political change.

6. Discussion and conclusion

Political turmoil and conflict have become a part and parcel of our day-to-day lives, and digital spaces and popular culture seem to play a vital role in the global spread of political unrest. Gone are the days when we used to solely engage with news and broadcast media. Nowadays words, images, videos, and digital popular culture contain power dynamics and ideologies, and we come to know about the political turmoils and unrest through social media feed scrolling, apps, videos, online comments, memes, GIFs, mash-ups, music videos, parodies, or comic strips. There is no doubt that the authoritarianism of Donald Trump or the protests in Gezi Park to acts of violence against China during COVID-19 gained momentum in digital popular culture (Way, 2021).

Linguistic features of both Bangladeshi and Nepali raps may be classified as the features of the hip-hop nation language (Alim et al., 2004) – a language with its own phonological, morphological, semantic, and syntactical features. Hip-hop artists use English and body gestures and postures associated with hip-hop culture usually from the West to identify themselves with greater hip-hop communities beyond the boundaries of their nation-states. The non-standard and regional varieties with their exaggerated stylized enunciation show that these varieties are the main source of activism for them. Taboo expressions, swear words, and provocative body gestures, which are socially denigrated by many, are extensively used in the hip-hop genre to draw attention to the corruption, dishonesty, and unlawful and undemocratic activities in their countries. The misogynistic expressions that exuberate toxic masculinity seem to be common, as shown in the swear words and curse words in Extract 1 and 2 in the context of Bangladesh. In other words, local languages and non-standard and regional varieties of national languages and swear words are used to engage with local issues, while English plays a vital role in connecting the local with the global and varied times and spaces.

The multimodal analysis also shows that English rap and hip-hop cultures are entangled with local issues. Digital rap can be conceived of as a 'third space' in the sense of Bhabha (1994) where the artists come to terms with the social, political, and economic struggles that occur at the margin, periphery, exterior, or border as spaces where protests against the dominant order can be articulated. The meshing of linguistic and semiotic resources thus allows individuals to create an alternative space where class, educational background, and socio-economic condition are questioned, and new identities can be performed. Diversi and Moreira (2009) identified the in-betweenness of the third space as the "constant site of struggle against forces of colonization" (pp. 207–208). Bhabha (1994), stated that "Third Space displaces the histories that constitute it, and sets up new structures of authority, new political initiatives" (p. 211). We see similar kinds of initiatives in the young rappers in Bangladesh and Nepal: through their musical activism, they want to transform society, while also creating new platforms for misogyny.

Notes

1 Traditional clothes worn by South Asian men.
2 I don't give a fuck to the student gang.
3 Translation: We just keep watching, we just keep watching.
4 A hook in rap is a catchy, repetitive, and memorable phrase or melody within a song designed to engage listeners and enhance the song's overall appeal.

References

Akindes, S. (2002). Playing it loud and straight. In M. Palmberg & A. Kirkegaard (Eds.), *Playing with identities in contemporary music in Africa* (pp. 86–103). Nordic Africa Institute.

Alim, H. S. (2009). Hip hop nation language. In A. Duranti (Ed.), *Linguistic anthropology: A reader* (pp. 272–289). Blackwell.

Alim, H. S., Ferguson, C. A., Finegan, E., Heath, S. B., & Rickford, J. R. (2004). Hip-hop nation language. In E. Finegan & J. R. Rickford (Eds.), *Language in the USA: Themes for the twenty-first century* (pp. 387–406). Cambridge University Press.

Alim, H. S., Lee, J., & Carris, L. M. (2010). "Short fried-rice-eating Chinese MCs" and "Good-hair-havin uncle Tom niggas": Performing race and ethnicity in freestyle rap battles. *Journal of Linguistic Anthropology, 20*(1), 116–133.

Al-Jezawi, H. K., Al-Abdulrazaq, M. A., Rababah, M. A., & Aldoory, A. H. (2024). Art voicing peaceful protest: Hip-hop and rap in the American and Arabic cultures. *International Journal of Arabic-English Studies, 24*(1), 57–72.

Androutsopoulos, J., & Scholz, A. (2002). On the recontextualization of hip-hop in European speech communities: A contrastive analysis of rap lyrics. *Philologie im Netz, 19*(2002), 1–42.

Azran, A. (2024). Bangladesh's disappointing position in TI corruption index. *The Daily Star.* https://www.thedailystar.net/news/corruption/news/bangladeshs-disappointing-position-ti-corruption-index-3532186

Baniamin, H. M., & Jamil, I. (2018). Dynamics of corruption and citizens' trust in anti-corruption agencies in three South Asian countries. *Public Organization Review, 18*, 381–398.

Bhabha, H. (1994). *The location of culture*. Routledge.

Bhatta, M. (2020). The decline of political trust in Nepal. In C. C. Echle & L. T. Waha (Eds.), *Trust in politics* (pp. 131–135). Konrad-Adenauer-Stiftung.

BJoseph. (2013). The 50 greatest sneaker references in rap history. *Complex.* https://www.complex.com/sneakers/a/brian-josephs/the-50-greatest-sneaker-references-in-rap-history

Bramwell, R., & Butterworth, J. (2019). "I feel English as fuck": Translocality and the performance of alternative identities through rap. *Ethnic and Racial Studies, 42*(14), 2510–2527.

Browning, B. (1995). *Samba: Resistance in motion*. Indiana University Press.

Cardozo, E. (2023). The poetics of Indian hip hop. In U. Anjaria & A. Nerlekar (Eds.), *The Oxford handbook of modern Indian literatures* (online ed.). Oxford University Press. https://doi.org/10.1093/oxfordhb/9780197647912.013.46

Chettri, K. (2024). "Straight outta Kathmandu": Hip-hop and youth culture in post-war Nepal. In E. Weesjes & M. Worley (Eds.), *Music, subcultures and migration* (pp. 203–216). Routledge.

Dattatreyan, G., & Singh, J. N. (2020). Ciphers, hoods, and digital DIY studios in urban India: Negotiating aspirational individuality and spatial collectivity. *Global Hip Hop Studies, 1*(1), 25–45.

Delis, P. (2022). Impoliteness in hip-hop music. African American and White artists' racist and sexist rhetoric. *Journal of Language Aggression and Conflict, 10*(1), 197–218.

Diversi, M., & Moreira, C. (2009). *Betweener talk: Decolonizing knowledge production, pedagogy, and praxis*. Left Coat Press.

Dodds, S. (2016). Hip hop battles and facial intertexts. *Dance Research, 34*(1), 63–83.

Escoto, M. A., & Torrens, B. M. (2012). *Rap the language*. The Open University Press. https://core.ac.uk/download/235864473.pdf

Evadewi, R., & Jufrizal, J. (2018). An analysis of English slang words used in Eminem's rap music. *English Language and Literature, 7*(1), 143–151.

Fascina, C. (2017). *The language of hip hop: A racial bridge? African American English (AAE) as interracial communication* [Doctoral thesis, Universita Deglu Studi Di Verina]. https://iris.univr.it/handle/11562/961034

Forchu, I. I. (2019). Actuality or misogyny? In A. O. Nwauwa & O. E. Anyanwu (Eds.), *Politics and identity formation in Southeastern Nigeria: The Igbo in perspective* (pp. 85–10). Lexington Books.

Gurubacharya, B. (2022). *Nepal voters seek change, younger generation leadership*. Associated Press. https://apnews.com/article/business-economy-nepal-kathmandu-5f1f6fa5c24103ba410772b21b2b22c0

Hachhethu, K., & Gellner, D. N. (2010). Nepal: Trajectories of democracy and restructuring of the state. In P. Brass (Ed.), *Routledge handbook of South Asian politics* (pp. 131–146). Routledge.

Hasan, M., & Kundu, P. (2022). Hip-hop music activism: A new phenomenon in Bangladeshi popular culture. In H. Khondker, O. Muurlink & A. Bin Ali (Eds.), *The emergence of Bangladesh* (pp. 405–417). Palgrave Macmillan.

Herd, D. (2009). Changing images of violence in rap music lyrics: 1979–1997. *Journal of Public Health Policy, 30*(4), 395–406.

Hunter, M. (2011). Shake it, baby, shake it: Consumption and the new gender relation in hip-hop. *Sociological Perspectives, 54*(1), 15–36.

Huq, R. (2001). The French connection: Francophone hip hop as an institution in contemporary postcolonial France. *Taboo: Journal of Education and Culture, 5*(2), 69–84.

Khatri, K. N., Khilji, S. E., & Mujtaba, B. (2013). Anatomy of corruption in South Asia. In S. E. Khilji & C. Rowley (Eds.), *Globalization, change and learning in South Asia* (pp. 63–81). Chandos Publishing.

Kitwana, B. (2004). The challenge of rap music from cultural movement to political power. That's the joint! In M. Forman & M. A. Neal (Eds.), *The hip-hop studies reader* (pp. 341–350). Routledge.

Kress, G. (2010). *Multimodality: A social semiotic approach to contemporary communication*. Routledge.

Lee, J. (2009). Open mic: Professionalizing the rap career. *Ethnography, 10*(4), 475–495.

Lipenga, K. (2023). *Rap culture and the youth in Malawi*. Palgrave Macmillan.

Lundqvist, M. (2021). Nep-hop for peace? Political visions and divisions in the booming Nepalese hip-hop scene. *International Journal of Cultural Studies, 24*(3), 454–469.

Moniruzzaman, M. (2009). Party politics and political violence in Bangladesh: Issues, manifestation and consequences. *South Asian Survey, 16*(1), 81–99.

Monroe, K. (2020). *Trans-Atlantic memories: Senegal's hip-hop griots and the Black radical tradition*. Council of American Overseas Research Centers. https://www.caorc.org/post/trans-atlantic-memories-senegal-s-hip-hop-griots-and-the-black-radical-tradition

Nzinga, K. (2022). Lyrical (re)citation: Remembering, recycling and revoicing bars from the rap canon. *Global Hip Hop Studies, 3*(1–2), 145–164.

Ogbar, J. O. G. (2007). *Hip-hop revolution: The culture and politics of rap*. University Press of Kansas.

Pennycook, A. (2007). *Global Englishes and transcultural flows*. Routledge.

Pennycook, A. (2010). Popular cultures, popular languages, and global identities. In N. Coupland (Ed.), *The handbook of language and globalization* (pp. 592–607). Blackwell Publishing Ltd.

Pennycook, A. (2022). Entanglements and assemblages of English. *Crossings: A Journal of English Studies, 13*(1), 7–21.

Quinn, E. (2024). Racist inferences and flawed data: Drill rap lyrics as criminal evidence in group prosecutions. *Race & Class, 65*(4), 3–25.

Shah, R. K. (2018). Corruption in Nepal: An analytical study. *Tribhuvan University Journal, 32*(1), 273–292.

Sharma, B. K. (2023). Translingual Englishes, participatory hip-hop and social media in Nepal. *World Englishes*, early view, 1–18. https://doi.org/10.1111/weng.12636

Shawel, T. (2023). "Out for presidents to represent me": Hip-hop, the breakfast club, and the 2020 presidential elections. In L. M. Bonette-Bailey & J. I. Gayles (Eds.), *Black popular culture and social justice* (pp. 95–108). Routledge.

Singh, J. N. (2021). Migration, hip hop and translation zones in Delhi. In T. K. Lee (Ed.), *The Routledge handbook of translation and the city* (pp. 308–325). Routledge.

Singh, J. N. (2022). *Transcultural voices: Narrating hip hop culture in complex Delhi*. Multilingual Matters.

Singh, J. N. (2023). Transcultural decoloniality and the study of global hip hop culture. In M. B. Solange & V. Resende (Eds.), *Coloniality in discourse studies: A radical critique* (pp. 136–154). Routledge.

Sultana, S. (2019). Linguistic and multi-modal resources within the local-global interface of the virtual space: Critically aware youths in Bangladesh. In T. Barrett & S. Dovchin (Eds.), *Critical inquiries in the studies of sociolinguistics of globalization* (pp. 1–19). Multilingual Matters.

Sultana, S. (2022). Translingual practices and national identity mediated in the semiotized digital spaces. *Journal of Australian Review of Applied Linguistics, 45*(2), 175–197.

Tamang, M. K., & Shrestha, M. (2021). Let me fly abroad: Student migrations in the context of Nepal. *Research in Educational Policy and Management, 3*(1), 1–18.

Tervo, M., & Ridanpää, J. (2016). Humor and parody in Finnish rap music videos. *European Journal of Cultural Studies, 19*(6), 616–636.

Transparency International. (2023). *Corruption perceptions index*. https://www.transparency.org/en/countries/nepal

Way, L. (2021). *Analysing politics and protest in digital popular culture: A multimodal introduction*. Sage.

Weitzer, R., & Kubrin, C. E. (2009). Misogyny in rap music: A content analysis of prevalence and meanings. *Men and Masculinities, 12*(1), 3–29.

Williams, Q. (2017). *Remix multilingualism: Hip hop, ethnography and performing marginalized voices*. Bloomsbury.

Zafarullah, H. M., & Rahman, M. H. (2002). Human rights, civil society and nongovernmental organizations: The nexus in Bangladesh. *Human Rights Quarterly, 24*(4), 1011–1034.

3
WORD-SOUND-POWER

Entanglements of Global Patwa in India

Jaspal Naveel Singh

1. Introduction

The lyrics ('word'), sonics ('sound') and politics ('power') of reggae vibrate across all four corners of the world and create distinctive opportunities for artists and fans to construct postcolonial identities and decolonial solidarities. Originating on the island of Jamaica in the mid-20th century, reggae is a spiritual and cultural music that played a crucial part in developing decolonial ideas and pan-African sensibilities in the Caribbean. As reggae became a global phenomenon in the 1970s, Jamaican music, culture, politics, religion, technology and language were transported into the world, leading to new transcultural formations and inspiring local decolonial struggles (e.g., in the South Pacific, see Shilliam, 2015). These global uptakes of reggae are thus not only musical but also linguistic and political. Artists and enthusiasts from around the world find ways to semiotically entangle globally circulating linguistic forms and meanings ('word') with musical technology and sonic aesthetics ('sound') to assume political positionality and create sociohistorical relationality ('power'). I use the term *Global Patwa* to refer to such *word-sound-power* entanglements, as well as their social evaluations, in reggae performances throughout the world.

Global Patwa is a performative type of musical speech or singing used by non-Jamaicans performing and celebrating reggae around the world. In such performances, non-Jamaican speaker-singers borrow, appropriate and approximate linguistic features of Jamaican Patwa (or Jamaican Creole) and blend them with local styles of speaking and local linguistic meanings.

In Jamaica, Patwa (also written as Patois or Patwah, also called Jamaican Creole) is a basilectal register of the Jamaican English creole continuum. It is considered the informal type of speech associated with the working-class, Black,

DOI: 10.4324/9781003441304-5

inner-city neighbourhoods of Kingston or Spanish Town that is markedly different in phonology, morpho-syntax and discursive features from more mesolectal or acrolectal registers of Jamaican English that are associated with middle-class and mixed-race Jamaicans and used in more formal contexts such as business, education and politics (Sebba, 1997). Due to its ideological associations with racialised working-class inner-city ghettos (and thereby also with the history of slavery), Jamaican Patwa was heavily stigmatised within postcolonial Jamaican society and the diaspora (Farquharson, 2007, 2015). Yet the national and international circulation of reggae and dancehall music, which heavily draws on forms of Patwa, has to some extent also valorised the register and gave it desirable, street-wise and/or spiritual indexical allure among Jamaican music and culture enthusiasts worldwide. There are currently efforts by Jamaican sociolinguists to give this covert prestige of Patwa some institutional support. For example, researchers at the University of the West Indies at Mona have established a research unit, the *Jumieka Langwij Yuunit*, and started to compile a dictionary. Rather than calling it 'Jamaican Patwa', some people and researchers started using the term 'Jamaican' or 'the Jamaican language,' a naming strategy that avoids treating Patwa as positioned at the lowest end of an English-based creole continuum (Farquharson, 2013). Moreover, several websites and social media accounts promote the institutionalisation of Jamaican, for example, a resourceful website designed by Jamaican hobby linguist Larry Cheng (http://www.jumieka.com/) or the Instagram page *Chat Patwah* (https://www.instagram.com/chattpatwah), which provides brief video lessons on specific Patwa lexical or grammatical features with over 80,000 followers worldwide. Whether such efforts are successful for creating a new standard for national identification remains to be seen. To some degree independent of such language-planning developments on the island of Jamaica itself, features of Jamaican Patwa have globalised and have become entangled within sociolinguistic realities of Jamaican as well as non-Jamaican reggae music artists and fans in different countries, such as the UK and India.

Typical linguistic borrowings used in Global Patwa include reggae and Rastafarian culture-specific lexical items (e.g., *dubplates, version, sound, Babylon, unity*) and phrases (e.g., *run it up, pull up, big up massive, give thanks and praises*), stylised Jamaican Patwa grammar (e.g., preposition *ina*, pronoun *dem*, *a*-prefixing) and approximations of Jamaican Patwa phonology (e.g., *idiot* [ˈiːdɪjʌt], *youths* [juːts]). These kinds of linguistic borrowings, appropriations and approximations are well documented in the sociolinguistic literature of global reggae (Gaudio, 2011; Moll, 2015; Levisen, 2016; Gerfer, 2018; Slade, 2018; Westphal, 2018). But more than simply a name for a specific linguistic style, repertoire or register, I understand Global Patwa as a dynamic social evaluation: its performance in a specific local context always ensues negotiations of gendered and raciolinguistic ideologies by audiences and other performers, both real and imagined ones. When non-Jamaican, and non-Black, artists and fans perform Global Patwa, they are to a greater or lesser extent subjected to social monitoring and evaluation, and even policing, by all kinds of audiences. In other words, performances of Global Patwa across the world are subject to diverse metapragmatic forces that regiment who can appropriate which elements of Jamaican Patwa for what kinds of linguistic, social and musical purposes. In my larger research project, I take a comparative view and study how and why Global Patwa performances are differently evaluated in Germany, in the UK and in India; three national contexts that have different histories of postcolonial Caribbean and Black migration and that are differently positioned in the colonial matrix of power.

In this chapter, however, I will focus my analysis of Global Patwa on one specific case study: the 2014 music video "Fever" by the Indian reggae selecta Delhi Sultanate. I use the Rasta spiritual analytic *word-sound-power* to offer decolonial sociolinguistic insights into how the song entangles global Englishes with musical technology, countercultural identities and sociohistorical relationality. I will first show how Delhi Sultanate, in his lyrics in "Fever," uses lexical and grammatical features of Jamaican Patwa and entangles them with local Indian concepts and global ways of using English, as well as with various kinds of linguistic citations. I will then show how the music video visually represents reggae culture as rooted in the local Indian ecosystem, amplified through the material technology of the soundsystem and connected to postcolonial world-systems of power/knowledge and resistance. I conclude with a reflection on analysing such semiotic entanglements.

2. Word-sound-power

Reggae music is the sonic medium of Rastafarianism, a decolonial minority religion that emerged in Jamaica in the 1930s and became popular throughout the world in the 1960s and 1970s. Reggae is thus not only a musical genre created for pop-cultural entertainment, but it is a channel for Rastafarians to express spiritual and political messages and it is also their method to attain higher states of consciousness. The concept of *word-sound-power* encapsulates this deep connection between Rasta and reggae.

Word-sound-power derives from Jamaican Rastafarian southern theory and captures the idea that "the vibrations of our speech, as well as music, have a real, tangible influence on the material world, not only in the sense of affecting social relationships" (Bean, 2014, p. 2). These material vibrations of language and music are in turn capable of contesting and resisting powerful colonial social orders of oppression, exploitation and racism. *Word-sound-power* chants down Babylon. Gomes (2021), studying Jamaican Rastafarians who repatriated to Shashamane Land in Ethiopia, explains how *word-sound-power* connects orality, performance and contestation of power to construct what the author calls Caribbean cosmopolitan sensibility:

> Ideas and sentiments of global belonging with Rastafari challenges to oppressive conditions globally and specifically in postcolonial Jamaica have been

expressed through word-sound-power, thereby demonstrating another component of a Caribbean cosmopolitan sensibility – one that is elucidated through orality. Situated within the ambiguity of creole social relations, performances of contrapuntal speech demonstrate the enactment of alternative value systems co-existing with dominant Eurocentric norms in the Caribbean – which persist in the postcolonial Caribbean with culturally dominant Afrocentric expressions inclusive of music. These forms are transnationally enacted among first- and second-generation Rastafari in Shashamane.

(Gomes, 2021, p. 28)

Similar to the transnational contrapuntal speech and the alternative value systems enacted by Jamaican Rastafarian repats living in Ethiopia, global reggae artists entangle music and language and power to construct unique cosmopolitan sensibilities for themselves and their subcultural communities. In a nutshell, we can say that the reggae *sound* can make the Rasta *word* vibrate across the world and contest unequal *power* relations induced by European colonialism. At the core of the entanglement, or better the resonances that achieves the entangling, is thus the notion of vibration, or vibe, a key cultural concept used by reggae artists throughout the world to describe how words and sounds can momentarily affect material conditions and give power to the people (for more on vibration, see Henriques, 2010; Deumert, 2023). It is important to keep in mind that the metaphor of vibration hints at the transitory or ephemeral nature of *word-sound-power* entanglements, which can only be analysed in the moment of their semiotic manifestation in the world, rather than understood as a permanently entangled structure.

Thus, the reggae cultural and Rastafarian spiritual analytic *word-sound-power* manifests as a momentary performative entanglement of language, materiality and sociohistorical relations that allows global reggae artists to construct solidarity across the postcolony and voice their identities vis-à-vis real or imagined others. I suggest that the triptych *word-sound-power* should not be read linearly or sequentially in a western fashion from left-to-right; as if the word was in the beginning (John 1:1) or in some kind of pre-discursive cognitive *origio* and then, only through human articulation, *becomes* the material sound, which then further transmits into some sort of social knowledge/power. Instead, I imagine the constellation *word-sound-power* to be linked in the manner of a rhizome, to speak with Deleuze and Guattari (1987), or, to speak closer to home with Pennycook (2017, 2020, 2024), in the form of an assemblage. Semiotic, material and social items that are part of an assemblage have no clear cause-and-effect trajectory but rather dynamically, reciprocally, rhizomatically and momentarily vibrate with one another in fairly unpredictable ways. They can even constitute one another, but one part can indeed also exist without the other parts of the assemblage and so the entanglements are not necessary conditions, but rather unexpectedly emergent vibrations, feedbacks or short circuits, which can result in excessive flows of power and power cuts. Recall the precariously tangled electrical wires above the

"Achieve Goal English" sign in Banilad, Cebu City in the Philippines, discussed in Pennycook (2020, pp. 224–225), which connect the message of the sign to various forms of power and, importantly, there is a constant risk of power cuts, or brownouts. Similarly, the *word-sound-power* entanglements of Global Patwa in India discussed in this chapter wire up linguistic performances with soundsystem technologies of voice and sound amplification and modulation that enable cultural and political messages to vibrate and connect people to celebrate global resistance to oppressive systems.

3. "Fever"

The song and music video "Fever" were released by the Indian reggae artist Delhi Sultanate in 2014. The artist is the front singer of the Indian ska band the Skavengers, but he is also the *selecta* ('selector', 'discjockey') of the soundsystem Bass Foundation Roots (BFR). Delhi Sultanate has built his own powerful set of loudspeakers that he drives around in a large van across India to play reggae music to urban youth, international travellers and local political activists (Al Jazeera, 2017). Apart from the loudspeakers, the soundsystem also comprises an amplifier, two turntables and a mixer, headphones, a microphone, dozens of cables and of course crates of seven-inch and twelve-inch vinyl records cut in Jamaica and around the world. The selecta plays reggae music on the turntables and uses the microphone to comment on the music, animate the crowd and spread political messages (see Figure 3.1). As is the case with "Fever", selectas occasionally also sing their own lyrics over *riddims* ('rhythms', 'instrumental music').

I chose to analyse "Fever" because it was among the first reggae music videos that were produced in the emerging Indian reggae scene. Although the Skavengers, playing ska music, had already released several professional music

FIGURE 3.1 Delhi Sultanate playing music on his soundsystem for the video of "Fever"

videos, "Fever" represents Delhi Sultanate and Begum X's first foray into promoting their reggae project and their BFR soundsystem, which draws on the subgenre of soundclash culture, as further explained in the following. To create the audio-visual worlds of "Fever", Delhi Sultanate, Begum X and their other collaborators created new local and global entanglements of *word-sound-power* that made it possible for viewers and listeners to imagine what Indian reggae, and soundclash culture, could sound and look like.

In his song "Fever", Delhi Sultanate sings lyrics over a riddim produced by REDS, a producer from London. The music video depicts an open-air music event, a so-called dance. Delhi Sultanate, the selecta, stands behind two turntables and a mixer, microphone in hand, singing in Global Patwa. In front of the sound system, several young Indian women and men dance to the music. Further down, I analyse the visual semiotics of the music video in more detail. In the first analytic section, though, I focus on the lyrics of the song to demonstrate how Global Patwa emerges from an entanglement of various forms of Englishes to construct cosmopolitan sensibilities that are at once connected to various sociohistorical relationalities spanning across the postcolony while also rooted in the local context.

The lyrics of "Fever" belong to a textual genre associated with a soundclash. A soundclash is a battle between two or more soundsystems who compete against each other in front of an audience that has the power to decide which soundsystem plays the better sound – better both physically through the size and the power of the soundsystem's loudspeakers as well as aesthetically through the quality of music they play. A crucial part of the soundclash is the lyrical performance of the competing selectas, who engage in verbal duels (Dundes et al., 1970) to aggrandise the self by associating one's own soundsystem with realness or cultural authenticity and denigrating (or metaphorically killing) the other soundsystem by associating it with commercialism and inauthenticity. Soundclash culture has its origins in Kingston's street nightlife culture (see, e.g., Henriques, 2010), and it is now popular around the world, including India, where several soundsystems regularly compete with each other in soundclashes.

3.1. Lyrical entanglements

The participation framework (Goffman, 1981, pp. 129–143) of the soundclash, namely the verbal duel between soundsystems in front of a listening and judging audience, gives the lyrics of "Fever" their indexical meaning. However, rather than a competition with an actual other soundsystem, the music and video of "Fever" shows how Delhi Sultanate engages in a verbal duel against an *imagined* other soundsystem, aggrandising BFR by associating it with authenticity and cultural knowledge and constructing the imagined other soundsystem as inauthentic and commercial. He achieves this lyrical construction of self and other by entangling various forms of global Englishes.

58 Entangled Englishes

In the lyrics to the song "Fever", we can find lexical, grammatical and phonological borrowings from Jamaican Patwa (underlined) as well as words and expressions that gain social meaning specifically in the Indian context (italicised). The lyrics also contain two different types of quotations, audio sampling and conversational sampling (in quotation marks). The following transcript is based on the transcript provided by the artist himself in the YouTube description, but it was expanded, ethnopoetically restructured and slightly modified by myself. When analytically relevant, I include perceptual phonetic transcriptions of lexical items.

Extract 1: Lyrics of "Fever" by Delhi Sultanate
Available at https://www.youtube.com/watch?v=gKuez2A1CIs

Audio sample of Jamaican selecta Ricky Trooper speaking

01   "Check out dem, dem nah know nuttin bout music"
02   "Computer pussy"
03   "Me a never let me sound back to dat bloodclat ear-service sound"
04   "Dem cyan tell me nuttin"
05   "Me have a true amplifier man a play sound from"

Delhi Sultanate:

06   Jah Jah
07   Fever
08   Ayo jump man sound
09   Fever
10   Tell dem

Ricky Trooper:

11   "Me a love dat some boombaclat man"

Delhi Sultanate:

12   Fever
13   Burn'em em em em make dem run for the thermometer
14   Hotter [ˈatə] than the water weh go boil ina mi *geyser*
15   Badder than anopheles mosquito weh give dem di malaria [məˈliːɹə]
16   A sound get bad up – beg fi di anaesthesia
17   Bring the news like *Al Jazeera*
18   Send dem ina di morgue we send dem deep down ina di freezer
19   Co- co- co- cold
20   My sound it have the city pon lock
21   Bare dubplates and heavy tunes we a go drop
22   Commercialists dem all a flip up and flop
23   Real sound ah real sound and idiot ah idiot [ˈiːdɪjʌt]

24   Remember: "sound no make sense if de selecta no deh behind it"
25   When Junior Reid said: "sound no make sense if de selecta no deh behind it"
26   Well let me tell you weh some real sound mean
27   Man a represent and we nah sell out fi di cream (i.e., money)
28   Plus we're down with *jungle, jal and zameen*
29   Strictly reggaematical soldier pon mi team
30   Remember: "sound no make sense"
31   We beg nothing from dem
32   Problem from the root to the fruit to the stem
33   Reggaematical truths [tɹuːts] for the youths [juːts] dem
34   And if a sound try and test – we gwine execute dem
35   Badang bang a billie bang
36   Shalalalalalaw
37   Shalalalalalalalaw

Delhi Sultanate's lyrics make heavy use of lexical items that can be regarded as borrowings from Jamaican Patwa and global reggae talk (see underlined words and phrases in the transcript). These include concept nouns such as *dubplates*, meaning records custom made for particular selectas, and *tunes*, meaning publicly available records (line 21); *reggaematical*, meaning a spiritual logic derived from reggae music (lines 29 and 33); and *sound*, meaning a soundsystem or a group of selectas running and representing a particular soundsystem.

   The lyrics of "Fever" also include morpho-syntactical features that are clearly indexical of Jamaican Patwa grammar. Prepositions such as *pon* and *ina*, pronouns like *weh* and *dem* and *a*-prefixing are used throughout the lyrics, as are morphological features such as the comparative adjective *badder* and Jamaican phrasal chunks such as *bad up*. Finally, there are also certain lexical items that are not borrowed from Jamaican *per se*, yet the way Delhi Sultanate pronounces them makes them indexical of Jamaican phonology. For example, the phonological realisations of the lexical items *hotter* [ˈatə], *idiot* [ˈiːdɪjʌt] or *youths* [juːts]. It is thus important for any analysis of Global Patwa lexical borrowing to consider also how words are pronounced by performers.

   The lexical items that I have identified as borrowed in some way or another from Jamaican Patwa are entangled in these lyrics in several further ways. For example, we can identify instances of citations or sampling. The song starts with an audio sample from Ricky Trooper, a legendary Jamaican selecta who is famous for his explicit disrespect against his opponents in the soundclash. The Ricky Trooper sample can be seen as a coda to the song "Fever", in the sense that it sets up the song as belonging to soundsystem culture, where verbal duels are to be expected. Trooper's use of explicit gendered language ("computer pussy") also constructs a discourse of techno-historical authenticity, in which selectas who use the latest computers and digital devices are emasculated as pussies, which carries the implications that those selectas who still use the original vinyl records and analogue soundsystems from back in the days, like Ricky Trooper and Delhi Sultanate, are in turn regarded as more authentic. We can find another form of citation in the lyrics, what Roth-Gordon (2009) has called conversational sampling. In this citational form, lyrics of famous artists are verbally quoted or paraphrased in conversations or musical performances. In lines 24, 25 and 30, Delhi Sultanate quotes a lyric by the famous Jamaican reggae artist Junior Reid, which much like the Ricky Trooper sample at the beginning, connects the song to soundsystem culture and discourses of authenticity. This performative sampling thus, in a Bakhtinian way, incorporates in the singer's own lyrical voice a voice of the other. By sampling the voices of legendary artists from Jamaica, Delhi Sultanate arguably authenticates his own Global Patwa competence by showcasing his knowledge of Jamaican artists and their ways of speaking. Citations are also a way to show respect to those who have come before him and have inspired him.

The Global Patwa performance of "Fever" not only orients to an exocentric norm of Jamaican Patwa through borrowing, approximation and citation but also uses at least three lexical items that are indexical of the local context in India: *geyser* (line 14), *Al Jazeera* (line 17) and *jungle, jal and zameen* (line 28). *Geyser* is the Indian English word for a device that generates hot water in houses, which is often called 'boiler' in other places. Delhi Sultanate uses the term to construct a simile that aggrandises his own soundsystem which is metaphorically hot and can metaphorically burn (line 13) other soundsystems. Whether or not Delhi Sultanate wanted to intentionally localise his lyrics within the Indian context by using the term *geyser* remains unclear. Poetically, it is clear that the term *geyser* rhymes with the song title *fever* and the other rhyming words used in the opening section of the song (lines 13–18). Moreover, in his own rendering of the lyrics, Delhi Sultanate spelled the term as *geezer*, which is a homophone of *geyser* but semantically refers to an undefined male person. In my re-transcription of the lyrics, I changed the spelling to *geyser* because in my mind it made more sense in the context of the lyrics. A second and semantically associated meaning of the word *geyser* is of course a hot natural spring, yet, given the possessive pronoun *me*, it is unlikely that Delhi Sultanate here refers to geysers in nature. Inspired by Pennycook's (2020) discussion of the supposedly Philippine English term *brownout*, I understand the aim of an analysis of entanglements to follow a sign's indexical traces, not to ontologically pin down its meanings or finitely determine its provenance.

The other two lexemes indexical of India, however, are much more likely candidates for intentional localisation. *Al Jazeera* is a global private news media company based in Doha, Qatar, which centres Middle Eastern, Arab and Islamic world issues. Over the last twenty years, Al Jazeera has been an important news media counterbalance to the global dominance of western media companies such as CNN or the BBC (Sadig & Petcu, 2019; Seib, 2008). In India, Al Jazeera has played an important role providing an alternative perspective within the country's mediascape, which can appear as either imitative of western media outlets or growlingly right-wing and Hindu nationalist. In fact, some Hindutva right-wing supporters and activists call to restrict Al Jazeera broadcasts in India because the channel's centring of Muslim issues is seen as disrupting social harmony between religions (Dhillon, 2023). The tune "Fever" was released in 2014, the year the Hindu nationalist party BJP, with Prime Minister Narendra Modi, came to power, which ensued a range of rhetorical, legal and sociocultural processes that aimed to marginalise India's Muslim population (Puniyani, 2018; Singh, 2020). Delhi Sultanate's choice of mentioning Al Jazeera as an example of a bringer of news can thus be seen as a counter-hegemonic strategy within the current Islamophobic context of Indian politics. In this way, Delhi Sultanate marks himself as attuned to the struggles of and solidarity with the Muslim population of India. Note also that the artist's name *Delhi Sultanate* refers to the late medieval Indo-Islamic empire that was established in India by renegade slave-generals of central Asian invaders. The historical Delhi Sultanate (1206–1526) was the first Indo-Islamic empire, the second being the Mughal Empire (1526–1857).

The third lexical item with localising indexicality is the phrase *jungle, jal and zameen*, which is Urdu/Hindi and means 'forest, water and land', and it is a slogan that encapsulates the three main demands of Adivasi (i.e., tribal or indigenous) communities who have populated India since thousands of years and who now find themselves surrounded by corporate interests of mineral extraction and occupied by a modern nation-state that privileges caste-Hindu culture and marginalises tribal life as backward and in need of development (Bharadwaj, 2019). Delhi Sultanate is an active supporter of Adivasi demands for autonomy and the demands of the revolutionary Naxalite movement, a Maoist insurgency group. By embedding this highly politicised slogan into his Global Patwa performance, Delhi Sultanate connects local Indian anti-colonial liberation movements to global reggae music's political message of resistance and unity, which is in itself rooted in Rastafarian and Jamaican calls for Black liberation and Pan-Africanism. In a published interview in the magazine *Critical Legal Thinking*, Delhi Sultanate discusses these (partly incidental) entanglements between Indian and Jamaican freedom struggles. He links the symbolism of the Rastafarian colours red, gold and green with the Adivasi and Naxalite demand for jungle, jal and zameen.

> For me there are also clear links between the forces that underpin Reggae music and things that are happening in India today. The colours red, gold and green have concrete meaning here, incidentally the first national flag of India or the flag of the revolutionary Gaddar [*sic.*] party also featured Red, Gold and Green. Red stands for the blood of the martyrs, green stands for natural abundance, and gold stands for the wealth that is inside the earth. To me, this is equivalent to the tribal slogan which is echoed by the Naxal movement of 'Jungle, Jal and Zameen' (forest, water and land). We need to take back control of the resources that sustain our lives. Maybe others will also perceive these conceptual connections and will also be able to draw strength and inspiration from it . . . and build networks of solidarity?
>
> *(Delhi Sultanate, quoted in Eslava & Pahuja, 2017, n.p.)*

The various lyrical entanglements – lexical, grammatical and phonological borrowings, citations, localising lexemes – that I have described in this section give us a glimpse of how global reggae artists use various globally circulating and locally rooted linguistic and sonic resources to construct unique postcolonial identities and decolonial solidarities and thereby contest dominant power structures. The soundsystem can thus be seen as a technological affordance for words and sounds to be amplified and vibrate together in order to circulate cultural and political messages of unity and resistance against colonial injustices. Such *word-sound-power* entanglements are also visually represented in the music video to "Fever", to which I turn next.

3.2. Visual entanglements

The music video to "Fever" depicts a *dance* (a gathering where reggae music is played) in an open-air space in India. The dance represents the people's momentary, ephemeral and embodied experience of word-sound-power, which the video aims to capture through its cinematography. The main protagonist is Delhi Sultanate, who stands behind two turntables and a mixer with a microphone in his hand singing the lyrics (see Figure 3.1). The video opens with a shot showing the unmanned soundsystem. In the visual semiotics of the video, the soundsystem technology thus becomes the given information (the theme) upon which the rest of the visual storyline (the rheme) builds (Kress & van Leeuwen, 1996, pp. 186–191). In this opening scene, we can see various technological devices connected with cables sitting on wooden furniture that is set up in front of the trunk of a large bodhi tree with its aerial roots (Figure 3.2).

The camera then pans up to focus on a langur monkey sitting on the branches of the bodhi tree (Figure 3.3). The monkey has a leash around the neck, which marks it as a domesticated animal, quite literally entangled with human life. The branch of the tree has a red cable wrapped up around it. The cable, the viewer later learns,

FIGURE 3.2 The soundsystem with cables in front of a bodhi tree with its aerial roots

FIGURE 3.3   A close-up of a langur monkey with a lead around the neck, sitting on the bodhi tree; a red cable connected to a microphone is wrapped around a branch

is used both as the electric channel and the suspension of the microphone used by Delhi Sultanate to sing his lyrics over the music.

Bodhi trees are a common sight in northern Indian cities and villages. These trees, with their distinctive aerial roots connecting the branches with the ground, can create vast spaces of shade. To avoid the hot sun during the day, one can often observe how iterant street vendors or artisans gather under bodhi trees, thus creating informal marketplaces where people come together to eat, drink tea, get haircuts and so on. The bodhi tree also has spiritual and historical significance in India because it is said that the Buddha received enlightenment when meditating under a bodhi tree (Jones, 2022). In fact, the tree derives its name from the Sanskrit word *bodhi*, which means 'enlightenment' or 'awakening'. In the geosemiotics (Scollon & Scollon, 2003) of the music video, the bodhi tree provides a stage-like backdrop for the main protagonist and entangles the soundsystem technology with the ecosystem of the place in which the dance is happening.

In the first part of the music video, we can see the *massive* (the crowd of dancers) of around ten young people dancing in front of the soundsystem, while Delhi Sultanate is controlling the sound and singing his lyrics into the microphone dangling from the branches of the tree (see Figure 3.4). The massive consists of men and women, dressed casually, dancing and enjoying themselves. Readers familiar with Indian reggae and hip hop artists might recognise familiar faces in the massive. For example, we can see Begum X, Delhi Sultanate's partner and the second half of the BFR soundsystem. We can also see Diggydang and Mr. Herbalist from the Reggae Rajahs, another Indian soundsystem, as well as B-Boy Ashu, a hip-hop breakdancer and event organiser. The dance is thus depicted as an intimate space where friends and fellow artists can come together to enjoy music.

In the second half of the music video, we can see the participants of the dance taking a break. Two women are shown sitting or lying on traditional Indian outdoor

64 Entangled Englishes

FIGURE 3.4 The massive dancing in front of the soundsystem

beds (*charpays*), reading critical decolonial literature: the Brazilian educator Paulo Freire's (1970/2001) *Pedagogy of the Oppressed*, the Indian historian Sumanta Banerjee's (1980) *In the Wake of Naxalbari: A History of the Naxalite Movement in India* and the Martinican psychiatrist and political philosopher Frantz Fanon's (1952/2008) *Black Skin, White Masks* (Figure 3.5). The choice of books depicted in this scene connects various histories of resistance against colonial oppression across the Global South. The scene of women reading critical decolonial books casts reggae dances not just as parties of embodied joy, musical celebration and masculine verbal duels but also as spaces of learning, contemplation and raising political consciousness. In an interview, Delhi Sultanate comments:

> The function of these exercises then would be to rupture and undermine the dominant discourse. To foster a sense of unity and strength in ourselves and our

Word-sound-power 65

FIGURE 3.5   Women reading revolutionary books

audience. To celebrate each other. To sing and to dance. Wherever we set up our sound system, we also set up a book stall with revolutionary books, films and stickers so a certain world of thought is always present at our dances.

(Delhi Sultanate, quoted in Eslava & Pahuja, 2017, n.p.)

The inclusion of signifiers of revolutionary thinking, in the form of books, films and political messaging, disrupts mainstream discourses that trivialise reggae as an insignificant youth pop-culture. Importantly, the choice of staging women as readers of these revolutionary books also disrupts reggae-internal discourses that associate reggae and especially soundclash culture with hegemonic masculinity.

In the final part of the video, the sun has set over the dance, and the massive has lit torches and put on anonymous masks (Figure 3.6), also called Guy Fawkes masks, that were popularised in the film *V for Vendetta* (McTeigue, 2005) and subsequently used by the Occupy movement, a global anti-capitalist awakening that emerged after the financial crash in 2008. The anonymous mask became a political icon of the so-called 99%, the vast majority of common people who are being exploited by the 1%, the super-rich finance elites, banks and multinational business magnates who accumulate most of the wealth of this world (Koch, 2014). The dancers' wearing of anonymous masks visually entangles the Indian reggae scene with contemporary global protest movements. The torches and the blazes of fire mark the dancers as revolutionaries getting ready to burn down colonial systems of oppression – burning down Babylon, a central theme of reggae music and Rasta consciousness (Cooper, 2004). Enticed by the power of the words and the sounds they hear emanating from the soundsystem during the day, and informed by their reading of revolutionary decolonial literature, the massive transforms the open-air

FIGURE 3.6 The selecta and the massive wearing anonymous masks and carrying torches

dance into a revolutionary space at night. This transformation from musical celebration to political uprising visually depicts how the vibrations of words and sound are entangled with resistance against systems of power and oppression.

4. Conclusion

The diverse lyrical and visual *word-sound-power* entanglements analysed in this chapter challenge positivistic models of semiotic analysis that suggest that we can fully disentangle the material effects of language use. While the very idea of 'analysis' of course involves some degree of dissection or disentanglement, semiotic entanglements should be handled carefully by analysts so as to avoid putting at risk the organically grown and locally rooted moments of resisting colonial power and tactics for creating autonomy. Trying to bring too much order or structure into semiotic entanglements runs the risk of causing power cuts and disenabling people on the ground to run their own systems, amplify their own voices and resist colonial injustice in ways that are unique to their cultural identities.

In this chapter, I have attempted an analysis of the *word-sound-power* entanglements in the lyrics and the music video of "Fever" by Delhi Sultanate without arriving at a conclusion of what these entanglements exactly mean or how exactly they work together. However, I hinted at what they might do for the participants in the moment of their vibration. I suggested that the semiotic entanglements allow Delhi Sultanate to construct postcolonial identities and decolonial solidarities. In the song and the video, language, music, materiality, technology and politics are entangled in ways that are both globally connected and locally rooted. Borrowing from the Jamaican language is only one – albeit an important – element of such entanglements of Global Patwa; references to Indian resistance politics, reading decolonial literature and using makeshift technology all play their part in allowing the entanglement to vibrate.

India and Jamaica share a common history of being subjected to British colonial and imperial rule. As a result, people in the two countries share world-political reference points, cultural tastes, such as love for cricket, as well as command over English-language resources, although in starkly different ways. In Jamaica, English has fully creolised into Jamaican Patwa and is the first language of most Jamaicans, while in India English is used mostly as an additional language. Another aspect worth considering here is that Indian indentured servants who were transported to Jamaica after the abolition of slavery might have had a direct influence on the establishment of the Rastafarian religion in the early 20th century. All this is to say that there are multiple sociohistorical links between India and Jamaica that Indian reggae artists like Delhi Sultanate can draw on to construct decolonial relationality and south-south solidarity through his lyrics and music. In my future research, I will investigate if and how such decolonial solidarities are differently established in the Global Patwa performances of German and British reggae artists, who speak-sing from very different positions in the postcolonial matrix of power.

Acknowledgements

I dedicate this chapter to the memory of Manuel Guissemo, Mozambiquan hiphopographer and sociolinguist, who left this earth way before his time. Rest in power. I would like to thank the British Academy and Leverhulme Trust for kindly funding my research project *Global Patwa: Raciolinguistic Appropriations of Jamaican Language Features in British, German and Indian Reggae Cultures* under award number: SRG23\231090.

References

Al Jazeera. (2017). *India's reggae resistance defending dissent under Modi*. Documentary. https://www.aljazeera.com/program/witness/2017/5/22/indias-reggae-resistance-defending-dissent-under-modi

Banerjee, S. (1980). *In the wake of Naxalbari: A history of the Naxalite movement in India*. Subarnarekha.

Bean, B. (2014). *"I-and-I Vibration": Word-sound-power in Rastafarian music and reasoning* [MA thesis, Goucher College, Philadelphia, PA].

Bharadwaj, S. (2019). Adivasi struggles in Chhattisgarh: "Jal, Jungle, Zameen". In V. Sachdeva, Q. Pradhan & A. Venugopalan (Eds.), *Identities in South Asia: Conflicts and assertions* (pp. 161–174). Routledge.

Cooper, C. (2004). *Sound clash: Jamaican dancehall culture at large*. Palgrave Macmillan.

Deleuze, G., & Guattari, F. (1987). *A thousand plateaus: Capitalism and schizophrenia* (B. Massumi, Trans.). University of Minnesota Press.

Deumert, A. (2023). Positive vibrations: Voice, sound, and resonance as insurgency. *Critical Inquiry in Language Studies*, *20*(4), 408–425.

Dhillon, A. (2023, July 16). Indian court halts airing of documentary on Muslim minority. *The Guardian*. https://www.theguardian.com/world/2023/jun/16/indian-court-halts-airing-of-documentary-on-muslim-minority

Dundes, A., Leach, J. W., & Özkök, B. (1970). The strategy of Turkish boys' verbal dueling rhymes. *The Journal of American Folklore*, *83*, 325–349.

Eslava, L., & Pahuja, S. (2017). A world of "sound" and "clash": An interview with Taru Dalmia. *Critical Legal Thinking: Law and the Political*. https://criticallegalthinking.com/2017/04/03/world-of-sound-and-clash-interview-with-taru-dalmia-part-1/

Fanon, F. (1952/2008). *Black skin, white masks*. Pluto.

Farquharson, J. T. (2007). Folk linguistics and post-colonial language politricks in Jamaica. In E. A. Anchimbe (Ed.), *Linguistic identity in postcolonial multilingual spaces* (pp. 248–264). Cambridge Scholars.

Farquharson, J. T. (2013). Jamaican. In S. M. Michaelis, P. Maurer, M. Haspelmath & M. Huber (Eds.), *The survey of pidgin and creole languages* (Vol. 1, pp. 81–91). Oxford University Press.

Farquharson, J. T. (2015). The Black man's burden? Language and political economy in a diglossic state and beyond. *Zeitschrift für Anglistik und Amerikanistik*, *63*(2), 157–177.

Freire, P. (1970/2001). *Pedagogy of the oppressed*. Bloomsbury.

Gaudio, R. (2011). The blackness of "Broken English". *Journal of Linguistic Anthropology*, *21*(2), 230–246.

Gerfer, A. (2018). Global reggae and the appropriation of Jamaican Creole. *World Englishes*, *37*(4), 668–683.

Goffman, E. (1981). *Forms of talk*. University of Pennsylvania Press.

Gomes, S. (2021). *Cosmopolitanism from the Global South: Caribbean spiritual repatriation to Ethiopia*. Palgrave Macmillan.

Henriques, J. (2010). The vibrations of affect and their propagation on a night out on Kingston's dancehall scene. *Body and Society*, *16*(1), 57–89.

Jones, D. T. (2022). The tree, the snake and the goddess: Symbols of the Buddha's relationship with nature. *Worldviews: Global Religions, Culture, and Ecology*, *27*(1–2), 25–56.

Koch, C. M. (2014). Occupying popular culture: Anonymous, Occupy Wall Street, and the Guy Fawkes mask as a political icon. *REAL Yearbook of Research in English and American Literature*, *30*(1), 445–482.

Kress, G., & Van Leeuwen, T. (1996). *Reading images: The grammar of visual design*. Routledge.

Levisen, C. (2016). The social and sonic semantics of reggae: Language ideology and emergent socialities in postcolonial Vanuatu. *Language and Communication*, *52*, 102–116.

McTeigue, J. (2005). *V for Vendetta* [film]. Warner Bros.

Moll, A. (2015). *Jamaican Creole goes web: Sociolinguistic styling and authenticity in a digital 'yaad'*. John Benjamins.

Pennycook, A. (2017). Translanguaging and semiotic assemblages. *International Journal of Multilingualism*, *14*(3), 269–282.

Pennycook, A. (2020). Translingual entanglements of English. *World Englishes*, *39*(2), 222–235.

Pennycook, A. (2024). *Language assemblages*. Cambridge University Press.

Puniyani, R. (2018). Muslims and the politics of exclusion. In A. Shaban (Ed.), *Lives of Muslims in India: Politics, exclusion and violence* (pp. 66–87). Routledge.

Roth-Gordon, J. (2009). Conversational sampling, race trafficking, and the invocation of the *gueto* in Brazilian hip hop. In H. S. Alim, A. Ibrahim & A. Pennycook (Eds.), *Global linguistic flows: Hip hop cultures, youth identities, and the politics of language* (pp. 63–77). Routledge.

Sadig, H. B., & Petcu, C. (2019). The history of Al Jazeera. In H. Sadig (Ed.), *Al Jazeera in the gulf and in the world* (pp. 1–33). Palgrave Macmillan.

Scollon, R., & Wong Scollon, S. (2003). *Discourses in place: Language in the material world*. Routledge.

Sebba, M. (1997). *Contact languages: Pidgins and creoles*. Macmillan.

Seib, P. (2008). *The Al Jazeera effect: How the new global media are reshaping world politics*. Potomac.

Shilliam, R. (2015). *The Black Pacific: Anti-colonial struggles and Oceanic connections*. Bloomsbury.

Singh, J. N. (2020). The sociolinguistic saffronisation of India. In I. Theodoropoulou & J. Tovar (Eds.), *Research companion to language and country branding* (pp. 57–71). Routledge.

Slade, B. (2018). Overstandin Idren: Special features of Rasta talk morphology. *Journal of Pidgin and Creole Languages*, *33*(2), 280–306.

Westphal, M. (2018). Pop culture and the globalization of non-standard varieties of English: Jamaican Creole in German reggae subculture. In V. Werner (Ed.), *The language of pop culture* (pp. 95–115). Routledge.

4
ENTANGLEMENTS WITHIN COVID-19 LINGUISTIC LANDSCAPES IN KYOTO, JAPAN

Yumi Matsumoto and Ivan Jin

1. Introduction

Beginning in early 2020, nearly everyone's lives were significantly impacted by the COVID-19 pandemic. Our languages, communicative practices, and lifestyles changed drastically. Despite this shared experience, many particularities of how people dealt with the pandemic – including how public health policies were enacted and communicated – probably differed based on each community's histories, linguistic and cultural norms, and local ideologies. This study explores how languages, cultures, embodiment, objects, spaces (including virtual space), histories, and ideologies are *entanglements* (e.g., Pennycook, 2020), which will be illustrated through an examination of the COVID-19 signage in Kyoto, Japan. More specifically, we closely analyze the complex intra-actions or interconnectedness of diverse languages, cultures, histories, objects, and ideologies – as assemblage – that are embedded within COVID-19 signs, situated in Kyoto during the most chaotic period of the pandemic in Japan (the summer of 2021).

Recently, a series of linguistic landscape (LL) studies (e.g., Dunn et al., 2021; Hopkyns & van den Hoven, 2021; Marshall, 2021; also see the special issues on COVID-19-related LL by Lou et al., 2022; Ogiermann, 2023) documented drastic changes in linguistic signage, for example, an abrupt shift to monolingual norms in various geographical contexts (e.g., Canada, Saudi Arabia) during the earlier phase of the pandemic, possibly due to travel restrictions, followed by a gradual shift to multilingual signage. In the case of Japan, however, there have been only a few investigations of COVID-19 LL phenomena (e.g., Ike & Hori, 2023; Nakamura, 2022), mostly focusing on quantitative analyses or examining the pragmatic aspects of signs. To get a better and deeper understanding of COVID-19 LL and sign meanings in Japan, specifically in Kyoto, we attempt to illuminate what kinds

DOI: 10.4324/9781003441304-6

of meanings and relations these COVID-19 signs encompass from the perspective of *entanglement* (e.g., Pennycook, 2020) and how these signs, as entangled assemblages, contribute to communicative practices – for example, for disseminating public health regulation information – during the summer of 2021.

Kyoto is a unique place renowned nationally and internationally for its distinctive culture, with a history of over 1,000 years as the ancient capital of Japan, serving as the representative of Japanese culture (see, e.g., International Relations Office, General Planning Bureau of Kyoto City, 2013). We analyze the LL of Kyoto, focusing on inscriptions of languages, cultures (e.g., religions), embodiment, material objects, histories, and ideologies that are intricately *entangled* within such signage, revealing ephemeral but nonetheless complex meanings and local people's stances toward the social changes brought by COVID-19 in the summer of 2021. Generally, the signage from our data seems to collectively demonstrate people's efforts to interpret and address COVID-19 phenomena by (re)contextualizing them into the specific history and culture of local communities and identities. This study suggests the benefits of employing entanglement, which enables us to reveal many possible layers (often invisible ones, which include language, materiality, spatiality, culture, history, and ideology) or relationships within signs that contribute to the meanings and communicative practices.

2. Studying COVID-19 linguistic landscapes through entanglement

In this section, we first discuss entanglement as a concept for analyzing and understanding multi-layered entities or relations within signage and their communicative practices. In the second section, we review LL research that examines impacts and consequences of various social phenomena, including language-related discourse (e.g., multilingualism) and ideological aspects (e.g., geopolitics, neoliberalism), and then discuss LL research on the COVID-19 pandemic in particular.

2.1. *Entanglements for examining the semiotic practices of signs*

Semiotic practices, including texts and public signs (which entail text-based and object-based ones), are indeed complex, situated phenomena (Scollon & Scollon, 2003). Signs, including public signs related to COVID-19 in this study, encompass complex and multilayered meanings. To study these signs and their meanings in depth, we employ the concept of *entanglement* (similar to sociomaterial *assemblages,* e.g., Toohey et al., 2015; also see Pennycook, 2020, for a discussion of associated concepts) as the major theoretical and analytical guide. In fact, entanglement and assemblage might differ due to their disciplinary origins (entanglement from quantum physics, see, e.g., Barad, 2007, and assemblage from philosophy, e.g., Deleuze & Guattari, 1987). Assemblage tends to highlight how a communicative event *relates to* the social world *at a particular moment* (a temporary, *ad hoc* amalgamation of heterogenous things), while entanglement often underscores how a communicative event is *intertwined with* various elements in the social world *over time* (historically constructed connections, connotations, and confluences). However, they share core principles. That is, both notions search for 'connections' and 'associations' within all elements (i.e., relational science), and they also question pre-existing categories/divisions and emphasize the extremely difficult nature of separating each entity, revealing the process of 'becoming' as a whole.

The notion of entanglement enables us to "shift the sociolinguistic focus towards a more profound sense of interconnectedness" (Pennycook, 2018, p. 225). Pennycook (2020) also argued that understanding the meaning of context from entanglement is different from the sociolinguistic meaning of context, which often involves a static relationship between (linguistic) settings and assumed languages (e.g., the default use of the Japanese language in Japan). Furthermore, the notion of entanglement aligns well with *new materialist* perspectives (e.g., Bennett, 2010), highlighting the critical role of nonhumans and objects in the meaning-making process. Therefore, it urges us to pay more attention to the complexity of sociolinguistic events or contexts, where a wide array of elements (languages, human bodies, physical and virtual environments, material objects, histories, ideologies, and more) – many of which are often invisible – are entangled with one another. Therefore, the notion of entanglement provides analytical power to examine local communicative practices of English(es) that involve many entities intertwined within signs. It enables us to consider many possible relationships deeply embedded in signs, which are usually difficult to disentangle through perspectives of World Englishes (Bolton, 2021; Kachru, 1992) or English as a lingua franca (e.g., Jenkins, 2015; Seidlhofer, 2011) that tend to mostly focus on studying linguistic aspects.

In short, through a lens of entanglement, signs are conceived as an amalgamation of things (e.g., languages, objects, embodiment, histories, cultures, spaces, ideologies including political relations) or simultaneous assemblage, situated in a specific place, at a specific time, and for specific people. Entanglement enables us to deepen our understanding of complex local 'context' that contributes to the meaning-making practices of signs (see also Blommaert, 2017). It can serve as a powerful framework for examining COVID-19 LL signs, disentangling complex meanings, and deepening an understanding of local communicative practices involving English and other languages (e.g., Japanese).

2.2. Researching linguistic landscapes in the time of the COVID-19 pandemic

LL research generally explores patterns of public signage (e.g., language choices, dominant and minority languages) and examines sign meanings situated in specific contexts and times, which include natural disasters (e.g., earthquakes, *tsunamis*, see Tan & Ben-Said, 2015; Uekusa, 2019) and protests (e.g., in Bosnia-Herzegovina, Bilkic, 2018; in the Philippines, Monje, 2017). Recently, due to the significant impact of COVID-19 on society, many researchers (e.g., Hopkyns & van den Hoven, 2021; Kalocsányiová et al., 2023; Zhang et al., 2020) have investigated the COVID-19 LL in various geographical contexts (e.g., Canada, China, the U.K.). Common themes that emerged from these studies include: (1) the prominence of English as a 'default' lingua franca (e.g., Marshall, 2021; Kalocsányiová et al., 2023), (2) access problems due to limited language choices in signage (e.g., Hopkyns & van den Hoven, 2021; Nakamura, 2022), and (3) the incorporation of local contexts (e.g., cultural, political, social) in producing signs (e.g., Douglas, 2022; Marshall, 2021).

While the prevalence of English in public signage has been common since the early days of LL research (e.g., Backhaus, 2006; Cenoz & Gorter, 2006), several COVID-19 LL studies showed that the pandemic further accentuated this trend. For example, both Marshall (2021) and Kalocsányiová et al. (2023) reported a lack of visibility of non-English COVID-19 signage in Canada and the U.K., respectively, despite the existence of diverse multilingual populations in those countries. Even in countries where English is neither the official nor the most-spoken language, English tends to be conceived as the default or ideal lingua franca in signage for disseminating important virus-related regulations and guidelines. In fact, researchers have suggested different views regarding the dominance of English in COVID-19 LL. Some (e.g., Lacsina & Yeh, 2022) argued that the use of English signifies a nation's or a city's effort to facilitate better communication among foreigners and survive global competition, while others (e.g., Hopkyns & van den Hoven, 2021; Marshall, 2021) interpreted it as an inevitable choice during times of crisis, but one that can contribute to linguistic inequality. We argue that simply acknowledging the dominance of English within signage might overlook the opportunity to fully examine the complex dynamics between English as a global language and other local language practices that co-exist in each context.

Therefore, it is critical for LL research to understand how English *interconnects* with other languages and semiotic elements *in situ* rather than examining only what is visible in signs on the surface. In this chapter, we build off the aforementioned studies (Douglas, 2022; Marshall, 2021) that focus on the integration of local characteristics into sign making processes, (re)contextualizing the COVID-19 phenomenon within the distinctive identities of each community. Such integration illuminates how signage can be interpreted as *assemblages* that bring together various elements, including cultural symbols, political relationships, and social practices in a cohesive manner. When examining signs as entanglement (Pennycook, 2020), we might be able to better interpret how signs embody social, cultural, material, ideological relations in a complex but integrated manner.

3. Research context and methods

Our study was conducted in Kyoto, one of the most famous cities in Japan. As suggested in the introduction, Kyoto attracts both domestic and international tourists due to its distinctive culture and history. However, the pandemic almost completely ceased international tourism in Kyoto because of travel restrictions (Onuki, 2020). Furthermore, the government in Kyoto imposed rigid measures on local shops, restaurants, and other businesses. At the time of our data collection (July and August 2021), restaurants were required to close at 8 pm and were prohibited from serving alcohol (Kyoto Prefectural Government, 2021), which severely affected their sales.

Three researchers (including the first author of this study) identified and collected 761 COVID-19 related signs from a downtown district of Kyoto called *Shijo Karasuma*. During data collection, we classified the 761 signs into two types: (1) 608 *individual* signs and (2) 153 *collage* signs, or a collection of signs that construct specific meanings as a whole. This classification allows us to understand signage as entangled assemblages even during the preliminary phase of our study. Out of the 608 individual signs, 489 signs are monolingual Japanese, and 119 signs are multilingual (entailing any language other than Japanese) (see Backhaus, 2006). It is evident that monolingual Japanese signs outnumber multilingual ones (e.g., English) in our data, likely related to the significant decline in tourism in Kyoto due to travel bans and restrictions at the time.

Semi-structured interviews with local sign producers (e.g., restaurant owners, government officials) and sign readers (e.g., local residents) were also conducted, providing additional *emic* perspectives (besides our analysts' views) on local meanings and community interactions with these signs. This ethnographic approach, combined with the theoretical and analytical lens of entanglement, allows us to understand how signs reflect local sociocultural realities during the pandemic and how those meanings are intricately related to many embedded elements (e.g., ideology, history, embodied practice) within signage.

4. Analyzing COVID-19 signs in Kyoto through entanglement

In this section, we analyze four COVID-19 signs in depth, zooming in on ones that reveal intriguing sociohistorical, cultural, spatial, political, and economic relations and connections. We specifically select signs that encompass elements that index local identities involving Kyoto and/or Japan by integrating researchers' and sign makers' and readers' perspectives (which are also conceived as entanglements).

We begin with an analysis of a sign posted at a bank in Kyoto that includes a phrase regarding new public health etiquette, which was promoted locally, nationally, and globally during the pandemic (Figure 4.1). The figure shows drawings of two of this bank's cute mascots participating in 'social distancing.' The characters are separated, or distanced, by a two-way arrow. The message above the arrow is "ソーシャルディスタンス" (*sōsharu disutansu*, meaning 'social distancing'); the message below the arrow is "距離をあけよう!" ('Let's keep our distance!'). In short, these two mascots are enacting a new embodied practice, social distancing, for protecting the public. The phrase, "ソーシャルディスタンス" ('social distance'), written in *katakana*, signifies its *foreign* origin (not from the Japanese).

Entanglements within COVID-19 linguistic landscapes in Kyoto 75

FIGURE 4.1 "ソーシャルディスタンス" ('social distance') at a bank; original (left) and translation (right)

One intriguing aspect related to entanglement is the fact that the phrase "ソーシャルディスタンス" is written in *katakana*. As mentioned, *katakana* is one of the Japanese writing systems used specifically for loanwords or words of foreign origin. It can be interpreted that this phrase originates from English, and this sign seems to have socio-historical and political undercurrents. Historically, Japan has had a dependent relationship and close ties with the United States in terms of trade, security, and politics (see, e.g., Rosecrance, 1993), which might also influence linguistic and communicative practices in Japan, particularly the ideological dominance of English and Western culture. The Constitution of Japan was enacted under the U.S. occupation after World War II (WWII), considering Japan's past imperialism and strong nationalism during WWII. During the time, the Japanese government directed the use of translated words instead of English loanwords, requiring the use of Japanese only.

In fact, the notion of 'Westernization/Americanization = modernization = internationalization' has long existed in Japan (see, e.g., Tsuda, 1990, 2003), as early as the Meiji Restoration (1986), and such an equation was further intensified after WWII. Japanese people have internalized this ideology, which might contribute to creating hegemonic relationships (Phillipson, 1992; Tsuda, 1990, 2003) and a hierarchy of Western/American linguistic and cultural values over others in society. One example is the prevalence of English loanwords in Japanese (see, e.g., Olah, 2007), and Japanese people have long desired to learn and acquire English for internationalization and global competition.

Zooming in on this sign, choosing the *katakana* representation, "ソーシャルディスタンス," instead of the equivalent phrase ("社会的距離" *shakaiteki kyori*) written in *kanji* (logographic Chinese characters, or another Japanese writing system, indicating Japanese origin), might relate to such ideological dominance of English and preference for Western values. Furthermore, this phrase in *katakana* is closely connected to the online space (e.g., social media), where new English words associated with COVID-19 public health (e.g., 'social distancing') were circulated globally (see Asif et al., 2021). In short, using the phrase, "ソーシャ

76 Entangled Englishes

ルディスタンス" in *katakana* represents not just simply incorporating English loanwords as Japanese (which is a *hybrid* language, see Rebuck, 2002) by reflecting social needs during the pandemic but also involves Japan's socio-historical relationships that highly value English and the U.S.

Another notable characteristic within this sign is the use of *cute* mascots for this bank. *Kawaii* (meaning 'cute') is a distinctive aspect of Japanese culture, which seems to be entangled within this COVID-19 sign. Simply put, *kawaii* describes things that are small, delicate, and immature (Allison, 2006; Burdelski & Mitsuhashi, 2010; McVeigh, 1996), and the cuteness-obsessed nature – including creating and using cute characters like Hello Kitty and mascots for companies' and governments' campaigns – is prevalent in Japan. Researchers have documented the critical roles of *kawaii* culture in Japan (see Dale, 2017; Sato, 2009), appealing to the sense of *pathos* (which elicits *affective, emotional* responses) in the audience through skillfully commodifying the sense of cuteness. Furthermore, it is also noteworthy that *kawaii* often indexes female identity (see, e.g., Asano-Cavanagh, 2014), possibly reinforcing the stereotypical female image (that needs protection because of smallness and delicateness) and power imbalance between males and females in Japan (e.g., Yukawa & Saito, 2004).

More specifically, cute, delicate, and immature objects, like these mascots in this sign, might trigger emotional responses in the audience's mind, possibly facilitating customers' acceptance of the bank's request for social distancing. The bank seems to employ these mascots as *intermediaries*, conveying their messages indirectly and persuasively through cute mascots rather than directly and formally from the institution itself. This sign is entangled with such Japanese hidden cultural norms (e.g., the importance of cuteness) for making a request for customers more persuasively. In short, the sign reveals the entangled relations, involving a phrase ('social distance') in *katakana* (i.e., associated with the dominance of English and superiority of Western culture since WWII), cute bank mascots (i.e., associated with *kawaii* culture and assigned *female identity*), commodification (i.e., making use of *kawaii* mascots for market/business purposes), an online platform that spread this new COVID-19–related manner word ('social distancing') globally, and much more.

The next sign, which was posted in front of a restaurant, entails a word associated with another form of etiquette (which involves locally specific and unique embodied practices) that emerged due to COVID-19 across Japan (Figure 4.2). This sign is requesting cooperation from the restaurant's customers, as it states "ご協力ください" (*gokyoyoku kudasai*, meaning 'Please kindly cooperate'), and then outlines what the customers are expected to do by using the phrase, "お控えください" (*ohikaekudasai*, meaning 'please refrain from . . .'). Specifically, this sign requests customers' cooperation with the guideline – not talking without a mask as a new manner and etiquette that orients and responds to the COVID-19 phenomena – since conversations during meals may increase the risk of spreading COVID-19 at restaurants. One should note that toward the top of the sign, the word "黙食" (meaning

Entanglements within COVID-19 linguistic landscapes in Kyoto 77

 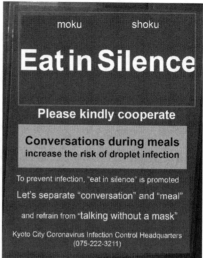

FIGURE 4.2 "黙食" (*mokushoku*, meaning 'eat in silence') at a restaurant; original (left) and translation (right)

'eat in silence') is written in *kanji* (logographic Chinese characters) in a large bold font. Also, note that "もくしょく" (*mokushoku*, meaning 'eat in silence') is written in *hiragana* (phonetic symbols) in small letters above the *kanji*. "もくしょく" is *furigana*, which provides the *pronunciation* of the kanji below.

In fact, one of the sign readers who is a Buddhist priest shared the following information: the word "黙食" is not entirely newly coined, but the same word (but with a different way of pronouncing the *kanji* as '*mokujiki*') has long existed as part of the Buddhist tradition and manner (interview on June 14, 2023). This word is associated with its particular embodied practice of 'eating without speaking or making any noise.' Therefore, it can be argued that *furigana* or "もくしょく" is provided here in this sign not only because of unfamiliarity with the term but also because of the necessity to disambiguate this new word from the old one, *mokujiki*.

Generally, Buddhism places an importance on the needs of *others* rather than those of ourselves, showing respect for all beings. This principle has largely influenced the creation and dissemination of *manners/etiquettes* (e.g., Be respectful of others; Remain as quiet as possible) in Japanese society, making social life comfortable for all and valuing being considerate for others. According to Drott (2023), religions in Japan, particularly Japanese Buddhism, are intricately embedded in people's everyday embodied practices (e.g., visiting temples, participating in seasonal festivals), and often Japanese people are not very aware of or do not reflect on religious belief when engaging in those daily practices. It can be interpreted that this sign with the word "黙食" is closely associated with such religious belief and discourse, promoting a considerate practice for others, which has been

78 Entangled Englishes

highly valued by Japanese Buddhism. However, it is important to note that neither '*mokushoku*' (used in this sign) nor '*mokujiki*' (the origin) are widely used in Japanese. Despite their long history connected with Japanese Buddhism, not many people are familiar with either word, akin to how they are not aware of the religious belief behind their everyday social, embodied practice. Thus, '*mokushoku*' might very well sound 'new' to many, and thus suit the abnormal situation of the pandemic.

Furthermore, according to the article "*Mokushokunosusume*" (2021), the word "黙食" (*mokushoku*) was first created and used by a small local restaurant owner in Japan to promote new COVID etiquette among his customers. Afterwards, the poster that used this word became widespread around Japan through social media; even other local governments, including Kyoto, adapted it for their posters. As discussed in relation to Figure 4.2, this sign and this word were also intricately entangled with the online space and discourse, where a new word *and* embodied practice associated with COVID-19 public health measures were circulated and disseminated widely. In short, this sign has religiously associated embodied relations that have long existed in Japan, which seem to be adapted and incorporated to serve to disseminate new COVID-19 manners and etiquette in Kyoto and all around Japan.

The next sign (Figure 4.3) was found at a subway station, which also seems to disseminate new pandemic manners and etiquette. It includes a cute drawing of a *ninja* who wears a mask (in the center), a title in English, "Be a Ninja" (on the top), and several catchphrases in Japanese that promote and educate appropriate manners and etiquette to subway passengers. The very use of a drawing of a *ninja* is layered with sociohistorical entanglements. *Ninjas* refer to specially trained, covert

FIGURE 4.3 "Be a Ninja" at a train station; original (left) and translation (right)

agents who used to work on secret missions during the feudal period in Japan. They emerged prominently during the Sengoku period (1467–1600), a time marked by social upheaval and constant conflict (see Turnbull, 1992). Historically, it is known that *ninjas* were well trained to perform serious missions, such as espionage, sabotage, guerrilla warfare, and assassination (Turnbull, 2003). After many years of legendary tales, the *ninja* has become an iconic figure in Japanese culture and history, particularly symbolizing their concealing and disciplined characters (e.g., Hayes, 2011). Like Japanese Buddhism in Figure 4.2, this sign also encompasses sociohistorical and cultural elements (*ninja*) for promoting good manners and etiquette for the public.

Zooming in on this sign's content, one can see how it skillfully connects appropriate "coughing etiquette" (coughing carefully in front of other people, for example, by wearing facemasks) to *ninja*'s mastery skills (the poster describes the "*Ninja*'s skill of concealing his mouth"). Such connection with the *ninja*'s character and culture within this sign encourages train passengers to take health measures seriously and engage in new embodied practices diligently, just as *ninjas* perform missions in secret (without being seen) and with mastery skills (without making mistakes through careful training). Simultaneously, like the bank mascots in Figure 4.1, the *ninja* in this sign is also illustrated in a cute, cartoon style, serving as a cultural and historical icon. In particular, such *kawaii* ninja as an entangled element might offer a sense of light-heartedness, making the message more friendly and less intimidating to diverse train passengers, including young people.

Also, importantly, this sign seems to be deeply intertwined with Japanese societal ideological emphasis or value on self-control and collective responsibility. The notion of "義理" (meaning 'duty') underscores the importance of fulfilling social obligations and maintaining harmony within the group (Davies & Ikeno, 2002). Such collectivism tends to be integral to social interaction and is reflected in various aspects of everyday life in Japan, including work, education, and community activities (Erez & Earley, 1993). It is worth noting that this sign was placed at a subway station with heavy human traffic. Thus, it relates to a strong ideological commitment to collective well-being over individual freedom, reinforcing the expectation that individuals should adopt their appropriate behaviors (e.g., wearing facemasks) for protecting others.

Finally, the use of English, "Be a Ninja," rather than a Japanese title is quite intriguing. As detailed in the analysis of a social distancing sign (Figure 4.1), selecting English here might relate to a close tie and affinity with the Western culture (particularly, the U.S.) influenced by post-WWII westernization and globalization (Hino, 2009). In addition, Japan has a long history of cultural hybridization, where traditional cultural elements are well blended with modern, often Western, influences (e.g., Jaimes et al., 2021). This type of blending, exemplified by the combination of a *ninja* image with an English slogan in this sign, can be interpreted as an ideological embracement of modernity as well as the maintenance of linguistic and cultural distinctiveness. Furthermore, such blending in English might also orient to the people who have limited knowledge of Japanese as the targeted audience. On the other hand, it is also possible to interpret that this sign *stylizes* and constructs the image of social 'coolness' through its indexicality. Furukawa (2014) argued that English is often used for fluid identity constructions and performances in Japan, signaling that English serves as part of a locally common resource that is also connected to the world outside of Japan.

In sum, this sign encompasses associations with *ninja* as a sociocultural and historical icon, cuteness (revealed in ninja's drawing), use of English as westernization and cool, creative, and fluid identity performance, the value of collectivism, and much more. So far, all the signs (Figures 4.1 to 4.3) appear to promote new words/phrases and/or new forms of etiquette for preventing COVID-19 and encompass diverse elements, some of which are locally specific based on Kyoto's and/or Japanese language, culture, and history. Such localized ways of sign-making (e.g., Marshall, 2021) might be effective for disseminating and promoting new public etiquette/manners to sign readers (e.g., local residents) since those signs refer to and signify shared local identities.

The next sign (Figure 4.4), which is quite distinctive from the other signs examined so far, was found in front of an *izakaya* (or Japanese-style bar) that voluntarily closed while we were collecting data (July and August 2021). As explained, the contextual information relevant for this sign is that the Kyoto local government enforced a strict measure at that time: restaurants were asked to close at 8 pm and were prohibited from serving alcohol (Kyoto Prefectural Government, 2021). This condition severely affected sales at many restaurants, particularly *izakayas*, which probably led to this *izakaya*'s decision to close temporarily.

FIGURE 4.4 "#Fuckucorona" at a closed *izakaya;* original (left) and translation (right)

According to this *izakaya* owner, this poster was downloaded *online* and posted because he thought "it is cool" (interview with the owner, on June 3, 2023). This indicates the impact of online space and discourse on this signage, which is similar to other signs (social distancing, Figure 4.1 and *Mokushoku*, Figure 4.2). However, unlike other signs with straightforward messages (disseminating and educating new pandemic manners), this sign differs because it does not explicitly demand any action (e.g., to follow new etiquette) from the sign readers. Instead, it seems to be symbolically resisting or fighting back at COVID-19, thus serving as a source of emotional support for those people battling against it.

On the lower part of this sign, the message "#kill you FuckuCoRoNA good-bye Japan" in English is located on the left and a panda in *kabuki* makeup is on the right. The English message "FuckUCorona" displays subversiveness and expresses strong emotions, especially anger (Jay & Janschewitz, 2008). Such negative affect constitutes a critical part of entanglements. As discussed in relation to other signs (Figures 4.1 and 4.3), selecting this curse word in English might relate to the notion of Westernization and Americanization. Also, the use of English for swearing in particular might serve as distancing from Japanese identities (Dewaele, 2004) or performing an alternative western persona. Thus, it is possible to project an abnormal, obscene self in a more playful manner. Note also that the panda is sending a similarly subversive message through the embodied act of raising its middle finger. This specific embodiment is usually interpreted as obscene and rude both in the West and in Japan. It is also noteworthy that the panda is wearing a mask, which conforms to pandemic-related public health norms and policies, belying his use of gestural and linguistic obscenities.

A closer look at the panda itself reveals intriguing, cultural elements embedded in this sign. As mentioned, this panda is wearing *kabuki* makeup, signifying Japanese classic culture and history. In other words, this sign connects back to traditional Japanese culture, particularly *kabuki*. *Kabuki,* a performing art, has a long history going back more than 400 years in Japan (Japan Art Council, 2023). Furthermore, the panda's *kabuki*-style makeup in red, along with his facial expression (with his slanted eyes), exhibits intense anger, likely orienting to government-imposed restrictions on opening hours and serving alcohol. In other words, *kabuki* culture, its makeup, the panda's embodiment, the emotion (anger), and the cursing word in English (FuckuCoRoNA) are all entangled within this sign, exhibiting the *izakaya*'s dis-aligning stances to the government regulation in specific and COVID-19 in general.

What is more, this poster itself can be interpreted as a genre of *art – caricature,* which constitutes a part of entanglements. A caricature involves a deliberate exaggeration of appearance or behavior in a humorous or critical manner. In fact, this caricature-style sign might have a connection with a famous caricature called *Choju giga* ('Frolicking Animals') that has belonged to *Kozanji* temple in Kyoto as an ancient cultural property (since the 12th and 13th centuries). This old, classic caricature consists of several volumes of satirical drawings that illustrate lively animals (e.g., rabbits, frogs, monkeys) who behave like humans (e.g., bathing in a river, wrestling) and is considered the foundation of modern comics (see The British Museum, 2018). The possible evidence of this connection is that they both employ *animals* (the panda in this COVID-19 sign) who act like humans, display a range of emotions, and express opinions and stances in an exaggerated manner. In short, this sign at the closed *izakaya* exhibits various relations, which include *kabuki* (its makeup style), embodiment (the panda's raising a middle finger), a curse word in English, online space (where this poster was originally found by the *izakaya* owner), emotion (intense anger expressed by the panda), and caricature. With all these entanglements, this sign expresses various meanings, demonstrating the *izakaya*'s playful but subversive stances toward the local government regulations and COVID-19.

5. Discussion and conclusion

Centering entanglement, this chapter examined how languages, cultures, histories, material objects, embodiment, spaces, and ideologies were intricately entangled within COVID-19 signs in Kyoto, Japan, during the height of the pandemic. This study revealed a wide range of elements embedded within those signs, which include languages (e.g., Japanese, including loan words; English), culture and/or history (e.g., *kabuki, ninja,* Buddhism, cuteness), emotion (e.g., anger), politics (e.g., a strong tie between the U.S. and Japan), ideology (e.g., cuteness related to female identity, social collectivism), economic beliefs, and much more. For example, the sign in Figure 4.2 includes the word *mokushoku*, which was widely used in Japan during the pandemic but originally referred to Buddhism and its embodied practices (*mokujiki* or concentrating on eating without talking) as its entanglement. Such history and culture became newly adapted for disseminating COVID-19 etiquette/manners not only in Kyoto but also around Japan.

Furthermore, the aforementioned signs contribute to communicative practices in a variety of ways. They serve to (1) circulate new words related to etiquette/manners (e.g., ソーシャルディスタンス, 'social distancing', 黙食, 'eating in silence') for public health education and/or (2) express stances and attitudes toward government regulations, manifesting alignment or dis-alignment with COVID-19–related policies and embodying identities as locals (e.g., locals in Kyoto, the Japanese). For instance, the sign in Figure 4.4 exhibits the *izakaya*'s owner's subversive, dis-aligned stance toward COVID-19 regulations and measures. It particularly illustrates the owner's emotion, especially anger, by creatively combining and infusing many elements, including Japanese cultural heritage (*kabuki* and *caricature*), a cool English curse word ("FuckuCoRoNA"), and obscene embodiment (the panda raising its middle finger). This sign as entangled assemblage appears to orient to the specific context when serving alcohol was strictly restricted by the local government. Despite some differences in how exactly each sign conveys reactions, our data overall demonstrated local efforts to understand and address COVID-19 phenomena in the way in which histories, cultures, ideologies, and identities are (re)contextualized across signs.

In the end, we propose some research implications. As revealed in our data analysis, it is more effective to examine several signs together as *assemblage* (in an integrated manner), not just studying each sign in an isolated manner. Indeed, by employing entanglement as an analytical lens, we can reveal many possible relations embedded within individual or multiple signs along with the complex communicative practices involving such signs. Specifically, entanglement urges us to analyze in depth how diverse entities, which are often hidden – including languages (Japanese loan words); cultures; histories (e.g., the dependent political relation with the U.S. since WWII); objects; and sociocultural, socioeconomic norms or discourse – are entangled within COVID-19 signs in Kyoto, revealing people's stance-takings during the chaotic time. Ultimately, we suggest the affordance of centering entanglement within LL studies more generally, which can be meaningfully applied *beyond Englishes*. This approach enables us to examine signs in a more complex, situated, and interconnected manner, transcending traditional structuralist boundaries (e.g., languages like Japanese) and revealing a juxtaposition of and interrelationship between languages, objects, embodiment, spaces, and ideologies involving signs.

Acknowledgements

The first author, Yumi Matsumoto, acknowledges the financial support from the Japan Foundation's Japanese Studies Fellowship.

References

Allison, A. (2006). Cuteness as Japan's millennial product. In T. Joseph (Ed.), *Pikachu's global adventure: The rise and fall of Pokemon* (pp. 34–49). Duke University Press.

Asano-Cavanagh, Y. (2014). Linguistic manifestation of gender reinforcement through the use of the Japanese term *kawaii*. *Gender and Language*, 8(3), 341–359.

Asif, M., Zhiyong, D., Iram, A., & Nisar, M. (2021). Linguistic analysis of neologism related to coronavirus (COVID-19). *Social Sciences & Humanities Open*, 4, 100201. https://doi.org/10.1016/j.ssaho.2021.100201

Backhaus, P. (2006). Multilingualism in Tokyo: A look into the linguistic landscape. *International Journal of Multilingualism*, 3, 52–66.

Barad, K. (2007). *Meeting the universe halfway: Quantum physics and the entanglement of matter and meaning*. Duke University Press.

Bennett, J. (2010). *Vibrant matter: A political ecology of things*. Duke University Press.

Bilkic, M. (2018). Emplacing hate: Turbulent graffscapes and linguistic violence in post-war Bosnia-Herzegovina. *Linguistic Landscape*, 4, 1–28.

Blommaert, J. (2017). Chronotopes, scales and complexity in the study of language in society. In K. Arnaut, M. Sif Karrebaek, M. Spotti & J. Blommaert (Eds.), *Engaging superdiversity: Recombining spaces, times and language practices* (pp. 47–62). Multilingual Matters.

Bolton, K. (2021). World Englishes: Approaches, models and methodology. In B. Schneider, T. Heyd & M. Saraceni (Eds.), *Bloomsbury World Englishes volume 1: Paradigms* (pp. 9–26). Bloomsbury Academic.

The British Museum. (2018). *Manga: A brief history in 12 works*. https://www.britishmuseum.org/blog/manga-brief-history-12-works

Burdelski, M., & Mitsuhashi, K. (2010). "She thinks you're kawaii": Socializing affect, gender, and relationships in a Japanese preschool. *Language in Society, 39*(1), 65–93.

Cenoz, J., & Gorter, D. (2006). Linguistic landscape and minority languages. *International Journal of Multilingualism, 3*, 67–80.

Dale, J. (2017). The appeal of the cute object: Desire, domestication, and agency. In J. P. Dale, J. Goggin, J. Levda, A. McIntryre & D. Negra (Eds.), *The aesthetics and affects of cuteness* (pp. 35–55). Routledge.

Davies, R. J., & Ikeno, O. (2002). *The Japanese mind: Understanding contemporary Japanese culture*. Tuttle Publishing.

Deleuze, G., & Guattari, F. (1987). *A thousand plateaus: Capitalism and schizophrenia* (B. Massumi, Trans.). University of Minnesota Press.

Dewaele, J.-M. (2004). The emotional force of swearwords and taboo words in the speech of multilinguals. *Journal of Multilingual and Multicultural Development, 25*, 204–222.

Douglas, G. C. (2022). A sign in the window: Social norms and community resilience through handmade signage in the age of Covid-19. *Linguistic Landscape, 8*, 184–201.

Drott, E. (2023, September 14). *Unraveling Buddhism's influence on the human body, brain, and beyond*. Sophia University. https://www.sophia.ac.jp/eng/article/feature/the-knot/the-knot-0129/

Dunn, J., Coupe, T., & Adams, B. (2021). *Measuring linguistic diversity during COVID-19*. Proceedings of the 4th Workshop on NLP and Computational Social Science (2020). https://arxiv.org/pdf/2104.01290.pdf

Erez, M., & Earley, P. C. (1993). *Culture, self-identity, and work*. Oxford University Press.

Furukawa, G. K. (2014). *The use of English as a local language resource for identity construction in Japanese television variety shows* [Unpublished doctoral dissertation, The University of Hawai'i at Mānoa].

Hayes, S. K. (2011). *The ninja and their secret fighting art*. Tuttle Publishing.

Hino, N. (2009). The teaching of English as an international language in Japan: An answer to the dilemma of indigenous values and global needs in the expanding circle. *AILA Review, 22*, 103–119.

Hopkyns, S., & van den Hoven, M. (2021). Linguistic diversity and inclusion in Abu Dhabi's linguistic landscape during the COVID-19 period. *Multilingua, 41*, 201–232.

Ike, S., & Hori, Y. (2023). COVID-19 discourse in linguistic landscape: Linguistic and semiotic analysis of directive signs. *Australian Journal of Linguistics, 43*(4), 375–396.

International Relations Office, General Planning Bureau of Kyoto City. (2013). *Kyoto, City of Kyoto, Printing no. 253230*. https://www.city.kyoto.lg.jp/sogo/cmsfiles/contents/0000062/62090/kyoto.pdf

Jaimes, A. C. E., Alvarez, L. D. M., Serrano, A. S., Arroyo, J. M. R., & De Zárate, M. R. O. (2021). Japanese postmodernism, anime and culture hybridations: An occidentalist aesthetic study of JoJo's Bizarre Adventure. *International Journal of Arts Humanities and Social Sciences Studies, 6*(3), 89–96.

Japan Art Council. (2023, December 2). *Kabuki for beginners. Kumadori Makeup*. https://www2.ntj.jac.go.jp/unesco/kabuki/en/feature/index.html

Jay, T., & Janschewitz, K. (2008). The pragmatics of swearing. *Journal of Politeness Research, 4*, 267–288.

Jenkins, J. (2015). Repositioning English and multilingualism in English as a lingua franca. *Englishes in Practice, 2*(3), 49–85.

Kachru, B. B. (Ed.). (1992). *The other tongue* (2nd ed.). University of Illinois Press.

Kalocsányiová, E., Essex, R., & Poulter, D. (2023). Risk and health communication during Covid-19: A linguistic landscape analysis. *Health Communication, 38*, 1080–1089.

Kyoto Prefectural Government. (2021, July 30). *Priority COVID-19 measures in Kyoto Pref.* https://www.pref.kyoto.jp/kokusai/documents/maneng07302_1.pdf

Lacsina, N., & Yeh, A. (2022). Keep social distance: The linguistic landscape of the major malls in Jeddah amid the COVID-19 pandemic. *Topics in Linguistics, 23*, 39–61.

Lou, J. J., Malinowski, D., & Peck, A. (2022). Introduction to the linguistic landscape of COVID-19. *Linguistic Landscape, 8*, 123–130.

Marshall, S. (2021). Navigating COVID-19 linguistic landscapes in Vancouver's North Shore: Official signs, grassroots literacy artefacts, monolingualism, and discursive convergence. *International Journal of Multilingualism, 20*(2), 189–213.

McVeigh, B. J. (1996). Commodifying affection, authority and gender in the everyday objects of Japan. *Journal of Material Culture, 1*(3), 291–312.

Mokushokunosusume. (2021, May 13). *Kobe Shinbun next.* https://www.kobe-np.co.jp/news/sougou/202105/0014322603.shtml

Monje, J. (2017). "Hindi Bayani/not a hero": The linguistic landscape of protest in Manila. *Social Inclusion, 5*, 14–28.

Nakamura, J. (2022). COVID-19 signs in Tokyo and Kanagawa: Linguistic landscaping for whom? *Asia-Pacific Social Science Review, 22*, 80–94.

Ogiermann, E. (Ed.). (2023). The interpersonal functions of public signs during the Covid-19 pandemic. *Pragmatics and Society, 14*(2). https://doi.org/10.1075/ps.14.2

Olah, B. (2007). English loanwords in Japanese: Effects, attitudes and usage as a means of improving spoken English ability. *Bukyou Gakuin Daigaku Ningen Gakubu Kenkyuu Kiyou, 9*(1), 177–188.

Onuki, S. (2020, June 18). *Decimated by pandemic, Kyoto tourism hinges on Japanese visitors.* Nikkei Asia. https://asia.nikkei.com/Business/Travel-Leisure/Decimated-by-pandemic-Kyoto-tourism-hinges-on-Japanese-visitors

Pennycook, A. (2018). *Posthumanist applied linguistics.* Routledge.

Pennycook, A. (2020). Translingual entanglements of English. *World Englishes, 39*, 222–235.

Phillipson, R. (1992). *Linguistic imperialism.* Oxford University Press.

Rebuck, M. (2002). The function of English loanwords in Japanese. *Nagoya University of Commerce and Business (NUCB) Journal of Language Culture and Communication, 4*, 53–64.

Rosecrance, R. (1993). The U.S.-Japan trading relationship and its effects. *Indiana Journal of Global Legal Studies, 1*(1), 139–153.

Sato, K. (2009). From Hello Kitty to Cod Roe Kewpie: A postwar cultural history of cuteness in Japan. *Asian Intercultural Contacts, 14*(2), 38–42.

Scollon, R., & Scollon, S. W. (2003). *Discourses in place: Language in the material world* (1st ed.). Routledge.

Seidlhofer, B. (2011). *Understanding English as a lingua franca.* Oxford University Press.

Tan, M. S., & Said, S. B. (2015). Linguistic landscape and exclusion: An examination of language representation in disaster signage in Japan. In R. Rubdy & S. Ben Said (Eds.), *Conflict, exclusion and dissent in the linguistic landscape* (pp. 145–169). Palgrave Macmillan.

Toohey, K., Dagenais, D., Fodor, A., Hof, L., Nuñez, O., Singh, A., & Schulze, L. (2015). That sounds so cooool: Entanglements of children, digital tools, and literacy practices. *TESOL Quarterly, 49*, 461–485.

Tsuda, Y. (1990). *Eigo shihai no kouzou.* Daisan Shokan.

Tsuda, Y. (2003). *Eigo shihai towa nani ka.* Akashi Shoseki.

Turnbull, S. (1992). *Ninja: The true story of Japan's secret warrior cult.* Firebird Books.

Turnbull, S. (2003). *Ninja AD 1460–1650.* Osprey Publishing.

Uekusa, S. (2019). Disaster linguicism: Linguistic minorities in disasters. *Language in Society*, *48*, 353–375.
Yukawa, S., & Saito, M. (2004). Cultural ideologies and Japanese language and gender studies: A theoretical review. In S. Okamoto & J. S. Smith (Eds.), *Japanese language, gender, and ideology* (pp. 23–37). Oxford University Press.
Zhang, H., Tupas, R., & Aman, N. (2020). English-dominated Chinatown: A quantitative investigation of the linguistic landscape of Chinatown in Singapore. *Journal of Asian Pacific Communication*, *30*, 273–289.

PART II
Entanglements of race

5
AN ENTANGLED UNEASE

Intrusive Englishes and allyship in Black feminism

Daniel N. Silva

1. Introduction

This chapter is an attempt to think of how semiotic resources normally dominated by elite groups might be appropriated by minorities and repurposed beyond usual frameworks of domination. My case study relies on Brazilian Black feminists recasting English, a language in the country usually associated with elite segments and practices, as a decolonial and liberating resource. Throughout this text, I use 'dominated' and 'domination' in specific ways. These terms are inflections of the verb 'to dominate,' which shares a root with, and is family-related to, the noun 'domain.' In linguistic anthropology, the geographical and political senses of domain – a sphere where an activity unfolds; a territory dominated by a group – is fundamental to thinking of the value and validity of linguistic ideologies and phenomena (Agha, 2007). Wortham (2008) synthesizes that all linguistic facts, including their use and evaluative models

> are recognized only by a subset of any linguistic community. . . . There is no one "macro" set of models or ideologies universal to a group. Instead, there are models that move across domains ranging from pairs, to local groups, all the way up to global language communities.
>
> *(pp. 45–46)*

In this sense, ideological constructs (e.g., standardized English) and linguistic tokens of these constructs (e.g., a form of pronunciation or writing labeled as 'Standard') are necessarily recognized only by a domain of people. No matter how universal or cosmopolitan a variety, language, or ideology purports to be, it will always be provincial (Bauman & Briggs, 2003), not least in this technical sense.

DOI: 10.4324/9781003441304-8

Further, domains are entangled with institutional and political forces. The New Oxford American Dictionary, for instance, defines 'domain' first as "an area or territory owned or controlled by a ruler or government" (Stevenson & Lindberg, 2010, n.p.). The domain where so-called standardized varieties of English are variously used and imagined is embedded in institutional politics and arrangements of domination relative to disputes located in time and space. But non-standardized varieties of English are also embedded in specific power games and institutional arrangements, even if such power and institutions are often erased in hegemonic domains. In keeping with the geographical and political nuances of the linguistic-anthropological concept of 'domain,' I engage in dialogue with Black feminists in Brazil to unpack their discourse about domains where English, a colonial language, may be repurposed as a tool to "potentially open up a decolonial space" (Awayed-Bishara et al., 2022, p. 1065).

We should note that the group of Black feminists that I am bringing for discussion reclaims linguistic resources that had been originally denied to their communities. In the Americas, Afro-diasporic communicative practices have been variously delegitimized and misrecognized. Further, Blacks in the Americas were generally deprived of alphabetic literacy in their forced displacement as enslaved people (Gilroy, 1993). Yet this has not prevented Black expressive cultures from having the strength and potency of today. Black organic intellectuals and expressive cultures have become known to the world primarily through oral culture and other embodied expressions, including hip-hop, jazz, reggae, samba and capoeira. In Brazil, thanks to affirmative action and the struggle of minority groups, including the Black Movement, there has been an increase in access to schooling and the university among the Black community and other minoritized groups (Gomes, 2019). However, their access to income redistribution, formal work and resources associated with social mobility, including institutional literacies and English, is extremely disproportionate to that of white segments (Dos Santos & Windle, 2021). Thus, the circuit of Black feminists that I discuss is not repurposing resources that are highly affordable on the symbolic market. The sense of unease in the title seeks to capture affects such as anger, defiance and discomfort that these intellectuals evoke in their trajectories of socialization into domains that are not normally imagined to include them. Instead of inclusion into social spheres where legitimized semiotic resources circulate, they often talk about *intrusion* into these arenas (see Lopes et al., 2017, p. 763). Additionally, these intellectuals do not frame their semiotic work of intrusion as individual projects. Rather, they project it as part of a collective struggle – as the imagination of semiotic domains that favor the redistribution of material resources and break with the devaluation of Black lives.

Moving away from a modern tradition that sees constructs such as language, nature and culture as circumscribed and independent entities (e.g., Bauman & Briggs, 2003), this chapter engages with a view of sociolinguistic resources as entangled to, "and part of, the material world" (Pennycook, 2020, p. 222). In proposing the concept of entanglements of English, Pennycook aims to focus on how English is interconnected to the material and social world in diverse ways. Further, this concept may help us to *disentangle*, however minimally, English from the colonial iteration of racial and other inequities. Methodologically, I draw on fieldwork with activists from Rio de Janeiro peripheries (see Silva & Lee, 2024). I focus on a collection of texts and talks by Black feminists who have been connected to these activists. Conceição Evaristo, Marielle Franco, Anielle Franco and Pâmella Passos have been, in different degrees, icons of progressive politics at large. In what follows, I discuss how they have disentangled hegemonic semiotic resources from a colonial past while also entangling these resources to a transperipheral (Windle et al., 2020) minority activism.

2. Expanding the ideological project of disentangling English from colonialism

Using a variety of instruments, including close analysis of interactions and engagement with reflexive discourse, linguistic anthropology and sociolinguistics have provided important insights into social life. This body of work has shown that the structure of a language is not independent from how speakers and institutions imagine it. Woolard (1998), for instance, suggested that "[t]he existence of a language as a discrete entity is always a discursive project, rather than an established fact" (p. 20). I am in dialogue here with authors who theorize alternative communicative practices to a well-known discursive project, that is, English as a colonial language (Canagarajah, 1999; Phillipson, 1992), indexically linked to ideological constructs debated in the sociolinguistic field, such as 'native speaker' (Holliday, 2005), 'white listening subject' (Rosa & Flores, 2017) or 'self-made speaker' (Rojo, 2019). Constituted with the aid of raciolinguistic ideologies – ideologies that "co-naturaliz[e] language and race" (Rosa & Flores, 2017, p. 621) – English as a colonial discursive project depended fundamentally on the imperial expansion of England, the United States and other colonial regions, in the contexts where globalization has spread and prevailed.

If we understand these elements as part of a (diverse, broad and contentious) 'discursive project,' then constructions of superior personhood and cosmopolitan society embedded in hegemonic imaginations of English are neither necessary nor natural. Further, seeing this project as part and parcel of ideologies implies that there will always be "an alternative [ideology] that somebody else, differently positioned, might hold" (Gal & Irvine, 2019, p. 13). Pennycook (2020) lays out entangled Englishes as a language ideology that contests this discursive project. Seeing English as entangled helps us render visible circuits of inequality that are usually erased, often naturalizing its autonomy. Pennycook thus aims to emphasize connections, formations and assemblages (including of humans and non-humans) that have entangled English with images of upper-class superiority, whiteness and 'triumph' of technology over nature. For Pennycook (2022), "the relations between English and discourses, ideologies, cultures, and economies are not inevitable"

(p. 17). These relations may be disentangled. Yet he is not suggesting "that English can somehow become unentangled" (p. 17) – a language severed from material and political connections. English can be ideologically reimagined, and for my purposes here, decolonial theories and practices enacted by social groups who have disproportionately suffered the effects of colonialism, such as Blacks in Brazil, are particularly suitable.

In Brazil, educational practices, including EFL teaching, have differently served as proxies of the surveillance of minorities (Machado & Bueno, 2023) or of a technical education that ignores social issues such as race, class and gender (Melo, 2015). This is reflective of a macro-political construction of 'security' as fighting an 'enemy' is reflected in the classroom (see Charalambous et al., 2020, for a discussion of (in)securitization as a practice of enemy-making that extends to the educational context). Examples of the instantiation of (in)securitization in the classroom include the obstacles to socialization in EFL brought about by the psychological effects of armed conflict (Rocha, 2016) and the invisibilization of marginalized groups in school literacy events involving EFL textbooks (Ferreira, 2019). Dos Santos and Windle (2021, p. 5) verify that "in Brazilian schools that serve Black and working-class students, learning English often involves a rejection of self, culture, and class identity." But the practices of resisting this rejection are also manifold. One of the participants in Dos Santos and Windle's (2021) study questioned not only the racial bias in curricular materials used in Brazil but also its very projection of English as a language that is authentically spoken only in the 'Inner Circle' (pp. 10–11). These Brazilian efforts to decolonize EFL teaching suggest that "in troubled or conflict-ridden educational contexts, English might offer a framework of voice that enhances agency and opens a space for contesting, rather than reproducing, linguistic, cultural, and political hegemonies and invisibilities" (Awayed-Bishara, 2024, p. 7). Let us now move to analyzing two empirical cases that demonstrate particular aspirations and nuances of this decolonial project among Black feminists.

3. "Our writing is not to put the masters' house to sleep but to wake them from their unjust sleep"

Here, I discuss unease as an affective stance embedded in the semiotic work of two women who have become icons of Black feminism in Brazil. My interlocutors in the field (and participants in the progressive field at large) often evoke the discourses on repurposing valorized semiotic resources voiced by Conceição Evaristo, a fiction writer born in a favela in Belo Horizonte, and Marielle Franco, a city councilwoman in Rio de Janeiro, also born in a favela (but brutally murdered in 2018, as discussed in the following). Favelas are neighborhoods built by residents. They were first formed by former enslaved peoples and their descendants following the end of slavery in Brazil at the end of the 19th century. Favelas are symbols of resistance because they were a practical solution to the lack of housing and labor policies for the poor. My work about the culture of survival in these spaces draws from

Derrida (1997), who originally suggested that surviving "goes beyond both living and dying, supplementing each with a sudden surge, deciding . . . life *and* death, ending them in a decisive . . . stop" (p. 89). In the semiotic work of Evaristo and Marielle, two women who grew up in favelas, a first place to investigate the affect of unease is in their engagement with practices of survival.

Marielle epitomizes the non-dichotomous interplay of life and death in contexts where the inequality of capitalism takes on a militarized and (in)securitized form, such as Rio de Janeiro. An advocate for human rights in favelas since her youth and a member of deputy Marcelo Freixo's progressive cabinet for ten years, Marielle was a Black woman elected to the city council in 2016. However, thirteen months into a mandate dedicated to defending minorities, Marielle was assassinated. Investigations indicate that the crime was planned by two brothers linked to *milícias*, groups of former and current police officers who compete with drug traffickers for control of certain favelas. For the crime, they hired former police officers Elcio Queiroz and Ronnie Lessa, who killed Marielle and her driver, Anderson Gomes, in an ambush. But dying did not prevent Marielle from being currently invoked by a broad progressive movement far beyond Rio de Janeiro. Marielle has been poetically summoned by protesters as a spectral return (Silva & Lee, 2021). Mantras such as *Marielle, presente* or 'Marielle, present,' along with discourses that recall her legacy, provide an authoritative repertoire for the fight against inequality. Sociolinguistically, Marielle survives in the form of a legacy of unique political significance in Brazil.

Survival is a trope that also appears in the work of Conceição Evaristo, a contemporary writer who has explored the appropriation by Black women of a resource denied to the enslaved: writing. Evaristo (2020) coined the term '*escrevivência*' to name this agentive appropriation. Morphologically, *escrevivência* is a combination of *escrever* 'to write' and *vivência* 'living.' The signifier also bears resemblance to *sobrevivência* 'survival.' In developing this concept, Evaristo draws on the diasporic experience of Black women whose ancestors were violently taken to Brazil. She explains that in the colonial system put in place by Portugal, Black women were often forced to take on the role of wet nurses. A sociolinguistic contradiction was that, while they were not free to speak, "to be silent, or to scream" (Evaristo, 2020, p. 30), they had to tell bedtime stories to their masters' children. Evaristo defines *escrevivência* as re-signifying this language regime:

> *Escrevivência*, in its initial conception, takes place as an act of writing by Black women, as an action that aims to blur, to undo an image of the past in which the body-voice of enslaved Black women also had its power of enunciation under the control of slave owners, men, women, and even children. And if yesterday not even the voice belonged to enslaved women, today the words, the writing, belong to us. They belong to us because we have appropriated these graphic signs, the value of writing, without forgetting the power of the orality of our ancestors.
>
> *(Evaristo, 2020, p. 30)*

In this passage, Evaristo elaborates on the domain of and access to writing among Black women. As they gain access to writing, a social domain expands. This new social domain is projected as 'blurring' and 'undoing' a past domain where the orality of Black women (i.e., "the body-voice of enslaved Black women") was controlled by Whites. The appropriation of writing (e.g., "we have appropriated these graphic signs") is crucial for this new domain.

Fundamentally, as an enregistered practice (i.e., a semiotic practice that links signs to images of person and social time-space, being relatively stabilized in a sequence of semiotic encounters, cf. Agha, 2007; Gal, 2018), writing co-occurs with sociolinguistic styles that facilitate the expression of unease. For example, for Evaristo (2020), although the *casa-grande* (the house where the masters lived on the colonial plantation) appropriated the Black woman's voice to lull their children, *escrevivência* today seeks to "wake [the *casa-grande*] from its unjust sleep":

> And if the voice of our ancestors had paths and functions that were delimited by the *casa-grande*, the same is not true of our writing. That is why I say: "our *escrevivência* is not to put those in the *casa-grande* to sleep, but to wake them from their unjust sleep."
>
> *(Evaristo, 2020, p. 30)*

Awakening whiteness from an unjust sleep suggests that *escrevivência* is also the enactment of anger at the present legacies of a colonial past. Anger is part of a wider discomfort embedded in *escrevivência* (see Carneiro, 2022). Evaristo (2020, p. 34), for instance, comments that this ideology of writing is "born out of a deep sense of unease with the current state of affairs." Yet unease, discomfort and anger are affects that are generally frowned upon in politics, especially when expressed by Black women (Deumert, forthcoming). Pâmella Passos (2023) writes that Black women in politics are often disqualified as 'angry' – their "political dissent, while troubling, is disqualified, singled out as immaturity, lack of skill, and further reduced to 'anger.'" But Passos counters this stereotype by laying out a citational chain linking the expression of this affect by political icons, including Marielle and political philosopher Audre Lorde. Passos reminds us that Lorde (2012) treated anger and other defiant affects in politics as a source of displeasure that nonetheless leads to transformation.

In interviews I conducted with Marielle's advisors and people who knew her, it was common for her to be described as *marrenta*, or 'tough.' She was recognized as a prototypical user of the *papo reto* activist register – a translational practice that sounds angry because it suspends politeness and favors a 'direct' mode of communication (Silva, 2022). This defiant sociolinguistic persona was also embedded in Marielle's account of her journey to 'occupy' English as a platform for transnational and feminist activism. In the following, I reproduce an excerpt from a speech Marielle gave to an audience of Brazilian Black women at Casa das Pretas hours before she was murdered on March 14, 2018. She speaks about two moments in her socialization in English: in college, in the late 1990s, when she confronted a professor who assigned texts in English (instead of Portuguese), and in the years 2016–2018, when she repositioned her epistemic and affective stance towards the language:

> [In college] I got into a fight with a teacher because he had assigned a bibliography in English. Obviously, the situation was different, the experience was different, the imposition and what was in dispute there too. There was not a dark cloud asking how many Black teachers were there. . . . Anyway, the letter, the movement that we made, at that moment regarding the language they were trying to impose on me, and today when I hear you speak Aline, I have a scholarship at Cultura Inglesa [an English course]. . . . I've been struggling for two years to learn English, and I think we have to occupy and know all these – the *feminist movement* [she utters the term in English]. Yeah – all the terms and to work and draft them in English really to occupy this space. I'm not saying we should subvert our culture but to manage to occupy this place.

This excerpt of talk is important because it signals a trajectory or a shift in the meaning of a sign (i.e., English) within a speech chain (Agha, 2007). Marielle invokes two different time-spaces in which English appears as a construct that gradually becomes a legitimate object in the political struggle of minorities. In the 1990s, Marielle says that "the situation . . . , the experience . . . , and what was in dispute [were different]." In other words, the most intense debate at that time was about affirmative action for Black students and other minority groups to enter the university. The national law on quotas was only consolidated in 2012. The permanence of these students at the university was crucial, and Marielle indicates that the debate at the time revolved around issues that included access to academic literacy in Portuguese. But by 2016, Marielle's political struggle had reached other spheres, and her entanglement to English changed. As we will discuss in the following, unlike her sister Anielle, Marielle had few opportunities for socialization in English, evidenced when she says: "I've been struggling for two years to learn English."

Sequentially, within an interaction that was predominantly in Portuguese, Marielle translingually mentions "the feminist movement" in English. She at once circumscribes and displays the social field of English that she wants to see "occupied." Marielle performed translanguaging at other moments in the debate, including in order to cite Audre Lorde's original words in English: "I am not free while another woman is a prisoner, even though her chains are different from mine." Indexically, these performances in English suggest that Marielle was interested in performing, rather than just mentioning, a domain she was invested in 'occupying.' Chronologically, in her speech, the social domain of (activist) English shifts – from a social range where English stands for a segregating academic language to one where it figures as a bridge between transnational Black activists.

4. "Can English connect worlds and struggles?"

In this section, I elaborate on the interdiscursive coherence between Conceição Evaristo's perspective on *escrevivência*, Marielle's trope of occupying English and Anielle Franco and Pâmella Passos's discourses and affective stances on connecting (and silencing) worlds and struggles through English. Anielle is Marielle's sister. Following her sister's murder, Anielle decided to embed the family's quest for justice into institutional networks of activism. In 2018, together with Marinete, her mother; Francisco, her father; and Luyara, her niece and Marielle's daughter, she founded the Marielle Franco Institute with the aim of "fighting for justice, defending [Marielle's] memory, multiplying her legacy and watering her seeds" (Instituto Marielle Franco, 2021, n.p.). In 2022, Lula da Silva, upon defeating Jair Bolsonaro in the presidential run, invited Anielle to become Brazil's Minister of Racial Equality – an index of the recognition of a movement where Anielle stands as an authoritative figure. But, as we will discuss, Anielle's trajectory of activism goes further back than these events, beginning with an unexpected experience: as a young adult, she was invited to work temporarily as a translator in a detention center in Texas, facilitating the interaction between detained undocumented Brazilians and members of the justice system.

Pâmella, a friend of Marielle and Anielle, is a professor of history and a human rights activist in Rio de Janeiro. Through her work at the university and her networked activism, Pâmella has projected an antiracist and progressive education, including through discussing far-right discourses coopting education (Passos & Mendonça, 2021) and designing human rights textbooks (Passos & Linhares, 2021). She was personally shaken when Marielle was murdered. Following Marielle's death, she sought refuge for a semester in Ireland, where she was a visiting fellow at Front Line Defenders, an NGO for human rights protection. In Dublin, her transformation of '*luto em luta*,' or mourning into struggle, iconized the repurposing of semiotic resources, including affects, that we are invested in studying here. Allow me to begin by unpacking Anielle's semiotic work.

4.1. "I'm the daughter of survival"

Anielle's trajectory of socialization into English is emblematic of its repurposing as a decolonial tool. The semiotic work of redesigning English involves a complex affective work. I unpack Anielle's metadiscourse through two events in which she describes her becoming an activist alongside her trajectory of learning English. The first is an online roundtable organized by the Brazilian Association of Applied Linguistics in 2021 (see ALAB, 2021) entitled "Língua inglesa e direitos humanos: pode o subalterno falar?", or "English language and human rights: can the subaltern speak?" The second event is the research project that Anielle submitted (and which was accepted) for the Doctorate in Applied Linguistics at the Federal University of Rio de Janeiro in 2021. Titled "Ei, você fala inglês? Escrevivências e usos antirracistas decoloniais de língua inglesa, através de um olhar feminista e negro" ('Hey, do you speak English? *Escrevivência* and decolonial uses of English, through a feminist and Black gaze'), Anielle's project aims to discuss "the empowerment and emancipation of Black people and Black women through decolonial and antiracist teaching" (Franco, 2021, p. 7).

In both events, Anielle reports that feelings of frustration and humiliation were part of her initial experience of learning the language. But an opportunity to attend college in the United States led her to reposition herself in relation to English. As a teenager, Anielle was a volleyball player. Her team, Botafogo, played Flamengo in a championship final. Some coaches from the United States had come to watch the final, hoping to recruit athletes for North American universities. Anielle was one of them. Here is a stretch of her account at the ALAB roundtable:

> In that final game, they had already said that they would like to take some people to live and study in the United States on a full college scholarship. And I was one of those selected. But my English at that time was only high school level. I'd never taken a *curso de inglês* [paid English course] in my life. I had only studied it in public school.... And my relation to it in school was very difficult because I really didn't like the language. I was like, "Dude, I'm not going to learn it, I can't learn it. It's very difficult." I saw people much more advanced than me who wanted to give up. And then this opportunity came up because of volleyball.

Anielle elaborates on a social problem in Brazil related to her class and racial group. Basic education in Brazil is a right offered at no cost for the entire population. Yet the structural conditions and quality of teaching vary enormously across locales, being more precaritized in social spaces like favelas (Koslinski et al., 2013). Further, upper-middle class and wealthy families create social distinction by avoiding public schools and instead enrolling their children in private schools (Roth-Gordon, 2017). Typically, students who display a higher proficiency in English are the ones whose families are able to afford *cursos de inglês*, English courses offered in paid language schools. Anielle evokes her lack of access to the latter to explain why her English was "high school level," that is, her socialization in English was constrained by the affordances of a public school in her community.

In her account, Anielle entangles the individual with the social and the internal affect with its external structuration. To unpack her entanglements, allow me to briefly refer to Bourdieu's (1985) pioneering key to studying affects and other dispositions to think, act and speak through their *habituation*. Habitus is one's incorporation of the social; through the habitus we simultaneously incorporate social norms and display our bodily uptake of them. Hanks (2005, p. 69) explains that for Bourdieu, habitus refers to "habits, dispositions to act in certain ways, and schemes of perception that order individual perspectives along socially defined lines" (p. 69). He adds that "[t]hrough the habitus, society impresses itself on the individual, not only in mental habits but even more in bodily ones." Anielle recounts myriad affects of discomfort with English, including feeling aversion to it ("I really didn't like the language") and inferiority ("I can't learn it, it's very difficult"). Following Bourdieu's key, this embodied display of affects in one's habitus is social, and thus Anielle points to the social regularity of the habituation of a norm, for example by citing similar experiences among her colleagues. These structural conditions, particularly Brazil's historical creation of social and racial distinctions through education (Roth-Gordon, 2017), underpinned Anielle and her colleague's dislike of the language and their desire to give up. But there is more to her early socialization in the language.

Prior to attending college in the U.S., Anielle's scholarship sponsored private English lessons in Rio de Janeiro. Anielle had to enroll at a *curso de inglês* located in Rio's wealthy Zona Sul. In her doctoral project, she further unpacks the societal and racial structuration of her unease:

> When I started my first English course at the age of 16, I remember the teacher talking only about travel, student exchanges, exquisite food, designer clothes, and the joy of experiencing it all. That was not my reality, and I felt like a complete stranger in that place, inhabited by people from neighborhoods I had never dreamed of being in.
>
> In addition, I was the only Black person in the class, I was a public school student, and I had no background in English.
>
> The differences between me and the other students in that class were striking: in my classroom materials, in my backpack sewn by my mother, in my nonstandard hair, but most of all, in my difficulty in assimilating the strange words that came out of the mouth of the teacher, a White woman who repeatedly expressed astonishment, unintentionally or not, when she heard me respond about my routine.
>
> The teenagers in my class seemed to have more financial power than my family. Stories of trips to Disney and Paris always came up as examples of ordinary vacations. It was painful. But I had a purpose, which was to study there and learn English so that I could go and live in the United States. Indeed, I was taking a private and standard *curso de inglês*, located in Rio de Janeiro's Zona Sul.
>
> It was six months of suffering that made me long for someone in that room to speak my language. Not English, because I still didn't have a grasp of it, but I was sure I would in my life in the United States. But the language of my reality, of empathy and care in teaching.
>
> That reality was mine and my family's alone. Not those students. Not this teacher. That's my story. This is one of the dimensions of *escrevivência*, as Conceição Evaristo teaches us: the experience of one in common.
>
> *(Franco, 2021, p. 2)*

In this excerpt, Anielle fleshes out the racial and class dimensions of her discomfort, this time by specifying the (violent) social difference produced in the *curso de inglês*. She begins by explaining that she felt a "complete stranger" in class: the teacher not only failed to accommodate Anielle's background, but unintentionally or not "expressed astonishment" when Anielle answered questions about her routine. Being displaced to a territory that did not welcome her, the 16-year-old Black girl experienced pain. There is a striking resonance between Anielle's pain and the emotions of fear, anger and frustration that Dovchin (2020) has documented with multilingual subjects who immigrate to Australia in search of work. Dovchin (2020) finds that, regardless of their high-proficiency in English, racialized international students in Australia are often " 'heard,' 'seen,' or 'imagined' speaking 'bad' or 'low proficient' English" (p. 804). These parallels suggest that, rather than purely internal and individual affects, pain and discomfort seem to be social and habituated emotions that respond to widespread inequalities in a colonial world.

Yet Black women like Anielle have thought to map out, and performatively reimagine, domains of English that allow for alternative affects and possibilities of cohabitation. In the previous excerpt, she writes: "It was six months of suffering that made me long for someone in that room to speak my language." Speaking this language did not mean speaking to her in the English she wanted to acquire – after all, she knew she would soon become proficient in it; rather, it meant acknowledging a multimodal and multisensory aggregate that Anielle describes as "the language of [her] reality, of empathy and care in teaching." Anielle explains that speaking (and listening) a language is much more than mastering a linguistic system; it means, first and foremost, building translingual dispositions conducive to listening to difference (Lee & Jenks, 2016), constructing comparable perspectives through resources that include, but are not reduced to, the structure of language (Hanks, 2018) and, above all, building 'safe spaces,' social domains in which the other can be heard (Dovchin, 2021).

Note that Anielle brings precisely one dimension of Conceição Evaristo's *escrevivência* into a relational and shared perspective of subjects who disproportionately suffer from the legacies of colonialism: "the experience of one in common." Further, more than describing a regular scenario of suffering among young Blacks learning English in Brazil, Anielle seeks to move beyond paralysis and build bridges between the common survival of Black people. She wants to expand the anti-racist domain of English in the peripheries of Brazil and beyond. In her project, Anielle says that the murder of her sister made her understand herself as a "daughter of survival" – a person who, in the face of precarity, seeks to find and mobilize communicative and economic resources to engage in a collective struggle. Following her studying in the U.S. and the traumatic experience of losing a sister to political violence, Anielle Franco (2021) has been engaged in repurposing domains of English (and other resources) "as a practice of resistance and emancipation for Black people and especially for Black women activists and human rights defenders" (p. 3).

4.2. "Listening in tongues"

Following Marielle's murder, Pâmella Passos decided to apply to a Rest and Respite program in Europe at the Front Line Defenders NGO in Dublin. It was not uncommon for Pâmella to hitch a ride with Marielle after events they both attended. She could have been in that car on the day of the murder of Marielle. Surviving the murder of her friend stirred up a combination of pain and guilt. In an article entitled "Listening in tongues: An invitation from a Brazilian defender," published on the Front Line Defenders website, Pâmella Passos (2021a) links her perspective on survival and vulnerability to the conditions of communicability of international defenders participating in programs such as Rest and Respite. Her article adds another layer to the decolonial refashioning of English that we have been discussing. In it, Pâmella challenges the very hegemony of English in institutions designed to protect and promote the work of those working to defend human rights. A painful sensation of not being properly heard accompanied Pâmella's experience in Dublin:

> As part of my training, I was welcomed by a Rest and Respite program in Europe.... I promised to myself that I would multiply that opportunity, but I didn't know that it would be so difficult to keep this promise without mastering the English language. In my case, in most of the activities I had the support of a person from the team who translated everything into Spanish. Although I am Brazilian, I understand and speak Spanish fairly well, which is not always a reality in my country. But still, I asked myself several times: why don't any people in Europe speak Spanish to me? Couldn't they learn Spanish or is there a naturalization that everyone must speak English?
>
> Despite all the welcome and rich learning I had in my experience as a defender abroad, in most activities I could not be heard in Portuguese or Spanish, and thus how genuinely could my genuine expression be heard? It was a very painful process.
>
> *(Passos, 2021a, n.p.)*

Pâmella draws attention to the "naturalization that everyone must speak English" in international human rights circles. Although she was provided with a translator to help her participate in activities, the feeling of not being heard in her "genuine expression" was painful. For a while, Pâmella thought about keeping this experience to herself, only recording it in her journals. But as her story resonated with others, she decided to make it public. She published "Listening in tongues" in Portuguese, Spanish and English on the Front Line Defenders website to discuss the incommunicability that can affect people in vulnerable situations like hers (see Passos, 2021b, 2021c).

Interestingly, Pâmella addresses her text to another racialized feminist, Gloria Anzaldúa, who entitled a letter to women writers as "speaking in tongues" (see Anzaldúa, 1983). Also known as glossolalia, speaking in tongues is practiced in religious and spiritual circles. To speak in tongues means to use a language unknown to oneself, often as part of rituals where others also speak (and listen) in tongues (Goodman, 2008). Note that Pâmella is not reclaiming to speak, but to be listened to, in tongues. Echoing feminist perspectives on listening to subaltern subjects

(Lopes, 2011), listening in tongues also implies a different temporality. While practices of listening such as watching videos on social media or understanding an utterance in our 'own' language suggest immediate uptake, listening in tongues opens up the possibility of slow listening. Rather than searching for a pre-defined meaning, this listening practice valorizes the resonances that the signifier produces in the body until it finally speaks to us (Marsilli-Vargas, 2022). Moreover, in reclaiming listening in tongues, Pâmella does not intend to abandon the reappropriation of English and other semiotic resources that we have been studying so far. As she aptly concludes her article: "I understand the importance of publishing this article in English, because even though this is an oppressor's language, I need it to speak with you" (Passos, 2021a, n.p.).

5. Conclusion

In this chapter, I engaged with Brazilian Black feminists and discussed how they have been projecting English and other valorized semiotic resources as a decolonial tool. I singled out the metapragmatic discourse of Conceição Evaristo, Marielle Franco, Anielle Franco and Pâmella Passos about their reclaiming of English and literacies. My discussion shows that projecting this domain is not something that Black feminists do without a strenuous affective work in confronting the legacies of colonialism. I thus tried to emphasize how unease and other likened affects, including anger and frustration, are entangled with their collective imagination of an alternative social domain.

In the two empirical cases, it is possible to discern an interdiscursive coherence. The four women locate their discourses in the terrain of survival. Conceição Evaristo created the concept of *escrevivência* (a signifier that echoes *sobrevivência*, 'survival,' in Portuguese) to talk about the defiant stance of Black women in appropriating writing to disturb the *casa-grande*. Marielle Franco was murdered, but her legacy lives on, through the collective vicarious reclaiming of causes she championed in life, including learning English to build bridges with international feminism. Anielle Franco considers herself a 'daughter of survival' and currently expands Marielle's legacy. Pâmella Passos struggles with the guilt of having survived her friend's assassination and problematizes the hegemony of English in circuits designed for activist survival.

It could be argued that such interdiscursive coherence results from them being part of a 'small' citational chain. After all, they all knew each other and shared a common struggle. But I would like to emphasize that there is also interdiscursive coherence between their reimagination and many other Black feminists in Brazil (Ferreira, 2019; Melo, 2015; Muniz, 2021; Souza, 2011). There are also resonances in other contexts, such as young Palestinians learning English in Israel (Awayed Bishara, 2024) or Mongolian immigrants in Australia (Dovchin, 2020). The peripheral unease in pursuing and reanalyzing English is therefore entangled. As theorists in linguistic anthropology have discussed, this perception of 'sameness' is an effect of the mobility and circulation of discourses (Agha, 2007; Gal, 2018). The interdiscursivity I have unpacked gestures to a socio-cultural type (Gal, 2018), or a common struggle that is nevertheless differently instantiated in global peripheries. The semiotic encounters described previously constitute an entangled and intrusive chain. That is, they are a local 'mark' (or a register) of minority participation in domains usually perceived as belonging to elite groups.

References

Agha, A. (2007). *Language and social relations*. Cambridge University Press.
ALAB. (2021). *Língua inglesa e direitos humanos: pode o subalterno falar?* https://www.youtube.com/watch?v=GwEXRfPx9qE
Anzaldúa, G. (1983). Speaking in tongues: A letter to 3rd World women writers. In C. Moraga & G. Anzaldúa (Eds.), *This bridge called my back: Writings by radical women of color* (pp. 165–174). Kitchen Table Press.
Awayed-Bishara, M. (2024). Linguistic citizenship as decolonial pedagogy: How minoritized language speakers contest epistemic injustices in EFL education. *Working Papers in Language & Literacies*, *324*, 1–18.
Awayed-Bishara, M., Netz, H., & Milani, T. (2022). Translanguaging in a context of colonized education: The case of EFL classrooms for Arabic speakers in Israel. *Applied Linguistics*, *43*(6), 1051–1072.
Bauman, R., & Briggs, C. L. (2003). *Voices of modernity: Language ideologies and the politics of inequality*. Cambridge University Press.
Bourdieu, P. (1985). The genesis of the concepts of habitus and field. *Sociocriticism*, *2*, 11–24.
Canagarajah, A. S. (1999). *Resisting linguistic imperialism in English teaching*. Oxford University Press.
Carneiro, A. S. R. (2022). Following the path of otherwise: Subalternized subjects, academic writing and the political power of discomfort. *Journal of Multicultural Discourses*, *17*(2), 138–157.
Charalambous, C., Charalambous, P., Zembylas, M., & Theodorou, E. (2020). Translanguaging, (in)security and social justice education. In J. A. Panagiotopoulou, L. Rosen & J. Strzykala (Eds.), *Inclusion, education and translanguaging* (pp. 105–123). Springer.
Derrida, J. (1979). Living on. In H. Bloom (Ed.), J. Hulbert (Trans.), *Deconstruction and criticism* (pp. 62–142). Continuum.
Deumert, A. (forthcoming). When things fall apart: On the dialectics of hope and anger. *Language in Society*.
Dos Santos, G. N., & Windle, J. (2021). The nexus of race and class in ELT: From interaction orders to orders of being. *Applied Linguistics*, *42*(3), 473–491.
Dovchin, S. (2020). The psychological damages of linguistic racism and international students in Australia. *International Journal of Bilingual Education and Bilingualism*, *23*(7), 804–818.
Dovchin, S. (2021). Translanguaging, emotionality, and English as a second language immigrants: Mongolian background women in Australia. *Tesol Quarterly*, *55*(3), 839–865.
Evaristo, C. (2020). A Escrevivência e seus subtextos. In C. L. Duarte & I. R. Nunes (Eds.), *Escrevivência: a escrita de nós. Reflexões sobre a obra de Conceição Evaristo* (pp. 26–46). Mina Comunicação e Arte.
Ferreira, A. J. (2019). Social identities of black females in English language textbooks used in Brazil and Cameroon: Intersectionalities of race, gender, social class and critical racial literacy. *Revista X*, *14*(4), 20–40.
Franco, A. (2021). *Ei, você fala inglês? Escrevivências e usos antirracistas decoloniais de língua inglesa, através de um olhar feminista e negro*. Research Project, Universidade Federal do Rio de Janeiro.

Gal, S. (2018). Registers in circulation: The social organization of interdiscursivity. *Signs and Society*, *6*(1), 1–24.

Gal, S., & Irvine, J. (2019). *Signs of difference: Language and ideology in social life*. Cambridge University Press.

Gilroy, P. (1993). *The Black Atlantic: Modernity and double consciousness*. Harvard University Press.

Gomes, N. L. (2019). *O movimento negro educador: saberes construídos nas lutas por emancipação*. Editora Vozes Limitada.

Goodman, F. D. (2008). *Speaking in tongues: A cross-cultural study of glossolalia*. Wipf and Stock Publishers.

Hanks, W. F. (2005). Pierre Bourdieu and the practices of language. *Annual Review of Anthropology*, *34*, 67–83.

Hanks, W. F. (2018). *Language and communicative practices*. Routledge.

Holliday, A. (2005). *The struggle to teach English as an international language*. Oxford University Press.

Instituto Marielle Franco. (2021). *Quem somos*. https://www.institutomariellefranco.org

Koslinski, M. C., Alves, F., & Lange, W. J. (2013). Desigualdades educacionais em contextos urbanos: Um estudo da geografia de oportunidades educacionais na cidade do Rio de Janeiro. *Educação & Sociedade*, *34*, 1175–1202.

Lee, J. W., & Jenks, C. (2016). Doing translingual dispositions. *College Composition & Communication*, *68*(2), 317–344.

Lopes, A. C. (2011). *Funk-se quem quiser: No batidão negro da cidade carioca*. Bom Texto.

Lopes, A. C., Silva, D. N., Facina, A., Calazans, R., & Tavares, J. (2017). Desregulamentando dicotomias: Transletramentos, sobrevivências, nascimentos. *Trabalhos em Linguística Aplicada*, *56*, 753–780.

Lorde, A. (2012). *Sister outsider: Essays and speeches*. Crossing Press.

Machado, M. I., & Bueno, J. R. (2023). "O tempo inteiro sob esse ar de punição": entre a docilização e a cultura de si em uma escola militarizada. *Retratos da Escola*, *17*(37), 225–243.

Marsilli-Vargas, X. (2022). *Genres of listening: An ethnography of psychoanalysis in Buenos Aires*. Duke University Press.

Melo, G. C. V. (2015). O lugar da raça na sala de aula de inglês. *Revista da Associação Brasileira de Pesquisadores/as Negros/as (ABPN)*, *7*(17), 65–81.

Muniz, K. (2021). Linguagem como mandinga: População negra e periférica reinventando epistemologias. In A. N. Souza (Ed.), *Cultura política nas periferias: estratégias de re-existência* (pp. 273–288). Fundação Perseu Abramo.

Passos, P. (2021a). Listening in tongues: An invitation from a Brazilian defender. *Front Line Defenders*. https://www.frontlinedefenders.org/en/blog/post/listening-tongues-invitation-brazilian-defender

Passos, P. (2021b). Ouvir em línguas: o convite de uma defensora do Brasil. *Front Line Defenders*. https://www.frontlinedefenders.org/pt/blog/post/listening-tongues-invitation-brazilian-defender

Passos, P. (2021c). Oír en lenguas: una invitación de una defensora de Brasil. *Front Line Defenders*. https://www.frontlinedefenders.org/es/blog/post/listening-tongues-invitation-brazilian-defender

Passos, P. (2023). Mulheres negras e direitos humanos: Dos tratados aos traçantes. *Le Monde Diplomatique Brasil*. https://diplomatique.org.br/dos-tratados-aos-tracantes/

Passos, P., & Linhares, T. (2021). *Quadrinhos por direitos*. Mórula Editorial.

Passos, P., & Mendonça, A. (2021). *O professor é o inimigo: Uma análise sobre a perseguição docente no Brasil*. Mórula Editorial.

Pennycook, A. (2020). Translingual entanglements of English. *World Englishes*, *39*(2), 222–235.

Pennycook, A. (2022). Entanglements and assemblages of English. *Crossings: A Journal of English Studies*, *13*(1), 7–21.

Phillipson, R. (1992). *Linguistic imperialism*. Oxford University Press.

Rocha, L. F. (2016). Políticas linguísticas para o ensino de língua estrangeira em Niterói: Um olhar crítico. *Cadernos de Letras da UFF Dossiê: Línguas e culturas em contato, 53*, 301–321.

Rojo, L. M. (2019). The "self-made speaker": The neoliberal governance of speakers. In L. M. Rojo & A. Del Percio (Eds.), *Language and neoliberal governmentality* (pp. 162–189). Routledge.

Rosa, J., & Flores, N. (2017). Unsettling race and language: Toward a raciolinguistic perspective. *Language in Society, 46*(5), 621–647.

Roth-Gordon, J. (2017). *Race and the Brazilian body: Blackness, whiteness, and everyday language in Rio de Janeiro*. University of California Press.

Silva, D. N. (2022). *Papo reto*: The politics of enregisterment amid the crossfire in Rio de Janeiro. *Signs and Society, 10*(2), 239–264.

Silva, D. N., & Lee, J. W. (2021). "Marielle, presente": Metaleptic temporality and the enregisterment of hope in Rio de Janeiro. *Journal of Sociolinguistics, 25*(2), 179–197.

Silva, D. N., & Lee, J. W. (2024). *Language as hope*. Cambridge University Press.

Souza, A. L. (2011). *Letramentos de reexistência: Poesia, grafite, música, dança: hip-hop*. Parábola.

Stevenson, A., & Lindberg, C. (2010). Domain. In A. Stevenson & C. Lindberg (Eds.), *New Oxford American dictionary* (3rd ed.). Oxford University Press. https://www.oxfordreference.com/display/10.1093/acref/9780195392883.001.0001/m_en_us1241435?rskey=InKr4s&result=1

Windle, J., Souza, A. L. S., Silva, D. N., Zaidan, J. M., Maia, J. D. O., Muniz, K., & Lorenso, S. (2020). Towards a transperipheral paradigm: An agenda for socially engaged research. *Trabalhos em Linguística Aplicada, 59*, 1563–1576.

Woolard, K. (1998). Introduction: Language ideology as a field of inquiry. In B. Schieffelin, K. Woolard & P. Kroskrity (Eds.), *Language ideologies: Practice and theory* (pp. 3–47). Oxford University Press.

Wortham, S. (2008). Linguistic anthropology of education. *Annual Review of Anthropology, 37*, 37–51.

6
"NO ENGLISH, NO ENGLISH"
Raciolinguistic entanglements in Czechia

Stephanie Rudwick

1. Introduction

In March 2023, Thabisa,[1] a young professional South African woman of Zulu descent,[2] walked into an upmarket boutique just off the grid from the 'old town' in Prague, Czechia. While the so-called 'old town' is frequented extensively by tourists, the boutique, although located in a central city area, caters primarily to Czech residents. Thabisa lives close by this boutique; the neighbourhood has been her home for a period of nearly ten years. Having skimmed the clothing in the shop, she found an item she liked and intended to buy without trying it on. With it in her hands, she walked towards a middle-aged salesperson standing close to the cashier. However, as she approached, the lady frantically and defensively crossed her hands in front of herself and said: "No English, no English!" Thabisa, who has a good working knowledge of Czech and merely intended to pay for the item was taken aback by this raciolinguistic profiling. After a moment of slight shock, and no further reaction from the lady, she angrily placed the item back on the rack and stamped out of the shop.

Thabisa recounted this experience to me when we met in a Prague café in late 2023. The reason I started this chapter with it is because it succinctly captures one of the many entanglements between language, in particular English, and race in Czechia.[3] As a person with sub-Saharan African heritage, one is mostly not expected to know the Czech language. This marks the country, and central eastern Europe (CEE) more generally, as distinctly different from most western European states, which have experienced extensive migration from ex-colonies for many decades. The term *Afropean* (Pitts, 2019) is increasingly accepted, and inherent in it is the understanding of Black European citizens as ordinary members of the European nation state. Czechia is different, and there are at least three distinct reasons

106 Entangled Englishes

for this. First, the country, unlike the UK, France, Germany, and others, never had a colony in Africa or elsewhere in the Global South. Second, the country (and CEE in general) was quite isolated under Soviet communism until the early 1990s and did not see the level of migration and mobility other European states witnessed throughout the 20th century. And last, CEE countries have been more recently (notably since 2015) reluctant to open up themselves to migration, something Kalmar (2022) conceptualised as 'central Europe's illiberal revolt.'

When exploring raciolinguistics in Czechia, it has to be pointed out that (pseudo)-race science was, as was the case all over Europe, at the core of the country's nation-building process. Despite the rejection of German race theories, the aim of white homogeneity was and is an important aspect of national identity making in Czechia (Shmidt, 2020). As an initial point of departure, it needs to be acknowledged that anti-Roma racism in Czechia is ubiquitous. While there is a sizeable community of Vietnamese people in the country, people from the African continent or people more generally with African heritage have not had a strong presence in Czechia. In 2021, there were approximately 4,000 individuals from sub-Saharan African countries registered as short- and long-term residents in the country.[4] At the same time, no data is available that would provide at least a rough idea about how many Czech individuals have one parent from the African continent or other Global South heritage. Against this background, it is perhaps not surprising that individuals with African heritage experience a strong sense of Otherness in Czechia (Rudwick & Simuziya, 2023; Rudwick & Nwagbo, 2024). Language and specifically English are crucial in the ways this racial Otherness plays out and is experienced by individuals.

Methodologically grounded in participant observation and extensive interviews, the chapter aims to develop a brief account of specific language and socio-political dynamics in this central eastern European space where whiteness and the Czech language are hegemonic and blackness and English index 'Otherness.' This chapter emerges as part of a larger qualitative research project that focuses on lived raciolinguistic experiences of Africans and Afroczechs in Czechia.[5] I provide a brief ethnographic perspective of how the perceptions of being 'Other' in the form of phenotypical blackness influence quotidian encounters of individuals and how English is entangled in these social realities. Through the ethnographic lens, we see the complexities of language dynamics emerging (Blommaert, 2010), and participant observation and extensive interviewing of long-term African residents and Afroczechs allows us to develop a nuanced account of language and socio-political dynamics in Czechia. While anthropologists have long acknowledged personal narratives as a legitimate source for research, Wei and Lee (2023) recently also emphasise the significance of individual stories in applied linguistics. Drawing from Bauman's (1996) conceptualisations of liquid identity, these scholars call for an understanding of anecdotes as a source of data that allow for "analytical premium on moments and momentarity" rather than patterns and systematicity (Wei & Lee, 2023, p. 7). This approach, and what anthropologists understand as minutiae of everyday life, provides the basis for this chapter in combination with a raciolinguistic lens. This study is ethnographic in a sense that I moved fluidly inside and outside the 'field' as participant observer over a period of about a year and a half, with the field being constituted by the capital of Czechia, Prague, and a smaller town by the name of Hradec Králové. Through ethnographic understanding, language identities and struggles for belonging can be fruitfully researched (Blommaert, 2010). Ethnographic activities involved a combination of informal field methods, such as involvement and participation in the activities of African individuals, events, and community meetings in order to holistically understand community dynamics and personal narratives. The primary data comprises 37 narrative interviews with people who have heritage from the African continent. Individuals were between 18 and 78 years old and came from various socio-economic and educational backgrounds.[6] The fieldwork was conducted between March 2022 and January 2024 and includes extensive observations and informal conversational data.

In order to make sense of what positions English held and holds in Czechia and how the language operates, it is necessary to initially provide a sociohistorical brief in connection with theoretical considerations in the next section. The subsequent section then focuses on two opposing English raciolinguistic dynamics that characterise encounters and experiences of Africans/Afroczechs with Czech strangers.[7] Both are rooted in the common perception that a person of colour (unless they are Roma or Vietnamese) is likely not to speak Czech. The first can be framed as *African person: 'English as a root of anxiety and rejection,'* the second one as *African person; 'English embraced as cosmopolitan lingua franca.'* In the discussion, I elaborate on the generational distinctions of these perceptions and juxtapose the entanglements between English and Czech before concluding.

2. English in Czechia through a raciolinguistic lens

When we research entangled Englishes (Pennycook, 2020, 2022), we are studying the multiple ways in which English and Englishes are connected to the world around us; the global and the local; and how this manifests in relation to culture, class, and nation. Almost four decades ago, the great South African writer Njabulo Ndebele (1987) aptly remarked that both the establishment and the labelling of English as '*the*' international language are quite simply the result of English imperialism. This explains the less dominant position of English in Czechia than elsewhere. The influence of the British Empire was negligible in Czech lands, where it was rather German and/or Russian which were more or less forcefully propagated. In fact, until late in the 20th century, English usage is described as 'atypical' and to 'arouse attention' in the territory of the Czechoslovakian nations (Nekvapil & Sherman, 2024). It was only when the communist regime fell in 1989 and the country opened towards the West that large numbers of foreigners arrived, in particular from the Anglo-American sphere of influence. Compulsory Russian acquisition in schools was quickly abandoned and opened up to increasing English tuition.

Nonetheless, it was not until 1997 that the English language became the most commonly taught language in Czechia's schools (Nekvapil & Sherman, 2024). While the instrumental value of English was then widely propagated in the new millennium (Nekvapil & Sherman, 2013), it did not change the fact that the overwhelming majority of middle-aged and older-generation Czechs (those roughly 45+ years today) did not experience much English acquisition throughout their schooling.[8] This detail is very significant for the purpose of this chapter because it explains why the majority of Czechs who were born before the 80s do not have great skills in the English language. Due to this, English also does not (yet) have clear international lingua franca status in the society, although it can be said to be the language closest to a lingua franca in Prague (Sherman, 2009). The context here is important in understanding that English, though commonly marked as 'superior,' certainly does not have dominant ground in everyday life in Czechia.

African migrants and long-term foreign residents in Czechia who have poor Czech language skills experience English as having limited use outside urban areas and among older generations (Rudwick & Simuziya, 2023). While many nonetheless live comfortably in the country and within their own social microcosms, this is often due to the bubble of expatriates and professional individuals with whom they have relations. Language politics are not a particularly prominent issue in the country, as Czech hegemony is an unspoken reality. Bourdieu (1991) has taught us that social identity politics are always about legitimacy and power and that this includes views and ideologies about language in the making and unmaking of groups. When it comes to primary and secondary education (with the exception of private schools), there is a very strong emphasis on grammatically correct, ideally unaccented Czech language skills (Obrovská et al., 2021). Hence, in this environment, English is clearly the language of an 'out-group,' and, at the same time, many English speakers are also acutely aware of the worldly linguistic and cultural hegemony implicated by the use of English (Sherman, 2009). And yet, as this chapter will show, the status and position of English are flexible and fluid depending on time, space, and context. It has also been noted that there is increasing superdiversity in the territory of contemporary Czechia (Sloboda, 2016), although this is hardly comparable to some other European nation states. For sure, there are distinct places, in particular in up-market wealthy city areas, where English has become ubiquitous. The language, hence, plays various roles in the country. Many Czechs consider English skills among their compatriots a sign of education and upward mobility. At the same time, however, the sole knowledge of English without Czech restricts life in Czechia in complex ways.

While sociolinguists have had a long-standing interest in the intersections of language and race and have long developed an understanding of these two variables as co-constituents in dynamics of power and inequality (Makoni et al., 2003; Harris & Rampton, 2003; Alim & Smitherman, 2012), more recent scholarship emerging under the label of 'raciolinguistics' (Flores & Rosa, 2015; Rosa & Flores, 2017;

Alim et al., 2016, 2020) has led to a proliferation of studies embracing the field. Succinctly summed up,

> the raciolinguistic perspective emphasizes 1) the colonial anchoring of racial and linguistic classifications and hierarchies, 2) the modes of perception through which race and language are jointly apprehended across contexts, 3) the production of naturalized typologies of racial and linguistic features, forms, and categories imagined to emanate from and correspond to one another, 4) the intersectional matrices of marginalization that dynamically (re)structure racial and linguistic hierarchies, and 5) the need for radically reimagined theories of change that move beyond modifying the linguistic practices of racialized populations to challenging colonial, imperial, and capitalist power formations that continually reproduce disparity, dispossession, and disposability.
>
> *(Rosa & Flores, 2023, p. 104)*

While there has been a focus on the Unites States and Hispanic contexts, raciolinguistic perspectives have increasingly been employed elsewhere in the world, and they are certainly relevant in the central eastern European context as well. However, it is important to be mindful of the fact that the ways in which people think about race might be different in this geopolitical region. After all, understandings of what race is and how it manifests are dependent on "the specific conditions . . . which concretize the notion of race" (Goldberg, 2006, p. 332) in any particular place and context. In Czechia there is still a prevalent discourse that if one acknowledges the existence of race as a meaningful social category, one might implicitly promote racism (Rudwick & Schmiedl, 2023). The 'evasiveness' to speak about race in the form of a "disavowment of race" (Migliarini, 2018, p. 453) or a shunning of race (Foner, 2018) continues to permeate Czech society. And yet race is deeply significant in societal power dynamics, both as social constructed category and in the form of phenotypical meanings. For the purpose of this chapter, I refer to the raciolinguistic perspective as a way of analysing the co-construction of language and race as a form of intersectional oppression rooted in coloniality and dominant whiteness. There has always been a close link between the linguistic and racial superiority of 'whiteness' (Ashcroft, 2001), and it is these intersecting meanings which continue to contribute to the production of inequality in any society. While this chapter focuses specifically on Czech sociolinguistic and cultural politics around the use of English, the Czech language obviously is entangled in this usage. Raciolinguistics also provides a useful theoretical framework and is an analytical tool through which perspectives on the role of national languages vis-à-vis English (as a lingua franca) play out in European politics of migration and mobility. Although not all paradigms from the Global North are applicable for the CEE region, hegemonic whiteness and linguistic and racial entanglements are evidently at play.

3. English raciolinguistic entanglements in Czechia

Due to Czechia's racial homogeneity, race also operates as a proxy for language (Czech vis-à-vis English and other languages) in the country. I focus on a dominant English raciolinguistic ideology in the analysis, which is rooted in the common idea among Czech people that people of colour, for example, individuals with African heritage, speak English (and no Czech). Kroskrity (2020, p. 80) argued that "most vernacular understandings of racism neglect or minimize the role of linguistically constructed racial categories and their associated hierarchies" and "attend to other linguistic practices and levels that are also involved in defamation and denigration." The ideology that people with African heritage speak English (rather than Czech), which is only one among many prevalent ones, enables an analysis of racialising practices and racism. English is, of course, entangled in multiple complex ways in Czech social life, and there is much language commodification (Duchêne & Heller, 2012) involved in a sense that, generally, upmarket areas exhibit more English(es). Markedly different from other contexts, however, the common conception that English is the language of the Global North is more complicated here. In Czechia, it can also be seen as the language of people from the Global South or, for instance, of people with African heritage. Nekvapil and Sherman (2024) recently argue that English largely maintains the status of a foreign language in Czechia even though many international corporate and upmarket spaces have increasingly adopted English as the lingua franca. However, the authors also show the more complex picture where they refer to a heavily discussed 2017 incident where a sign was placed at the Czech City Hall which stated "You are in Czech office, so you have to be able to speak Czech. Or you have to come with translator" (Sattler, 2017, cited in Nekvapil & Sherman, 2024). No doubt, there are still many services, both public and private, in Czechia that are simply not available in English.

In this chapter, I limit my discussion to the unspoken fact that to be addressed in English, or to be expected to only speak English, is an absolute quotidian experience among Africans and Afroczechs in the country. I am pointing this out because in most western European countries, the number of Afropeans is much higher, and people of colour are not regularly spoken to in English. Every single one of the 37 interviewees reported multiple experiences of immediately being spoken to in English rather than in Czech. As stated, this is evidently rooted in the fact that Czech society is predominantly white, and people with sub-Saharan heritage are widely seen as 'other.' One particularly haunting memory was recounted by Alex, a professional Zambian man with long-time residence in Czechia and solid Czech language skills. On a Sunday afternoon, he sits in the train, reading an English book and sharing the compartment with a Czech mother and her child. He overhears the mother making racist remarks in Czech about him to her child, assuming he does not speak Czech. Nigerian-Czech Samuel also has a plethora of comments he 'collected' about people making negative and racist remarks in front of him, assuming he does not know Czech. As this research shows, Afroczechs and Africans who speak good Czech have multiple experiences of overhearing people speaking about them to others in Czech, assuming they do not understand (because they are not white and are perceived as non-Czech). For women it is often in the form of verbal sexual harassment; a Kenyan woman, for instance, recalled hearing when passing a crowd of men in a bar: "Guys look at the black girl, I would not mind getting her to bed." Exoticisation is a huge problem for women of colour in the country, while men are often perceived as a threat.

In the following section, I focus on a perspective linked to the African-English association framed as *African person = English is foreign* (and a root of anxiety leading to rejection). How this plays out will be illustrated through diverse lived experiences and narratives from African and Afroczech individuals.

3.1. African person: 'English is foreign'

The anecdote provided at the outset of this chapter speaks directly to this association, framed as *African person = English is foreign*, and a root of anxiety leading to rejection. It is symptomatic of the assumption that an African person speaks English and probably no Czech. In analysing these raciolinguistic dynamics resulting from the perspective that English is foreign and by no means a lingua franca, it is difficult to know in how far the unpreparedness and apparent anxiety to speak English by some Czechs is only due to English language incompetence or might also carry a component of racial rejection. All of the non–Czech-speaking interviewees remembered instances when after asking a stranger or even a sales assistant something in English they were immediately dismissed, sometimes with a rather rude hand gesture, basically waving them away. But this does not only happen to people of colour in Czechia. What marks the difference is that people with African descent are often denied a service or rejected before they even have a chance to open their mouth. Ben, a young Rwandan professional, remembers, "before I learned Czech, life was so hard here, I cannot count the times people would simply ignore me, or tell me to go away; 'no English' was the common statement." In a similar vein, Sofie says, "It's really not easy to navigate this place with English only, people are scared to speak it, or they really don't speak it, or they don't like blacks." At the same time, however, she conceded that all her corporate friends and the places and restaurants they frequent in Prague fully cater to English speakers. Extreme gentrification of some areas in the city has also resulted in more and more English becoming part of the linguistic landscape. And yet, even in gentrified parts, there are places where English might not be spoken, such as a post office, for instance.

There are some situations which participants described as quite positive in mitigating what they interpreted as initial racial or raciolinguistic profiling in relation to English. A doctoral student from Zambia, Mdu, who has intermediate Czech skills, reflected on an incident where he sat on public transport and an elderly man looked at him with what Mdu interpreted as some contempt. Mdu remembers how after saying "Dobry den pane" ('Good day mister'), "there was a smile, a strange relief in the guy's face." There is no doubt that on the one hand and in some instances, racial Otherness can be mitigated through Czech language skills. On the other hand, however, there are also distinct limits to the power of language against ideologies of race. Several Afroczech individuals described situations where they had spoken to a person on the phone in their unaccented first-language Czech, and the person, upon meeting them physically, could not hide their 'shock' about their appearance. One participant commented on how his white British friend does not experience the same kind or level of unwillingness to interact with him among people when he speaks in English. At the ministry of foreign affairs, paradoxically, one interviewee described how the clerk at the counter refused to interact in English, specifically adding "no Africa English" [sic]. The comment suggests that the association between English and Africa has a distinct raciolinguistic component which ignores that a Black British person, for example, might have never set foot on the African continent. Conversely, most of the African student interviewees reported that visa extensions are a source of great discontent and even anxiety. Several participants noted that there are employees of the foreigners' police and registration office who are not proficient in English or are unwilling to make use of the language. Nandi described in great detail the emotional and psychological stress she felt weeks ahead of reapplying for her visa. Instances of being screamed at, having her passport thrown back at her, and a general feeling of humiliation mark her experiences. "I cannot help feeling that my race has something to do with it as well" is her concluding statement.

There was reasonable consensus among the Afroczech interviewees that an initial negative encounter in which it was assumed that they spoke only English could be mitigated by speaking Czech, especially what is perceived as 'good' Czech. Often, however, the preceding response also opened up racial 'Othering' dynamics such as the notorious question "Where are you from?" This question is strongly indicative of the idea that the person is not regarded as 'fully Czech' due to their skin colour and hence provides further evidence for the perceived hegemony of whiteness in the country. Samantha, a young Angolan Czech woman, described that her claim to Czechness would, in some instances, trigger resistance. She cited an elderly lady responding to her by saying "But this is not what a Czech person looks like." Among African people who, due to their experience of English as limiting make efforts to acquire Czech, there was variation in how individuals experienced these efforts, with some feeling positively surprised and others having experiences which disheartened them. Among one of the disheartening experiences was the insistence of others to speak to them in English. This embracing of English leads to the second language approach, identified as English as the cosmopolitan lingua franca.

3.2. African person: 'English is a cosmopolitan lingua franca'

The role English and English speakers take up in Czechia can be linked to Pennycook's (2022, p. 8) conceptualisation of the worldliness of English, which refers "both to its local and to its global position, both to the ways in which it reflects and constitutes social relations" and how it is "always global and local, part of local struggles for communication and recognition, bound up with class, race, culture, gender, and education." Various participants described how they encounter many people, especially young and upwardly mobile Czech people, who want to profile themselves as cosmopolitan and are keen to demonstrate their well-spoken and sophisticated English. While this is welcomed in most instances, some Afroczech individuals in the sample also experience the repeated addressing in English as what some scholars would conceptualise as a microaggression. As Petr remarked, "you know it is so annoying that people make assumptions on the basis of my skin colour," or Samantha, a young Afroczech woman of Angolan-Czech descent, notes, "I know they mean well when they talk to me in English, and they are more welcoming than others but then again – for me it is always a reminder how different I am, how I just don't quite fit in." While growing up in rural Czechia, Samantha experienced some heinous acts of racism in her childhood which she has been trying to grapple with through years of therapy.

While the embracing of English among some Czech people in encounters with Africans and Afroczechs is clearly not always welcomed, Tom, a 68-year-old Nigerian who came to study in Czechia in the 1970s to acquire a PhD, looks at it more positively: "in the 1990s no one spoke English and Neo-Nazis were roaming the streets of Prague. Now we have lots of people who are embracing diversity – I see nothing wrong with it [the immediate speaking of English to Africans]." He also conceded, however, that he feels for his children and grandchildren, who continue to be 'othered' quite a lot in their everyday life despite them feeling more Czech than anything else. Lara, a middle-aged successful entrepreneur who is originally from Uganda and came to Czechia in her early 20s, concludes our conversation about English in Czechia with the sentence: "At last Czechia is really becoming worldly," which is a nice fit for Pennycook's (2022) conceptualisations of the worldliness of English. There are also complex gender dynamics that lie outside of a focus on English and cannot be considered in detail due to the limited scope of this chapter. Suffice it to say the fieldwork indicates that African and Afroczech women are frequently exoticised and sometimes sexually harassed, while African/Afroczech men are often the victims of blatant racism.

Although the term 'microaggression' is not commonly known in Czech society, individuals with African heritage are frequently aware of the term due to their more global reading on racial injustices. Students from African countries who study for a semester or longer in Czechia often comment on the 'relentless staring' they experience, especially outside of the main cities. All in all, Prague must be seen as distinct from the rest of Czechia due to its extensive tourism industry, large expat communities, and status as a world metropole. People in Prague are more diverse, and most Czechs are much more ready to speak English than people who reside in the Czech countryside. In fact, as one of the participants, who is a PhD student from Ghana who lives in a middle-sized town with just under 100,000 inhabitants, remarked: "I always relax when I travel to Prague because people are so ready to speak in English; it is not like in Hradec Králové." While many foreigners welcome the increasing openness to speak in English in Prague and other Czech cities, it is also not surprising that being permanently addressed in English rather than Czech can be a frustrating experience for Afroczechs whose L1 is Czech and who want to feel at home in Czechia. It can lead to what has been conceptualised as *restricted affiliation* (Rudwick & Nwagbo, 2024) to the country and its broader society. The experience of permanently being 'othered,' despite one's own sense of rootedness in Czechia and Czechness, comes with certain costs and influences mixed-race individuals in terms of their sense of belonging to the country. At the same time, many Africans who live in Czechia and have little to no knowledge of Czech welcome the openness of Czech strangers to speak in English. Those, however, who make a concerted effort to learn Czech might also get frustrated with people who insist on speaking English to them while they are aiming to improve their Czech.

4. Conclusion

There is an indexical connection between people with African migration backgrounds and English language usage in Czechia. Raciolinguistic dynamics which involve English are complex and differ greatly depending on space and context. This chapter focused on specificities of the context where whiteness and the Czech language are hegemonic, while blackness and English are signifiers for 'Foreignness' or 'Otherness.' On the one hand, there is a language ideology, held primarily by urban, educated, and upwardly mobile people, that sees English as a global lingua franca. As a result of this, one can argue that there is an increasing willingness to speak English in certain spaces and certain contexts, such as international corporate environments, in gentrified city neighbourhoods and upmarket restaurants and cafés, and in particular in Prague. At the same time, however, many Czechs of the generation 45 years old and up do not have good English skills and are unable and sometimes also unwilling to provide services in English. Also, more broadly, people in smaller cities and in the country are not well prepared for English customers and simply cannot offer services in English.

This chapter has also sought to draw attention to the fact that English is not an all-inclusive lingua franca in the country and that understanding its associations and entanglements requires good knowledge of the particular language history of the country. Findings from the ethnographic research suggest that there are distinct generational changes in language and racial attitudes, but much more research is necessary in order to provide a nuanced account of this. This chapter also elaborated further on the social ambiguity of English as a lingua franca with reference to Czech society (Rudwick, 2021). On the one hand, there exists an evident connection between English and colonialism (Pennycook, 1998), and this impacts the "modes of perception through which race and language are jointly apprehended across contexts" (Rosa & Flores, 2023, p. 104). This plays out in perceptions among some

Czech locals, in particular from older generations, who feel that English-speaking foreigners neo-colonise their spaces. On the other hand, there are extensive trans-cultural exchanges and a distinct level of metrolingualism emerging (Pennycook, 2007; Otsuji & Pennycook, 2010). Research into these issues is in Czechia in its infancy and hopefully will receive more attention in the upcoming years.

Within both English raciolinguistic dynamics described previously, that is, 1) *African person: 'English is foreign'* and 2) *African person: 'English is the cosmopolitan lingua franca,'* there are challenges and opportunities involved for Africans and Afroczechs in the country. In fact, most Afroczech interviewees bear witness to the fact that as a Czech who phenotypically looks African/Black, one is conditioned to a level of 'Othering' which, in some instances, involves English. Although the national language (Czech) can be considered a deeply significant constituent of Czech nationality, the lived experience of Afroczechs demonstrates that it often does not suffice in Czech national identity-making (Rudwick & Nwagbo, 2024). But this is not unusual for CEE contexts, where other scholars have already shown that non-white people are 'outside' of the imagined racial image of the society, for instance, in Poland (Balogun & Joseph-Salisbury, 2021; Ohia-Nowak, 2016). The perception of hegemonic whiteness also translates into language politics in which English is identified as a language of the racial Other. But English in this context can also open up opportunities for joint struggles (Pennycook, 2017). It might trigger some counter-articulations in the context described previously and within rebellious acts, which might contribute to further social and racial justice.

Notes

1 All names provided are pseudonyms in order to ensure the anonymity of the participants.
2 Forty-seven-year-old female from South Africa.
3 Given my preference for emic categories, I employ the term 'Czechia' rather than 'the Czech Republic,' as this is the preferred term among most Czech academics who write in English.
4 Czech Statistical Office (ČSÚ). 2021. "T02 Foreigners by Category of Residence, Sex, and Citizenship–31December2021."https://www.czso.cz/documents/11292/27914491/2112_c01t02.xlsx/27555e04-231a-4d6c-96ae-b07c4ca16ce8?version=1.0
5 I hereby acknowledge funding from the Czech Research Council, *Grantová Agentura Česke Republiky* [22-19820S]. I also would also like to thank the two anonymous reviewers of this manuscript for their constructive comments.
6 Participants are further distinguished between Africans from the sub-Saharan part of the continent and Afroczechs, who are mostly but not only of mixed heritage with one Czech parent and one parent from the African continent. There are, however, also self- and other-identified Afroczechs with both parents from the continent but a minimum of 15 years residence in Czechia. The latter have very good, often native-like knowledge of the Czech language and feel, at least to some extent, that they belong to Czechia.
7 For reasons of scope, the focus lies on these two dynamics. However, they are certainly not the only ones emerging.
8 Many older people still speak some German, but the teaching of the language has been steadily declining in Czech schools (Dovalil, 2018).

References

Alim, S., Reyes, A., & Kroskrity, P. (Eds.). (2020). *The Oxford handbook of language and race*. Oxford University Press.
Alim, S., Rickford, J. R., & Ball, A. F. (Eds.). (2016). *Raciolinguistics: How language shaped our ideas about race*. Oxford University Press.
Alim, S., & Smitherman, G. (2012). *Articulate while Black: Barack Obama, language, and race in the US*. Oxford University Press.
Ashcroft, B. (2001). Language and race. *Social Identities*, 7(3), 311–328.
Balogun, B., & Joseph-Salisbury, R. (2021). Black/white mixed-race experience of race and racism in Poland. *Ethnic and Racial Studie*s, 44(2), 234–251.
Bauman, Z. (1996). From pilgrim to tourist – or a short history of identity. In S. Hall & P. Du Gay (Eds.), *Questions of cultural identity* (pp. 18–36). Sage.
Blommaert, J. (2010). *Sociolinguistics of globalization*. Cambridge University Press.
Bourdieu, P. (1991). *Language and symbolic power*. Polity.
Dovalil, V. (2018). Qual der Wahl, or spoiled for choice? English and German as the subject of decision-making processes in the Czech Republic. In T. Sherman & J. Nekvapil (Eds.), *Volume 5: English in business and commerce: Interactions and policies* (pp. 276–309). De Gruyter Mouton.
Duchêne, A., & Heller, M. (Eds.). (2012). *Language in late capitalism: Pride and profit*. Routledge.
Flores, N., & Rosa, J. (2015). Undoing appropriateness: Raciolinguistic ideologies and language diversity in education. *Harvard Educational Review*, 85(2), 149–201.
Foner, N. (2018). Race in an era of mass migration: Black migrants in Europe and the United States. *Ethnic and Racial Studies*, 41(6), 1113–1130.
Goldberg, D. T. (2006). Racial Europeanization. *Ethnic and Racial Studies*, 29(2), 331–364.
Harris, R., & Rampton, B. (Eds.). (2003). *Language, ethnicity and race reader*. Routledge.
Kalmar, I. (2022). *White but not quite: Central Europe's illiberal revolt*. Bristol University Press.
Kroskrity, P. (2020). Theorizing linguistic racisms from a language ideological perspective. In H. S. Alim, A. Reyes & P. Kroskrity (Eds.), *The Oxford handbook of language and race* (pp. 68–89). Oxford University Press.
Makoni, S., Smitherman, G., Ball, A., & Spears, A. K. (Eds.). (2003). *Black linguistics: Language, society and politics in Africa and the Americas*. Routledge.
Migliarini, V. (2018). "Colour-evasiveness" and racism without race: The disablement of asylum-seeking children at the edge of fortress Europe. *Race, Ethnicity and Education*, 21(4), 438–457.
Ndebele, J. (1987). The English language and social change in South Africa. *The English Academy Review*, 4, 1–16.
Nekvapil, J., & Sherman, T. (2013). Language ideologies and linguistics practices: The case of multinational companies in Central Europe. In E. Barat, P. Studer & J. Nekvapil (Eds.), *Ideological conceptualizations of language discourses and linguistic diversity* (pp. 85–117). Peter Lang.
Nekvapil, J., & Sherman, T. (2024). English in the Czech Republic. In K. Bolton (Ed.), *The Wiley Blackwell Encyclopaedia of World Englishes* (1st ed.). Wiley-Blackwell.
Obrovská, J., Jarkovská, L., & Lišková, K. (2021). "Since they are here in Czechia, they should talk in Czech": Ethnicity in peer groups at school. *Intercultural Education*, 32(1), 62–82.
Ohia-Nowak, M. A. (2016). In Black and White: Reflections from studies about Black people in everyday Polish language and in media discourse in Poland. *Africa and Eastern/Central Europe Series, Africa in Words*. https://africainwords.com/2016/12/19/in-black-and-white-reflections-from-studies-about-black-people-in-everyday-polish-language-and-in-media-discourse-in-poland/

Otsuji, E., & Pennycook, A. (2010). Metrolingualism: Fixity, fluidity and language in flux. *International Journal of Multilingualism, 7*(3), 240–254.
Pennycook, A. (1998). *English and the discourses of colonialism*. Routledge.
Pennycook, A. (2007). *Global English and transcultural flows*. Routledge.
Pennycook, A. (2017). *The cultural politics of English as an international language*. Routledge.
Pennycook, A. (2020). Translingual entanglements of English. *World Englishes, 39*(2), 222–235.
Pennycook, A. (2022). Entanglements and assemblages of English. *Crossings: A Journal of English Studies, 13*(1), 7–21.
Pitts, J. (2019). *Afropean: Notes from Black Europe*. Penguin.
Rosa, J., & Flores, N. (2017). Unsettling race and language: Toward a racial linguistic perspective. *Language in Society, 46*(5), 1–27.
Rosa, J., & Flores, N. (2023). Rethinking language barriers & social justice from a raciolinguistic perspective. *Daedalus, 152*(3), 99–114.
Rudwick, S. (2021). *The ambiguity of English as a Lingua Franca: Politics of language and race in South Africa*. Routledge.
Rudwick, S., & Nwagbo, A. (2024). Restricted affiliation: The costs of otherness among Afroczechs. *Journal of Ethnic and Racial Studies, 47*(15), 3259–3279.
Rudwick, S., & Schmiedl, M. (2023). "It's not our problem": Czech online discourse on kneeling in football and Black Lives Matter. *Sport in Society, 26*(10), 1701–1722.
Rudwick, S., & Simuziya, N. J. (2023). African diasporic narratives from the Czech Republic: Focus on language and race. *Diaspora Studies, 16*(3), 264–286.
Sherman, T. (2009). Managing hegemony: Native English speakers in the Czech Republic. In J. Nekvapil & T. Sherman (Eds.), *Language management in contact situations: Perspectives from three continents* (pp. 75–96). Peter Lang.
Shmidt, V. (2020). Race science in Czechoslovakia: Serving segregation in the name of the nation. *Studies in History and Philosophy of Biological & Biomedical Sciences, 83*, 1–13.
Sloboda, M. (2016). Transition to superdiversity in the Czech Republic: Its emergence and resistance. In M. Sloboda, P. Laihonen & A. Zabrodskaja (Eds.), *Sociolinguistics transition in former East Bloc countries: Two decades after the regime change* (pp. 141–183). Peter Lang.
Wei, L., & Lee, T. K. (2023). Transpositioning: Translanguaging and the liquidity of identity. *Applied Linguistics*, amad065. https://doi.org/10.1093/applin/amad065

7
RE-/IMAGINING RACIALIZED ENTANGLEMENTS OF ENGLISHES AND PEOPLES

A call for a quantum ethos

Patriann Smith

1. Introduction

In 2023, Angela Bassett, an American actress for 40 years best known for portraying Black women who made history, became an Oscar nominee for the Marvel film *Black Panther: Wakanda Forever*. This Oscar/Academy Award nomination, constituting a second award that she was nominated for but did not receive (i.e., for her performance in the 1993 Tina Turner biopic *What's Love Got to Do with It*), emerged amidst a discourse of #OscarsSoWhite: a place where "81% of voters identify as white and 67% as male" (Kendall, 2023, n.p.). For many, Angela Bassett's inability to be recognized as an Oscar award winner functioned as a stark reminder of the work required of racialized people of Color, navigating in perpetuity an often veiled but nonetheless indelibly printed 'abyssal line' (de Sousa Santos, 2007). In describing this line unveiled by de Sousa Santos (2007), García and colleagues (2021) assert that such "abyssal thinking . . . creates a line establishing that which is considered 'civil society,' and declares as nonexistent those colonized knowledges and lifeways positioned on the other side of the line, thus relegating them to an existential abyss" (pp. 203–204). They add that "colonial logics stemming from abyssal thinking have been so well established that they are not readily apparent" (García et al., 2021, pp. 203–204). It is these colonial logics undergirding what many have viewed as an always shifting and impossible standard that raised questions concerning what was believed to be the impossibility of Bassett's impeccable performance, no matter how great, to meet the requirements for an Oscar. It must be acknowledged here that whether Angela Bassett deserves an Oscar or not, though, is a question that escapes my capacity to evaluate or to determine, given that the film industry and those who select individuals who deserve to be recognized in it extend beyond the scope of this chapter.

DOI: 10.4324/9781003441304-10

Notwithstanding, as history shows, and as I first came to learn from a *Time* magazine essay, "public racism at the Oscars dates back to Hattie McDaniel, the first Black person to win an Oscar, being seated at a segregated table the year that she won the award for Best Supporting Actress" (Kendall, 2023, n.p.). In the opinion of some, "progress has removed segregation in seating at the Oscars but not much else" (Kendall, 2023, n.p.). "After all," they claim, "since awards were first handed out in 1929, only 22 [of 3,140] Black actors have won, though many more including Bassett have been nominated over the decades" (Kendall, 2023, n.p.). Moreover, these persons point to the corresponding perpetual erasure of colonial hurt and pain on the part of individuals such as the human, Angela Bassett, who, though visibly heartbroken and snubbed at the Oscars in 2023, was immediately painted as having reacted inappropriately – a reflection of Black peoples as progenitors of 'rage' and 'hate' (Black & Mowatt, 2024).

Arguably, in Angela Bassett's phenotypical representations of what manifested as colonial hurt and pain in an actress racialized as Black in America, we see a human who has – for four decades – been intertwined with semiotics, including language and film. She challenges a dualism that: (1) has placed her on a side of history where she may not equitably be considered for an Oscar and must seemingly work to transcend the 'abyssal line,' even as the almost impossible standard keeps shifting (i.e., evident before and after filming *Black Panther: Wakanda Forever*), but that (2) has also placed her on a side of history where she is a lauded actress who knows that she must perpetually leverage her individual linguistic and broader semiotic repertoire (García & Li Wei, 2014; Lin, 2019) to challenge duality and coloniality, and to transcend this invisible line. In this dynamic, though Bassett knows she will almost always be met with the shifting of an impossible standard, she persists anyway (i.e., evident before, during, and after the Oscars). In the 'racialized entanglements' (presented and discussed later) of Angela Bassett, we see that she is intertwined with the Englishes and broader semiotics that position her and her kind as undeserving of recognitions such as the Oscars but, at the same time, inextricably linked to those that position her as seemingly successful, an esteemed actress who has *done well* and who must persist to demonstrate that she is worthy.

It is out of the raciolinguistic dynamics (Alim et al., 2016; Rosa & Flores, 2017) of operating perpetually on such constantly shifting margins of precarity as invoked by the use of Englishes, languaging, and broader semiotics by racialized peoples, that this chapter emerges. Observing clear similarities between the intricacies of Angela Bassett's experiences and the Black immigrant and transnational peoples with whom I have worked for the past decade inspired an interweaving of theory and practice. Thus, drawing from the notion of *translingual entanglements of Englishes* (Pennycook, 2020, 2021) in conjunction with a *transraciolinguistic approach* (Smith, 2019; see also Alim et al., 2016; Rosa & Flores, 2017 for the foundational bases of this term) based on quantum conceptions, I introduce *racialized entanglements of Englishes*: a concept alluding to a dynamic space located neither within Englishes nor within racialized bodies. In this context, the interaction between racialized individuals and variations of English is mutual, where both influence each other significantly. Constantly defined and redefined by positioning and repositioning based on evolving understandings arising from individual-global analyses (Blommaert et al., 2005; Rosa & Flores, 2017; Smith, 2019), I discuss how this *dynamic space* of racialized entanglements of Englishes and peoples – and not human bodies, or Englishes – is necessary as a key unit of analysis if research is to "challenge the [abyssal] line" that rejects the linguistic repertoires of (trans) racialized communities "rather than simply help[ing] people live with or overcome it" (García et al., 2021, p. 3).

Relying in part on the previously published research of Caribbean youth and educators, racialized and transracialized as Black, who migrated to the United States (e.g., Smith, 2024, in press), I use transraciolinguistics to illustrate three conceptual premises:

1. entanglements occur in specific ways between Englishes and *ethnicized* English-speaking Caribbean nationals based on their ethnicities as Caribbean, which occur in conjunction with how they are inadvertently racialized as Black (with the Caribbean perceived as a predominantly 'non-White world');
2. entanglements emerge in unique ways between Englishes and *racialized* Caribbean migrants based on how their transracialization (Alim, 2016) occurs globally in the United States (perceived as predominantly 'White world'); and
3. entanglements are constantly being defined and redefined as the dynamic spaces between and among Englishes and *racialized* as well as *ethnicized* bodies based on both institutional and local norms within and across local and global contexts (with US and Caribbean perceived as 'White and non-White worlds') (Smith, 2022).

Through these illustrations, I demonstrate how *unequal Englishes* (Tupas, 2015; Tupas & Weninger, 2022) emerge as the racialized bodies of Black Caribbean immigrants in the United States interact in a different locale (i.e., U.S.) with the same languaging (i.e., Englishes), creating a dynamic space of interaction between the body and Englishes that is redefined based on the privilege ascribed globally to certain nation-state norms (i.e., Eurocentric). I also demonstrate how unequal Englishes evolve as the racialized body interacts with the same language (i.e., English) but what are perceived as various dialects (i.e., Englishes) in specific Caribbean contexts. However, in doing so, I demarcate where interaction between the body and Englishes is redefined based on the privilege ascribed locally as well as globally to institutional norms. Given these indications, I argue for a methodological dislocation of Englishes as independent from the body and vice versa (i.e., body as independent of Englishes and Englishes as independent from the body) – a quantum *disentanglement* (not *unentanglement*) – and for the need to locate the research, theory, and practice of examining and addressing the pathways between racialized Englishes and the individual bodies that generate them (i.e., *language* →

personhood space) as units of analysis that function constantly as dynamic *spaces of change*. Re-/imagining how racialized bodies constantly and consistently change Englishes while they too are changed by Englishes via a study of such spaces, I argue, can provide opportunities for novel ecologies of quantum knowledges that institutions may use to decolonize multilingual practice and research across multiple fields.

In the sections that follow, I first operationalize translingual entanglements of Englishes as articulated by Alastair Pennycook, with a focus on Black immigrant and transnational humans as a unique population whose intersections of race, language, and immigration allow for novel insights into how these entanglements function. I then highlight transraciolinguistics as steeped in transdisciplinarity, raciolinguistics, and transracialization for reimagining these entanglements as racialized. Subsequently, I propose racialized entanglements of Englishes and peoples as a function of translingual entanglements of Englishes and the quantum world. Implications for research and practice – (1) invoking language → personhood space, (2) disentangling, and (3) bridging – are outlined.

2. Entanglements of Englishes and Black immigrant and transnational humans

My initial interest in Angela Bassett as a human in the media stemmed simultaneously from my daughter's embarking on a college degree in film production, which had immersed me at least peripherally in this world. I had also recognized the distinctly similar sources for often observed nuances that emerged between Bassett's experience with aspiring to excellence and that of the lives of Black immigrants and transnationals with whom my scholarship is largely concerned. Though not perceived as famous, these individuals constantly grapple with 'becoming Black' (Ibrahim, 1999), becoming immigrant, becoming what they are often made to believe is a 'non-native English' speaker even as they work towards what many view as 'success' and the 'American dream.'

The representations of Englishes and languaging in the lived and literate experiences of Black immigrants – transnationals of the Majority World (Pence & Marfo, 2008; otherwise referred to as 'Global Majority') – is increasingly documented, though largely untapped as a basis for teaching and learning within schools and the academy. Broadly, from research such as that of Agyepong (2013), Ukpokodu and Ojiambo (2017), and Kumi-Yeboah (2018), there is evidence that Black immigrants wrestle with invisibility (Watson et al., 2024), facing perceptions of inferiority tied to their Blackness and Africanness, which are often shaped by how they are racialized within the framework of the Black–White binary in the U.S. More specifically, from other insights into the extant literacies, Englishes, and broader languaging of Black immigrants and transnationals (e.g., Kiramba et al., 2023; Smith, 2022, 2023a), there have been calls for a problematization of popular narratives of immigrant youth from West Africa and for a humanizing of the Black immigrant body (Watson & Knight-Manuel, 2017, 2020; Watson, Knight-Manuel et al., 2024; Watson, Smith et al., in press; Watson et al., 2022). Additional calls have invited a centering of race in examining their migratory experiences across borders (e.g., Bryan, 2020; Nalubega-Booker & Willis, 2020; Smith, 2019) and in presenting their lived experience as a function of Afrocentric practice (Braden, 2020; Braden et al., 2022). The transnationalism often undergirding the process of migrating with certain enactments of named languages such as Englishes whose distinctly associated privileged perceptions often supersede the recognition of individual linguistic repertoires of Black immigrant and transnational peoples (e.g., see Milu, 2022; Skerrett & Omogun, 2020; Smith, 2023b) further complicates such conversations that intersectionally foreground race, language, and immigration.

The processes observed with Black immigrants become even more salient when considered in relation to their experiences with languaging in their own countries (e.g., in locales such as the Caribbean and Africa) as well as within the broader context of the Black–White binary in spaces such as the United States. Across these contexts, though differentially, peoples racialized as Black appear to function in response to varied degrees of self-awareness concerning how racism can be perpetuated individually, historical knowledge that makes visible how White supremacy has functioned across time, and political knowledge that enables understandings of how laws and policies perpetuate racial inequity (Kendi, 2019; O'Brien et al., 2021; Simmons, 2019). These spaces, explained by critical race theory (CRT) as being structurally and ideologically informed by race, have long since functioned – *largely through the conaturalization of language and race* (Rosa & Flores, 2017) – as detrimental to peoples racialized as Black. For Black immigrants and transnationals, like their African-American counterparts, it becomes possible to see what it means to become overtly racialized in a largely anti-Black world such as the U.S. as an extension of what is often covert racism in individuals' home countries. By extension, it is possible to observe how they become bodies further entangled with Englishes and other languages that insist they reinforce their own pain even as they are overtly made to function as intergenerational bearers of trauma, so often miscast as 'rage' and 'hate,' as was the case with Bassett.

From the perspective of Pennycook (2020, 2021), the intertwining of the Englishes and bodies of Black immigrants and transnationals undertaken in this chapter makes it possible to consider how Englishes and bodies become one even as the pathways constituted between them remain present. According to Pennycook (2021), we do not observe Englishes out there and study them apart from us, because as we examine them, we examine ourselves. Pennycook (2020) asks us to reconsider our focus on observing the world, or Englishes and languages, for that matter, as humans, and to instead recognize that we are entangled in that world as material. In other words, as articulated by Pennycook (2021), the natural or material world is part of us, and we are part of it. Thus, Englishes are part of us, and we are part of them, and by extension, languages and broader semiotics are part of us and we are part of them. Given this conundrum, in Pennycook's (2021) estimation, Englishes will always be part of the problem.

So what does it mean then when I use the phrase 'racialized entanglements of Englishes and peoples'? I am suggesting that we imagine spaces for teaching and research that are neither located within Englishes nor within racialized bodies. In such spaces, where it often appears that the racialized body exerts as much influence on variations of English as those variations of English impact the racialized body, Englishes and the racialized body are one. Thus, (a) the pathway from the racialized body to the Englishes and broader semiotics it generates as well as (b) the pathway from the generated Englishes and broader semiotics to the perpetual reconstitution of the racialized body via languaging remain invisible and thus, are yet to be fully explored.

In the sections that follow, I delineate why it is important to consider the role of racialization in the languaging of peoples by relying on the lived experiences of Black immigrants, nationals, and transnationals of Afro-Caribbean origin. This delineation, I argue, can form a basis for conceptualizing language personhood space and how it makes possible, through transraciolinguistics, the capacity to focus on such space as entanglements of this population with their Englishes by considering how they are transracialized across borders (see Alim, 2016). I conclude by inviting an imagination of language personhood space, continuously shaped and reshaped by norms prevalent in institutions and society where Englishes and racialized bodies are instantiated as one, ultimately arguing that that we cannot possibly observe or teach language as a construct that is out there, isolated from the racialized body and vice versa, but instead, might find it useful to consider how quantum realities can silence invisibilities (Watson et al., 2024) surrounding racialized languaging and peoples.

3. Transraciolinguistics

'Trans-' from the perspective of transdisciplinarity encompasses phenomena that exist concurrently in the realms between, across, and beyond traditional disciplinary boundaries (Nicolescu, 2010; Smith, 2013). Raciolinguistics articulates a 'conaturalization' of race and language where race shapes the construction of language, while concepts surrounding language influence race, thereby creating raciolinguistic ideologies that often result in delegitimization of racialized speakers despite attempts to conform to perceived or prescribed language standards (Alim, 2016; Rosa & Flores, 2017). Its extension, a raciolinguistic perspective, as outlined earlier, reflects:

> (i) historical and contemporary co-naturalizations of race and language as part of the colonial formation of modernity; (ii) perceptions of racial and linguistic difference;(iii) regimentations of racial and linguistic categories; (iv) racial and linguistic intersections and assemblages; and (v) the contestation of racial and linguistic power formations.
>
> *(Rosa & Flores, 2017, p. 3)*

'Trans-' and 'raciolinguistics' combined form 'transraciolinguistics,' which encompasses phenomena that exist in the spaces between, across, and beyond different representations of raciolinguistics. In turn, a *transraciolinguistic approach* is based on a desire to see between, across, and beyond raciolinguistics to understand how racialized (im)migrant participants "simultaneously engaged inthinking about their thinking about race – *metaracial*; thinking about their thinking about culture – *metacultural*; and thinking about their thinking about language – *metalinguistic*" – the three Ms (Smith, 2022, p. 4). Through a transraciolinguistic approach, racialized (im)migrant/transnational students can be understood to use "metalinguistic, metaracial, and metacultural understanding of their experiences with race and language, and by extension, culture, to determine how to function effectively within non/academic settings in ways that [do] not completely sacrifice their personhood" (see Smith, 2019, p. 5). They reflect 'flexibility' and 'duality' with racialized language use (see Smith, 2019), leading them to demonstrate 'raciosemiotic architecture' (Smith, 2022, 2023a, 2023b; see also Flores, 2020 on 'language architecture').

By raciosemiotic architecture, I refer to the manipulation of "multiple modalities" (e.g., audio, visual, tactile) "for specific purposes while engaging racialization based on how [students] understand choice and meaning to be related via their socialization into cultural, linguistic, and racial community practices" (Smith, 2023a, 2023b). This notion extends the metaphor of language architecture proposed by Flores (2020):

> Using the dichotomous framing of academic language might lead an educator to conclude that close reading and writing for specific tasks, purposes and audiences require academic language that is completely dichotomous from the non-academic home language practices of racialized students. In contrast, adopting the perspective of language architecture frames these students as already understanding the relationship between language choice and meaning through the knowledge that they have gained through socialization into the cultural and linguistic practices of their communities.
>
> *(p. 25)*

With language architecture, there is no goal to build "bridges between academic and non-academic language practices" but to instead "[begin] from the premise that the language architecture that ... children from bilingual communities engage in on a daily basis is legitimate on its own terms and is already aligned" to mechanisms such as the U.S. Common Core State Standards (Flores, 2020, p. 28). In previous studies of Black immigrant and transnational youth (e.g., Smith, 2019), it is evident that these youth used raciosemiotic and language architecture to transcend "limitations of others' negative constructions based on intersections between their Englishes and race [as immigrants] to develop agency" (p. 139), while institutional norms based on the White listening subject (Rosa & Flores, 2017) challenged their constantly repositioned personhoods across borders (see also Smith, 2022 for a visual and in-depth depiction of a transraciolinguistic approach).

Transraciolinguistics here is thus positioned as a function of racialized entanglements of Englishes and peoples (Alim, 2016; Pennycook, 2020, 2021; Rosa & Flores, 2017; Smith, 2019) but also as a function of quantum entanglements (Smith, 2022) where transdisciplinarity is considered from the perspective of quantum physics and molecular biology as the basis for addressing diversity using a new kind of education (Nicolescu, 2005, 2010; Smith, 2013). According to a transraciolinguistic approach (Smith, 2022), racialized entanglements exist between each individual racialized person and their languaging (e.g., Englishes). In other words, every time a person's languaging (e.g., Englishes) is impacted by self or others, they are impacted. And every time a person is impacted, their languaging (e.g., Englishes) is impacted (see Smith, 2022 for a visual depiction of a transraciolinguistic approach).

To further illustrate the role of the quantum in entanglements and thus, transraciolinguistics, I draw next from. Nicolescu's discussions of transdisciplinarity based on the laws of quantum physics used to usher in a new kind of education that focuses equally on the body and emotions as it does the mind and the intellect. I do this by engaging with former propositions that the laws of quantum physics be applied to multiculturalism for equity. In turn, this paves the way for demonstrating, in part, how transraciolinguistics in conjunction with illuminated insights from the quantum world makes it possible to imagine and to reimagine how racialized quantum entanglements of peoples and Englishes, and by extension, languaging and broader semiotics can be envisioned through the lens of peoples largely racialized as Black and ethnicized as Caribbean (see Smith, 2013 for a full discussion). I now briefly discuss the elements of transdisciplinarity as a function of the quantum world that make it possible to consider entanglements of racialized peoples and Englishes.

4. Racialized quantum entanglements of Caribbean peoples and Englishes

My reliance on the research of Nicolescu almost a decade ago provided a pathway for discussing how the axioms of transdisciplinarity are positioned uniquely to address arising concerns with achieving the goals of multicultural education and thus were integral to arriving at transraciolinguistics. Specifically, delving into understandings of quantum physics and molecular biology as enacted in the material world, I argued that understanding the concepts of the ontological axiom, logical axiom, and complexity axiom could allow for approaches to thinking about diversity in multicultural teacher education that remained largely omitted from broader discussions of equity (Nicolescu, 2005; Smith, 2013). Initially, I was concerned more broadly with the potential of transdisciplinarity for transforming the education system by informing one's "learning to know," "learning to do," "learning to live together with," and "learning to be" (Nicolescu, 1999, p. 4). However, more recently, as visible in a transraciolinguistic approach, I have been focused on how the axioms of transdisciplinarity allow for a consideration of languaging and specifically, Englishes, in relation to humans, that can allow for an evolution of thought which in turn addresses what are often materialized as dichotomies.

4.1. Axioms of transdisciplinarity

The three axioms – ontological, logical, and complexity – emerging from constantly evolving understandings of sciences such as quantum physics and molecular biology can be considered as follows.

4.1.1. Ontological axiom

Here, levels of reality of nature and knowledge as well as levels of perception of a person are central. By levels of reality of nature and knowledge, I refer to "a set of systems which are invariant under certain laws" observed in natural systems – macrophysical, microphysical, and cyber-space-time levels (Nicolescu, 2005, p. 7). Nicolescu (2005) insists there are "multiple levels of Reality" due to the fact that the "laws governing a certain level of reality do not apply to other sets of systems" (cited in Smith, 2013, p. 31). He "observes that for every system, there are particularly different laws" (p. 31) and "describes this inapplicability of laws from one level of reality to another as 'discontinuity in the structure of the levels of Reality'" (cited in Smith, 2013, p. 31). This "proposed definition of levels of Reality permits human beings to move beyond levels of reality present only in natural systems to those which hold in other systems (e.g. social systems)" – "levels of perception of a person" (Smith, 2013, p. 31).

In addition, he draws on the principle of relativity which allows for the "incomplete nature of each level of reality" where one reality can enhance the understanding of another, arguing that there are distances in separation of one level of reality from another and that there is a potential because of these distances, for an infinite number of levels of reality where knowledge is positioned as limitless (Smith, 2013, p. 31; see also Nicolescu, 2005).

4.1.2. Logical axiom

Here, a contradiction is derived as a result of what Nicolescu (2005) discusses as the "classical logic" – a logic which governs habits of the human mind and which in turn is based on three axioms (p. 11): (1) the axiom of identity which states that 'A is A'; (2) the axiom of non-contradiction which states that 'A is not non-A'; and (3) the axiom of the excluded middle which states that no third term 'T' exists which is simultaneously 'A' and 'non-A' (Nicolescu, 2005, p. 11). According to Nicolescu (2005) as cited in Smith (2013):

> the excluded middle is transformed into an "included middle in which the third term 'T' exists at the same time as both 'A' and 'non-A'". This transformation

is made possible by the affordances of "levels of Reality" as identified within the ontological axiom.... Given experimental evidence faced at any new given level of reality, the third term "T" assumes self-contradiction on the new level and knowledge of "T" must be reexamined.

(p. 32)

The idea of an included middle and a third 'T' implies therefore that it is largely impossible to arrive at theoretical conceptions of knowledges presented as theories that are 'complete and exclusive' because the logic of the included middle requires openness to continuous revelation. As proposed, "knowledge in this sense [therefore] is 'forever open'"(Smith, 2013, p. 12; see also Nicolescu, 2005).

4.1.3. Complexity axiom

Nicolescu's (2005) complexity axiom refers to vertical complexity which is in turn "rooted in the principle of universal interdependence" – a principle that "highlights simplicity in the interaction of all the levels of reality" (cited in Smith, 2013, p. 32). As observed by Nicolescu (2005):

a distinguishing feature of this axiom is that symbolic language which holistically reflects human beings' thoughts, feelings and emotions, is indispensable to maintaining the interdependence present among individuals.

(cited in Smith, 2013, p. 32)

Knowledge based on this axiom is interdependent (Nicolescu, 2005).

Though admittedly multifaceted, transdisciplinarity's axioms present *levels of reality* that enhance levels of perception of a person, the *logic of an included middle* that inhibits finality of knowledge, and a *principle of universal interdependence* that maintains interconnectivity, all of which together signal opportunities for considering how humans racialized as Black across borders are constantly positioned and repositioned based on the entanglements that they reflect with their Englishes.

4.2. Quantum entanglements

In quantum physics, it is said that entangled particles remain connected so that actions performed on one affect the other, even when these entangled particles are separated by great distances. In fact, Albert Einstein found this so fascinating that he referred to it as "spooky action at a distance" (Caltech Science Exchange, 2024), though emerging insights as articulated by Thomas Vidick suggest there is nothing 'spooky' about this and that it is merely correlation occurring in the absence of communication such that particles "can be thought of as one object" (Caltech Science Exchange, 2024, n.p.). In other words, entangled objects are thought to be merely single objects and entanglements to thus "occur among hundreds, millions, and even more particles . . . throughout nature, among the atoms and molecules in living species and within metals and other materials" (Caltech Science Exchange, 2024, n.p.). In tandem, the rules of quantum physics state that an unobserved entity such as a photon "exists in all possible states simultaneously but, when observed or measured, exhibits only one state" (Tate, 2013, n.p.). Thus, there are supposedly many quantum entanglements but one state, invoked upon observation of an entity.

Considering the notion of translingual entanglements of Englishes as articulated by Pennycook (2020, 2021) in conjunction with the conception of transdisciplinarity by Nicolescu (2005) and quantum entanglements as offered by quantum physics (Caltech Science Exchange, 2024), it is possible to consider the ways in which peoples racialized as Black migrating as transnationals to the United States reflect entanglements with Englishes via three conceptual premises as delineated earlier. It is also possible to see how harnessing data that involves the experiences of such peoples with Englishes signals methodological opportunities for better characterizing the entanglements of people migrating across borders.

5. Conceptual premises characterizing racialized entanglements of Caribbean peoples and Englishes

The extensive examinations of the Englishes of West Indian peoples, functioning as nationals, immigrants, and transnationals across the U.S. and Caribbean, and in which I have been immersed thus far (e.g., see Smith, 2023b, 2024, in press) indicate, as mentioned earlier, that there are three premises characterizing entanglements of Englishes and peoples migrating while Black: (1) entanglements occur in specific ways between Englishes and ethnicized English-speaking Caribbean nationals based on their ethnicities as Caribbean, which occur in conjunction with how they are inadvertently racialized as Black (perceived as predominantly 'non-White world'); (2) entanglements emerge in unique ways between Englishes and racialized Caribbean migrants based on how their transracialization (Alim, 2016) occurs globally in the United States (perceived as predominantly 'White world'); and (3) entanglements are constantly being defined and redefined as the dynamic spaces between and among Englishes and racialized as well as ethnicized bodies based on both institutional and local norms within and across local and global contexts (perceived as 'White and non-White worlds') (Smith, 2022). Specifically, the indications from Black immigrant educators and youth suggest the following.

5.1. Peoples ethnicized as Caribbean in country of origin

Entanglements occur in specific ways between Englishes and *ethnicized* English-speaking Caribbean nationals based on their ethnicities as Caribbean, which occur in conjunction with how they are racialized within their home countries. Their ethnicities create a dynamic where they believe they are legitimate speakers of approximations of Englishes designated by European colonization as superior but also often illegitimate when they leverage Englishes that do not approximate these norms. At the heart of the beliefs that govern their ethnicization as Caribbean peoples is a racialization of languaging based on colonialization that functions locally, though often covertly based on institutional norms, while also in turn impacting how they deploy their personhoods based on transnationally informed norms.

In such an instance, the racialized body interacts with variations of the same named language – Englishes – in specific spaces based on a person's belief that they either possess legitimacy or illegitimacy as a Caribbean user of Englishes. This happens when interaction between the body of the Caribbean national and the Englishes that they leverage is constantly defined and redefined based on positioning by self, others, and spaces (see Smith, 2019 on the application of 'positioning theory' in conjunction with 'raciolinguistics'), given the privilege and power ascribed to local institutional norms based on ethnicity in the country of origin. Such a dynamic in turn creates entanglements with unequal Englishes at the local level that are restricted in their capacity to be known in a given moment and also can never be fully known until the racialized body becomes further entangled given that knowledge functions as limitless.

To clarify, it is possible to consider the research participant David (pseudonym), a Caribbean immigrant youth to the U.S. featured in my previous works (Smith & Warrican, 2021), who, having resided in the Bahamas before migrating, makes visible such a dynamic. In one instance, ethnicized as an English-speaking Afro-Caribbean national, David believes himself to be a legitimate speaker of an English designated by European colonization as superior – Bahamian Standard English – but also an illegitimate speaker when he leverages Englishes that does not approximate these norms. In another instance, David believes himself to be a legitimate speaker of an English designated by European colonization as inferior – Bahamian Creole English, but also intentionally refuses, in certain circumstances, to leverage Bahamian Standard English that does not align with these norms.

In reflecting these English ideologies, David holds what seem like competing positions about his use of Englishes. The decisions he makes about his Englishes are in a constant state of paradox. He dichotomously appears to believe and function with the entanglements that he possesses in ways that allow him to ascribe both legitimacy and illegitimacy to his language use despite the inferior–superior dynamic created by white listening subject norms. We know that his positioning (Blommaert et al., 2005) and repositioning which shift and change his English practice based on his operation across spaces helps to create this response but what we do not know is what is happening between his racialized body and the Englishes that he leverages as he engages with making these shifts. Thus, the question arises: *"What opportunities exist via the quantum world to examine David's individual language (L) → personhood spaces as a function of his ethnicization as a Caribbean national given the hypothesis that knowledge concerning his individual language (L) → personhood spaces is limitless?"*

5.2. Peoples racialized as Black in country of destination

Entanglements emerge in unique ways between Englishes and racialized Caribbean migrants based on how their transracialization (Alim, 2016) occurs globally (e.g., Caribbean to the United States) regardless but also as a consequence of ethnicity, often overtly as a function of institutional norms. In such an instance, the racialized body of a Caribbean person interacts with variations of the same named language – Englishes – but interaction between the body and Englishes is constantly defined and redefined based on positioning by self, others, and spaces given the power privilege ascribed to certain nation-state norms in the country of destination (e.g., United States). This creates what I am proposing as entanglements with unequal Englishes at the global level, requiring an openness to continuous revelation about how migrants are entangled with Englishes as a function of their racialization given that "knowledge in this sense" is "forever open" and "limitless" (Nicolescu, 2005, p. 12).

To clarify, it is possible to consider the research participant Juliana (pseudonym), a Caribbean immigrant and transnational youth to the U.S. featured in my previous works (Smith, 2023b) and having resided in Jamaica before migrating, as one such individual whose lived experiences reflect this dynamic. On the one hand, while racialized as an English-speaking Afro-Caribbean national, Juliana believes herself to be an illegitimate speaker of an English designated by European colonization as superior – Mainstream American English – but also an illegitimate speaker when she leverages Englishes that do not approximate these white listening subject norms. On the other hand, Juliana believes herself deserving of a space where her illegitimate use of both Englishes deserves to be leveraged acceptably, a direct rejection of these norms.

In subscribing to these English ideologies, Juliana presents, like David, what appears to be a paradoxical position concerning her uses of Englishes, but in this case, as a function of her racialization in the country of destination. Based on her positioning (Blommaert et al., 2005) and repositioning (Smith, 2019), the question becomes: *"What opportunities exist via the quantum world to examine Juliana's individual language (L) → personhood spaces as a function of her racialization as a Black Caribbean immigrant and immigrant to the U.S. given the hypothesis that knowledge concerning her individual language (L) → personhood spaces is forever open and limitless?"*

5.3. Peoples racialized and ethnicized across country of origin and country of destination

Entanglements are constantly being defined and redefined as the dynamic spaces between and among Englishes and racialized as well as ethnicized bodies based on both institutional and local norms within and across local and global contexts. In such instances, the racialized body interacts with variations of the same named language (again, Englishes), but interaction between the racialized body and

Englishes is constantly defined and redefined based on positioning by self, others, and spaces (see Smith, 2019) given contested power and privilege ascribed to certain nation-state norms in the country of destination as well as the country of origin. This creates entanglements with unequal Englishes at the transnational level based on interaction between the racialized body and Englishes. However, because knowledge is 'interdependent' while at the same time 'forever open' and 'limitless,' what is known about these dynamic spaces between Englishes and racialized bodies is never static but, in fact, becomes representative only of the individual perceptions or observations that are obtained at a given point in time.

To clarify, it is possible to consider the research participant Samantha (pseudonym), a youth of Afro-Caribbean origin having lived in the Bahamas and then in the U.S., and featured in my previous works (Smith, 2023b), as one such individual who makes visible such a dynamic. In one instance, ethnicized but also racialized as an English-speaking Caribbean national, Samantha longs for the illegitimately perceived speaking of an English designated by European colonization as superior – Bahamian Creole English – insisting that her father leverage it as well. In another, she craves the legitimately perceived Bahamian Standard and Mainstream American English as a racialized Black speaker in the U.S. in total adherence to white listening subject norms.

In reflecting these English ideologies, Samantha appears to ascribe legitimacy to Englishes deemed illegitimate by society as an ethnicized national in the Bahamas in much the same way that society ascribes this legitimacy to her Bahamian Standard English as a racialized immigrant in the U.S. It seems to be the case that her ethnicized and racialized positioning (Blommaert et al., 2005) across the Caribbean and the U.S. are together creating a dynamic where Samantha is deciding to transgress norms of delegitimacy (Smith, 2020), creating a situation where she reinstates her Bahamian Creole English as a legitimate part of her linguistic repertoire. Considering these dynamics, the question arises: *"What opportunities exist via the quantum world to explore Samantha's individual language (L) → personhood spaces as a function of her racialization and ethnicization as a Caribbean immigrant functioning as a transnational within the context of a hypothesis that knowledge concerning her individual language (L) → personhood spaces is forever open, limitless, and interdependent?"*

5.4. Extending spatial conceptions of languaging

The first two conceptual premises presented above focus on entanglements of differentially ethnicized youth, whom, though racialized as Black, operate in entirely different cultural locales, based on individual language (L) → personhood space dynamics. In contrast, the third conceptual premise represents entanglements arising from the ethnicized and racialized populations across cultural locales as a function of individual language (L) → personhood space. Accordingly, the basis for entanglements between Englishes and racialized Caribbean peoples as indicated by personal research undertaken across multiple studies thus far – whether racialized as migrants in the U.S. or ethnicized as nationals in their home countries – suggests the need for moving beyond static notions of how Englishes are racialized based on race to analyses of individual language (L) → personhood spaces, where Englishes become the racialized person and the racialized person becomes Englishes.

In other words, given the indications from Caribbean nationals and migrants and the theoretical advancements put forward by Pennycook (2020, 2021), I am suggesting that there is a need to shift the focus away from the racialized bodies *or* their Englishes to the entanglements as units of analysis to the individual language (L) → personhood spaces and vice versa of constant positioning and repositioning that signal how Englishes and the racialized body remain in a constant and perpetual dance as a single object – a racialized entanglement of Englishes and people. Blommaert et al. (2005) asserted that "space is context and therefore a potential for semiotization" and thus a basis for generating "indexical meanings" that "are scalar" and which "involve important differences in order and scope," with "some being purely situational and others translocal" (p. 213). The goal in delineating the role of space within multilingualism by Blommaert and colleagues appeared to focus on shifting away from "what individuals have or lack" to what "the environment, as structured determination and interactional emergence, enables and disables them to deploy" (p. 213). Here, I extend beyond conceptions of space in previous discussions where "multilingualism is structured and regimented by spaces and relations between spaces" (Blommaert et al., 2005) and which dictate "that how people use language is strongly influenced by the situation in which they find themselves" (e.g., Labov, 1972), all of which demonstrate greater concern with people's roles, competence, and so on in interactional spaces using language (see also research on scales, Blommaert et al., 2005; Chomsky, 1965 on linguistic competence; Hymes, 1972 on communicative competence). In doing so, I acknowledge that knowledges generated about racialized multilingual peoples' uses of language as dictated by space have often tended to be based on "assumptions about shared knowledge and stable communities" that are "problematic" (Blommaert et al., 2005, p. 211).

Instead, I am concerned in this proposition with the quantum and yet unexplored possibilities of how racialized peoples' bodies make the largely invisible journey from their personhoods to languaging as well as broader semiotics and vice versa (i.e., language (L) → personhood spaces) to create ways of being with language that are forever open and limitless and reflect an interdependence between who racialized humans are and the languaging as well as broader semiotics that they are consistently being positioned and repositioned to negotiate. In such a proposition, concern is not merely focused on "those who regularly inhabit spaces and who can be said in some sort of way to 'own' them" (Blommaert et al., 2005, p. 209) (e.g., peoples racialized as white), on space as already present there before an activity begins, or on space as "inhabited, appropriated, shaped and (re)configured by occupants for the purposes of and during social activities" (Blommaert et al., 2005, p. 206). The focus is instead on determining exactly how each racialized body creates unique entanglements between their personhoods and the Englishes that they leverage as well as broader semiotic repertoires that they use.

Focusing on this language (L) → personhood space by engaging the quantum, though not yet unraveled fully in terms of the possibilities that it holds, can potentially function as an interlocutor for better understanding the many entanglements possible as a function of how Englishes engage with racialized bodies across varied contexts and vice versa. It can also thus present a more logical unit of analysis for consideration in research by standing in stark contrast to locating analysis in: (a) what we think of independently as language; or (b) a perpetually fixed racialized body based on knowledge that is closed, limited, and disconnected. Here racialization of the body is continuously redefined by Englishes and Englishes by the racialized body. The dislocation of Englishes as separate from the body and vice versa and the need to locate the theory and practice of Englishes in the dynamic of change is thus made possible through a focus on individual language (L) → personhood spaces of repositioning (Smith, 2019), that is, in how the racialized body constantly and consistently changes Englishes while they too are changed by ever-evolving Englishes – *repositioned Englishes*.

6. Re-/imagining racialized entanglements of Englishes and peoples

In this chapter, I began with an insight from renowned American actress Angela Bassett, compelled to engage, given her precarious positioning (Blommaert et al., 2005) on the periphery, with the instantiations of her multiple entanglements with her Englishes and broader semiotics which caused her to be snubbed by some and historically overlooked as a symbol by others. Introducing the concept of 'racialized entanglements of Englishes' as a space neither located within Englishes nor within racialized bodies such that the racialized body impacts the Englishes as much as the Englishes impact the body, I articulated how this constantly shifting space, through positioning and repositioning (Smith, 2019), is continuously shaped and reshaped by norms within institutions and society. Based on this discussion, the lingering question remains: *How might we explain, through affordances of the quantum world, the mutually constitutive relationship between ethnicized bodies* redefined as *Black in their locales of origin* after transnatiionalization *and the Englishes they leverage*? Based on the indications from this research, I highlight three implications for researchers: (1) invoke *individual language→ personhood space*; (2) disentangle, not unentangle; and (3) create a bridge.

With racialized entanglements of Englishes and peoples, it is possible to consider the individual language→ personhood space as the focus for change and not the person or the Englishes or languages (see Smith et al., 2017 on locating a focus on diversity between as opposed to 'within' persons). But in order to do this, we need to first understand the dynamic occurring between Englishes and the racialized body. Why? Because though Englishes or the Eurocentricity of languages can be disentangled from peoples, they will never be unentangled from the racialized body nor the racialized body from those Englishes/languages. And this is, I argue, because Englishes are constantly being redefined by the racialized body and the racialized body by Englishes. Locating change in the individual language→ personhood space can allow for institutional change to target how Englishes interact as part of racialized bodies, and vice versa, as opposed to trying to change Englishes themselves and traumatizing the racialized bodies of which they are a part. This acknowledges and also extends beyond the call for "simply help[ing] people live with or overcome" the rejection of the linguistic repertoires of racialized communities (García et al., 2021, p. 3).

Creating a bridge through considerations of 'both-and' Smith (2016) (not *both-sides,* which is arguably dissimilar) requires an imagining and re-imagining of racialized entanglements, possible via the quantum world, to bridge the gap between the linguistic and semiotic "parts of our broken psyche" as racialized peoples of Color "that work to institutionally and societally reject the trauma imposed on our enslaved ancestors . . . and those elements of our personhoods that long to instantiate the inheritances of the Master with which we are already entangled, to create new worlds where our psyche heals, via an extending beyond" (Waldron et al., 2023, p. 62). In turn, this can facilitate a disentangling that restores, not an unentangling that destroys an often already broken racialized human.

Methodologically examining individual language (L) → personhood spaces of racialized entanglement allows for imagining and re-imagining racialized entanglements as constantly shifting language→ personhood space while situating examination of such spaces of racialized entanglement as just one possible state. Focusing on the possibility of how this space constantly evolves and changes based on positioning, repositioning, transracialization, and the limitations of observation as just one state can facilitate disentangling, which can be done through a focus on institutionally addressing English language arts standards; individually supporting the creation of storylines and relationally connecting racialized populations and their peers through engineered lessons using the 'three Ms' (see previously) in classrooms; and enhancing relations among racialized populations across local, national, and international contexts (Smith, 2022). Through a greater emphasis on invoking individual language (L) → personhood space as a unit of analysis, there is opportunity for quantum insights to be engineered that allow for a view of the pathways constituting individual entanglements of Englishes and peoples as constantly being positioned and repositioned by the self and by others (Smith, 2019). Much like it has been possible to see how Angela Bassett was entangled with the Englishes and broader semiotics that positioned her as undeserving but simultaneously inextricably linked to those positioning her as successful, it is possible, through a careful quantum examination of individual language (L) → personhood space, to extend beyond dichotomous solutions regarding languaging and peoples to instead embrace the deictic complexity that undergirds them.

References

Agyepong, M. (2013). Seeking to be heard: An African-born, American-raised child's tale of struggle, invisibility, and invincibility. In I. Harushimana, C. Ikpeze & S. Mthethwa-Sommers (Eds.), *Reprocessing race, language and ability: African-born educators and students in transnational America* (pp. 155–168). Peter Lang.

Alim, H. S. (2016). Who's afraid of the transracial subject. In S. Alim, J. R. Rickford & A. F. Ball (Eds.), *Raciolinguistics: How language shapes our ideas about race* (pp. 34–50). Oxford University Press.

Alim, H. S., Rickford, J. R., & Ball, A. F. (Eds.). (2016). *Raciolinguistics: How language shapes our ideas about race*. Oxford University Press.

Black, T., & Mowatt, R. A. (2024). *Laundering Black Rage: The washing of Black death, people, property, and profits*. Taylor & Francis.

Blommaert, J., Collins, J., & Slembrouck, S. (2005). Spaces of multilingualism. *Language & Communication*, 25(3), 197–216.

Braden, E. (2020). Navigating Black racial identities: Literacy insights from an immigrant family. *Teachers College Record (1970)*, 122(13), 1–26. https://doi.org/10.1177/016146812012201310

Braden, E., Boutte, G., Gibson, V., & Jackson, J. (2022). Using Afrocentric praxis as loving pedagogies to sustain black immigrant racial identities. *International Journal of Qualitative Studies in Education*, 35(6), 569–587. https://doi.org/10.1080/09518398.2022.2025495

Bryan, K. C. (2020). "I had to get tougher": An African immigrant's (counter) narrative of language, race, and resistance. *Teachers College Record*, 122(13), 1–28.

Caltech Science Exchange. (2024). *What is entanglement and why is it so important?* https://scienceexchange.caltech.edu/topics/quantum-science-explained/entanglement

Chomsky, N. (1965). *Aspects of a theory of syntax*. MIT Press.

de Sousa Santos, B. (2007). Beyond abyssal thinking: From global lines to ecologies of knowledges. *Review (Fernand Braudel Center)*, 45–89.

Flores, N. (2020). From academic language to language architecture: Challenging raciolinguistic ideologies in research and practice. *Theory into Practice*, 59(1), 22–31.

García, O., Flores, N., Seltzer, K., Wei, L., Otheguy, R., & Rosa, J. (2021). Rejecting abyssal thinking in the language and education of racialized bilinguals: A manifesto. *Critical Inquiry in Language Studies*, 18(3), 203–228.

García, O., & Wei, L. (2014). *Translanguaging: Language, bilingualism and education*. Palgrave Macmillan.

Hymes, D. (1972). On communicative competence. In J. B. Pride & J. Holmes (Eds.), *Sociolinguistics* (pp. 269–293). Penguin.

Ibrahim, A. K. M. (1999). Becoming Black: Rap and hip-hop, race, gender, identity, and the politics of ESL learning. *TESOL Quarterly*, 33(3), 349–369.

Kendall, M. (2023). Angela Bassett's face said everything. *Time Magazine*. https://time.com/6262473/angela-bassett-reaction-oscars-2023-loss/

Kendi, I. X. (2019). *How to be an antiracist*. One World.

Kiramba, L. K., Kumi-Yeboah, A., & Sallar, A. M. (2023). "It's like they don't recognize what I bring to the classroom": African immigrant youths' multilingual and multicultural navigation in United States schools. *Journal of Language, Identity & Education*, 22(1), 83–98.

Kumi-Yeboah, A. (2018). The multiple worlds of Ghanaian-born immigrant students and academic success. *Teachers College Record*, 120(9), 1–48.

Labov, W. (1972). *Sociolinguistic patterns*. University of Pennsylvania Press.

Lin, A. M. (2019). Theories of trans/languaging and trans-semiotizing: Implications for content-based education classrooms. *International Journal of Bilingual Education and Bilingualism*, 22(1), 5–16.

Milu, E. (2022). Toward a decolonial translingual pedagogy for Black immigrant students. In T. Do & K. Rowan (Eds.), *Racing translingualism in composition: Toward a race-conscious translingualism* (pp. 123–142). Utah State University Press.

Nalubega-Booker, K., & Willis, A. (2020). Applying critical race theory as a tool for examining the literacies of Black immigrant youth. *Teachers College Record, 122*(13), 1–24. https://doi.org/10.1177/016146812012201309

Nicolescu, B. (1999). *The transdisciplinary evolution of learning*. Paper presented at the American Educational Research Association Conference. Montreal, Quebec.

Nicolescu, B. (2005). Towards transdisciplinary education. *TD: The Journal for Transdisciplinary Research in Southern Africa, 1*(1), 5–15.

Nicolescu, B. (2010). Methodology of transdisciplinarity: Levels of reality, logic of the included middle and complexity. *Transdisciplinary Journal of Engineering & Science, 1*(1), 9–38.

O'Brien, M., Fields, R., & Jackson, A. (2021). *UCSF: Anti-racism: A toolkit for medical educators*. https://ucsf.app.box.com/s/27h19kd597ii66473parki15u0cgochd

Pence, A. R., & Marfo, K. (2008). Early childhood development in Africa: Interrogating constraints of prevailing knowledge bases. *International Journal of Psychology, 43*, 78–87. https://doi.org/10.1080/00207590701859143

Pennycook, A. (2020). Translingual entanglements of English. *World Englishes, 39*(2), 222–235.

Pennycook, A. (2021). *Entanglements of Englishes*. Keynote speech by Professor Alastair Pennycook, Sydney. https://www.youtube.com/watch?v=MRURk-tw_G0

Rosa, J., & Flores, N. (2017). Unsettling race and language: Toward a raciolinguistic perspective. *Language in Society, 46*(5), 621–647.

Simmons, D. (2019). *How to be an antiracist educator*. https://ascd.org/el/articles/how-to-be-an-antiracist-educator

Skerrett, A., & Omogun, L. (2020). When racial, transnational, and immigrant identities, literacies, and languages meet: Black youth of Caribbean origin speak. *Teachers College Record, 122*(13), 1–24. https://doi.org/10.1177/016146812012201302

Smith, P. (2013). Accomplishing the goals of multicultural teacher education: How about transdisciplinarity? *Curriculum and Teaching Dialogue, 15*(1), 27–40.

Smith, P. (2016). A distinctly American opportunity: Exploring non-standardized English (es) in literacy policy and practice. *Policy Insights from the Behavioral and Brain Sciences, 3*(2), 194–202.

Smith, P. (2019). (Re) Positioning in the Englishes and (English) literacies of a Black immigrant youth: Towards a transraciolinguistic approach. *Theory Into Practice, 58*(3), 292–303.

Smith, P. (2020). "How does a Black person speak English?" Beyond American language norms. *American Educational Research Journal, 57*(1), 106–147. https://doi.org/10.3102/0002831219850760

Smith, P. (2022). A transraciolinguistic approach for literacy classrooms. *The Reading Teacher, 75*(5), 545–554. https://doi.org/10.1002/trtr.2073

Smith, P. (2023a). Beyond dichotomies in the quest for raciosemiotic architecture: Black immigrants in the United States. *Teachers College Press Blog*. https://www.tcpress.com/blog/dichotomies-quest-raciosemiotic-architecture-black-immigrants-united-states/

Smith, P. (2023b). *Black immigrant literacies: Intersections of race, language, and culture in the classroom*. Teachers College Press.

Smith, P. (2024, in press). *Literacies of migration: Translanguaging imaginaries of innocence*. Cambridge University Press.

Smith, P., Richards, J., Gutierrez, S., Schaffer-Rose, J., & Kumi-Yeboah, A. (2017). Shifting from diversity in multicultural populations to teacher/student interactions within transcultural spaces in an online literacy teacher education course. *Literacy Practice and Research, 42*(3), 7–15.

Smith, P., & Warrican, S. J. (2021). Migrating while multilingual and Black: Beyond the "(bi) dialectal" burden. In E. Bauer, L. Sánchez, Y. Wang & A. Vaughan (Eds.), *A transdisciplinary lens for bilin-gual education: Bridging translanguaging, sociocultural research, cognitive approaches, and student learning* (pp. 102–128). Routledge.

Tate, K. (2013). *Livescience.* https://www.livescience.com/28550-how-quantum-entanglement-works-infographic.html

Tupas, R. (Ed.). (2015). *Unequal Englishes: The politics of Englishes today*. Springer.

Tupas, R., & Weninger, C. (2022). Mapping out unequal Englishes in English-medium classrooms. *Journal of Language, Identity & Education, 21*(5), 347–361.

Ukpokodu, O. N., & Ojiambo, P. O. (2017). *Erasing invisibility, inequity and social justice of Africans in the diaspora and the continent.* Cambridge Scholars Publishing.

Waldron, C. H., Willis, A., Tatum, A., Salas, R. G., Coleman, J. J., Croom, M., Deroo, M. R., Hikida, M., Smith, P., & Zaidi, R. (2023). Reimagining LRA in the spirit of a transcendent approach to literacy. *Literacy Research: Theory, Method, and Practice, 72*(1), 50–73.

Watson, V. W., & Knight-Manuel, M. G. (2017). Challenging popularized narratives of immigrant youth from West Africa: Examining social processes of navigating identities and engaging civically. *Review of Research in Education, 41*(1), 279–310.

Watson, V. W., & Knight-Manuel, M. G. (2020). Humanizing the Black immigrant body: Envisioning diaspora literacies of youth and young adults from West African countries. *Teachers College Record, 122*(13), 1–28.

Watson, V. W., Knight-Manuel, M. G., & Smith, P. (Eds.). (2024). *Educating African immigrant youth: Schooling and civic engagement in K–12 schools.* Teachers College Press.

Watson, V. W., Reine Johnson, L. E., Peña-Pincheira, R. S., Berends, J. E., & Chen, S. (2022). Locating a pedagogy of love: (Re)framing pedagogies of loss in popular-media narratives of African immigrant communities. *International Journal of Qualitative Studies in Education, 35*(6), 588–608. https://doi.org/10.1080/09518398.2021.1982057

Watson, V. W., Smith, P., & Brown, A. (in press). Diasporic tellings of race, literacies, joys, and geographies in the lives of Black African immigrant youth. *Research in the Teaching of English*.

PART III
Entanglements of practice

8
ENTANGLED BODIES, ENTANGLED IDEOLOGIES

The case of Bikram yoga practitioners

Kellie Gonçalves

1. Introduction

Recent work within the field of interactional sociolinguistics, applied linguistics, and critical sociolinguistics has been committed to studying individuals' repertoires and resources of meaning-making that extend beyond just language to include other modes and material artifacts (Angouri et al., 2017; Blackledge & Creese, 2017; Gonçalves, 2020; Gonçalves & Schluter, 2024; Pennycook & Otsuji, 2015). Language is therefore no longer viewed as a structure or abstract entity but as an activity that we do and considered as a material part of social and cultural life (Pennycook, 2010) that is complexly intertwined with an array of other entanglements and assemblages (Pennycook, 2020, 2023). Locating language in the material world isn't a new idea (Scollon & Scollon, 2003), and the link between language and materiality has been acknowledged by early sociolinguistic work by Williams (1977). However, it has received renewed interest in the past decade within the fields of applied linguistics, linguistic anthropology, and critical sociolinguistics (Cavanaugh & Shankar, 2017; Pennycook & Otsuji, 2015; Pietikäinen, 2021; Shankar & Cavanaugh, 2012). Most recently, scholars are exploring an array of "material and nonhuman phenomena that contribute to interaction and meaning-making – among them sounds, visual signs, animals, images, digital devices, bodies, and movements – in order to stimulate new thinking surrounding the question of what language is from a posthumanist perspective" (Schneider & Heyd, 2024, p. 1).

It is no surprise therefore that studies on language and the workplace have turned to analyzing the deployment of material objects and semiotic resources (one of which is language) (Gonçalves & Kelly-Holmes, 2021; Pennycook & Otsuji, 2015; Pietikäinen, 2021), allowing for a richer understanding of how linguistic, multimodal, and semiotic repertoires and non-verbal practices (Gonçalves, 2020; Kusters et al., 2017, 2021) within particular workplaces (Marra et al., 2022) cannot be separated but need to be looked at simultaneously in order for meaning-making to occur and successful communication to be achieved. In this chapter, I explore the discourses of work and leisure by taking account of the embodied and linguistic ideological entanglements and assemblages of yoga practitioners in a Bikram yoga studio located in Oslo, Norway, where I carried out an ethnographic study from 2018–2020. I draw on Pennycook's (2023) SEMIOSIS framework to uncover the complex semiotic relations that exist between people, language, bodies, and place. In this chapter, I am interested in finding out how individuals' language ideologies manifest in embodied practices and what complex relations of semiotic signs are involved in such processes.

2. Bikram yoga: a demanding form of embodied practice

Bikram yoga is considered "a demanding form of yoga" (Hauser, 2013, p. 109) that was invented by Bikram Choudry, a Bengali Indian who migrated to the United States in the 1970s. Unlike other forms of hatha yoga, Bikram is a set sequence of 26 postures composed of 24 asanas and two pranayama breathing exercises that is fixed and does not allow for variation. In 1994, the Bikram sequence was copyrighted (Hauser, 2013, p. 115), allowing Choudry to tap into and capitalize on this form of yoga on a global scale. For Bikram practitioners, this means that regardless of one's physical place and the language used for instructive purposes, the embodied sequence takes precedence. Bikram classes are conducted over a 90-minute period in a room heated to 40 degrees Celsius, with relative humidity of 40 percent to ensure the release of 'toxins' and individuals' ability to stretch deeper with the aim of avoiding injury. Bikram also relies primarily on verbal instruction from teachers, who have mastered a fixed 46-page script that must be executed within the 90-minute class. As a result, students must listen very carefully to teachers' quick oral instructions. While there is considerable variation in terms of gesture use among teachers, teachers do not simultaneously practice and teach. As such, instructors do not serve as embodied examples for students to follow. Rare exceptions to this rule are when 'silent courses' are offered, when the only word uttered by the instructor is 'change,' informing practitioners when to begin and end a posture. Due to the lack of embodied instruction, Bikram yoga rooms are equipped with large, mirrored walls so that students can constantly check their alignment and postures (see Figure 8.1). Another difference is that there is just one type of Bikram class offered to students regardless of individuals' level. While this may at first appear to index inclusivity and diversity, status differences become apparent and are also visually manifested in a hierarchical order, with more experienced and advanced practitioners (who also happen to be wearing less clothing) located in the front and intermediate and beginners located toward the back. The objective of this hierarchy is for beginners to look and learn from more experienced students.

FIGURE 8.1 Bikram yoga room and the visual hierarchy

3. Methods: embodied ethnography at Bikram Yoga Oslo

Bikram Yoga Oslo (BYO) is located in central Oslo and was established in 2011 by an Indian Australian migrant to Norway. At the time of my fieldwork, the studio had 4,000 students (including drop-ins) and 7 teachers, including 1–2 traveling staff. My interest in this studio as a research site had to do with the mobile and international staff, languages, and gestures used in class, teaching, and spatial style, as well as the consumption of material and thus embodied culture of the practice. Similar to other researchers who have investigated sports within sociolinguistics (Madsen, 2015), my pre-research knowledge of Bikram as a long-time practitioner and certified hot yoga instructor was a major impetus for carrying out this ethnographic study. Drawing on ethnography was crucial as it allows for a rich and deep understanding of local semiotics, where the sociocultural meaning of embodiment can be recognized and "thick description" made (Geertz, 1977, p. 10). For this study, I collected diverse data sets consisting of spoken, written, and visual data over a two-year period from 2018 to 2020, as listed in Table 8.1.

I began my Bikram practice at BYO in 2017 and had been engaged in a regular practice there for an entire year before beginning my research. The reasons for this had to do primarily with gaining trust from prospective participants, many of whom were part-time instructors at BYO. Upon receiving consent from the company owner, we discussed possible pseudonyms for the studio, which she did not approve of and suggested I use the studio's 'real name,' as the project might attract prospective clients and be beneficial to her business (see Madsen, 2015 for a discussion on using real names in research). My next step was to inform teachers

TABLE 8.1 Diverse data sets

Type of data	Data description	Data length
Spoken data	11 open-ended interviews	60-90 minutes in length
Spoken/visual/ embodied data	Eight recorded 90-minute yoga classes	12 hours in total
Observational data	Participant observation and participation in yoga classes myself resulted in field notes	320 hours
Visual data	Digital ethnography by means of screenshots	Studio website and Lululemon website[1]
Visual/semiotic data	Changing signage and artifacts in BYO studio	Pictures
Visual/semiotic data	Participation in FB group	Images and screenshots
Written data	Bikram script	46 pages

about the owner's consent in order to receive permission to record their classes, which was granted. This meant that I also received consent from every student in the recorded classes. Those students who were not comfortable being recorded signed consent forms but were physically placed in the studio beyond the video recorder's frame to guarantee that they were not included in the recordings.

4. Theoretical framework: embodied practices, ideologies, and assemblages

Studies focusing on communication and the body are not new in research on language and social interaction (Nevile, 2015; Streeck et al., 2011), gesture studies (Gullberg, 1998, 2011; Kendon, 1990, 2004; McNeill, 1981, 2005), interactional sociolinguistics (Canagarajah & Minakova, 2022; Keevallik, 2010, 2013; Mondada, 2014, 2016, 2019), or social semiotics (Beilharz, 2011; McDonald, 2013; Murray, 2005), but they have received a renewed interest within the field of sociolinguistics prompted by the call from Bucholtz and Hall (2016). According to them, "embodiment is enlisted in a variety of semiotic practices that endow linguistic communication with meaning ranging from the indexicalities of bodily adornment to gesture, gaze, and other forms of movement. And just as bodies produce language, language also produces bodies" (Bucholtz & Hall, 2016, p. 173). Interestingly, for Woolard (2021), embodied practices are also closely tied and connected to language ideologies. For her, "language ideologies occur not only as mental constructs and in verbalizations but also in embodied practices and dispositions and in material phenomena such as visual representations" (p. 2). This line of argumentation resonates with the work of Pennycook (2017), who refers to *semiotic assemblages*, which include "the importance of things, the consequences of the body, and the significance of place alongside the meanings of linguistic resources" (p. 269). As such, the notion of *semiotic assemblages* captures the complexity of various modes, resources, mobile bodies, and materials that need to be accounted for in any sociolinguistic study attempting to push the theoretical boundaries of language-society relations (Coupland, 2016). For Blommaert (2017), this means accounting for ethnographic explorations of complexity while broadening our understanding of signs that go beyond purely 'linguistic' signs where the 'total linguistic/semiotic fact' must be considered. For Blommaert (2017), this means taking account of these facts while not losing sight of "cultural ideology" and "sociolinguistic stratification" (p. 58). In an attempt to bring these multiple factors together around people, place, and things, Pennycook (2023) has recently developed an analytical framework for considering a wide array of semiotic relations through the acronym SEMIOSIS admitting that "while it is evident that we can never arrive at a full account of the total linguistic or semiotic fact, it is nonetheless important to consider carefully what is at stake" (p. 596). The set of semiotic relations developed by Pennycook are indicated in Table 8.2.

The SEMIOSIS acronym stands for several complex relations within social interaction where meaning emerges and is negotiated. Applying this framework to some of my data sets highlights the ways in which many factors must be considered at once while also indexing that any analysis is always partial. Moreover, while the framework demarcates factors individually for reasons of analytical clarity, most of these factors are intertwined, entangled, and thus seen as a larger assemblage in its own right.

5. Dialogue and heat: embodied ideologies of pleasure and pain

Doing yoga is a performative and thus embodied act that requires people, the teacher's voice and guided instructions, yoga mats, water bottles, and, in the context of Bikram, also a heated room at 40 degrees equipped with full-length mirrors to check participants' alignments. As such, the material objects like mirrors and mats together with set room temperatures that facilitate stretching and sweating combined with the teacher's oral guidance required for such an embodied practice emerge as significant factors that allow individuals to claim doing Bikram while simultaneously serving

TABLE 8.2 SEMIOSIS framework (Pennycook, 2023)

SEMIOSIS	
Social relations	Social background in interaction
Emotion and affect	Affective domains
Multilingual practices	Metrolingualism and space
Iterative activity	Language as social practice
Objects and assemblages	Networks of artefactual relations
Spatial repertoires	Available semiotic resources
Interactivity	Posture, gesture, and interaction
Sensory relations	Social and semiotic role of senses

146 Entangled Englishes

as an index of an authentic Bikram yoga identity. Doing yoga in a heated and humid room for 90 minutes while receiving military yoga commands of this particular yoga style also contributes to the sensory relations of this practice which tap into affective domains of individuals' emotions that are influenced by practitioners' mental and physical states within a certain time and place. In all of my interviews, the Bikram dialogue entangled with individuals' language ideologies and heated room temperatures emerged as key factors that contributed to participants' discursive and embodied experiences of their particular practice.

The Bikram script is a fixed 46-page oral instruction manual that teachers must master during their teacher training and then subsequently deliver within the 90-minute class once they begin to teach. Given that Bikram is done primarily through instructors' dialogue rather than embodied demonstration, language becomes a key factor of class instruction. During the time of my fieldwork in Oslo, I experienced various classes that were taught in English or Norwegian only, which were also advertised online for prospective students to consult. The following is a sample schedule of yoga classes at BYO categorized by date, time, yoga type, instructor, and language of instruction:

	Class	*Instructor*
Mon May 13, 2019		
10:00 am–11:30 am	Hot Bikram Yoga 90min	Martin – Norsk
12:00 pm–1:15 pm	Hot Vinyasa Flow Yoga 75 min	Aki – English
5:00 pm–6:30 pm	Hot Bikram Yoga 90min	Jimmy – English
7:30 pm–9:00 pm	Full Pakke 90min	Jimmy – English
Tue May 14, 2019		
7:00 am–8:30 am	Morning Flow 55min	Naja – Norsk
9:00 am–10:30 am	Hot Bikram Yoga 90min	Linn K – English
3:30 pm–5:00 pm	Hot Bikram Yoga 90min	Henrik – English
6:00 pm–7:30 pm	Hot Bikram Yoga 90min	Jimmy – English
8:00 pm–9:00 pm	Hot Yin Yoga 55 min	Aki – English
Wed May 15, 2019		
9:30 am–11:00 am	Hot Bikram Yoga 90min	Susanne – Norsk
11:30 am–12:45 pm	Hot Vinyasa Flow Yoga 75 min	Aki – English
5:00 pm–6:30 pm	Hot Bikram Yoga 90min	Bjørg – English
7:30 pm–9:00 pm	Hot Bikram Yoga 90min	Jimmy – English
Thu May 16, 2019		
9:00 am–10:30 am	Hot Bikram Yoga 90min	Susanne – Norsk
11:30 am–12:30 pm	Hot Yoga Therapy 60min	Kari – Norsk
6:00 pm–7:00 pm	Hot HIIT	Josephine – English

During my fieldwork, I took Bikram classes in both languages and found that many instructors often stuck to one language only (resonating with the One Parent One Language (OPOL) strategy in family language policy studies; see Gonçalves & Lanza, 2024 for a thorough discussion), but some instructors also mixed languages depending on where they were from and their multilingual repertoires. There were of course exceptions to the one teacher–one language policy, since a few teachers were able to teach their classes in either Norwegian or English depending on the students and situation. In several instances, I attended classes that were originally advertised to be in Norwegian, as indicated by the studio's online website, but were then carried out in English due to walk-ins (practitioners from abroad) who did not understand Norwegian.

This gives us insight into the diverse entangled and multilingual practices being done within this particular space while simultaneously revealing individuals' levels and teachers' command of the script in diverse languages. Given that the Bikram script is a set sequence that does not allow for variation, long-time practitioners usually know the sequence by heart. This is also a main reason that when silent classes are offered at Bikram studios, advanced practitioners are encouraged and allowed to join, while beginners are not. Silent classes are for practitioners who have mastered the set sequence of the Bikram series, but need guidance in terms of time, that is, how long postures are held for. In silent classes, instructors only call out the name of the posture and the command 'change' when students are expected to switch postures. They do not deliver the 46-page Bikram dialogue. Theoretically, language choice for advanced practitioners might therefore not matter since the sequence is set, and whether class is taught in English, Spanish, or Mandarin, the postures and time allotted for each posture remain the same. For beginner and intermediate students, however, language choice is much more important, as they may not be familiar with the set sequence nor be able to anticipate what postures are done in chronological order. Beginner and intermediate students must therefore pay very careful attention to the dialogue in order to set up their posture correctly in the first set before holding the pose for the allocated time in the first and second set. As a result, ideologies about language and embodied practice become further entangled and emerge as both relevant and irrelevant to individuals based on their temporal experiences with Bikram.

Interestingly and somewhat paradoxically, the Bikram script is referred to as a 'dialogue'; however, it is more of a monologue, as students are not allowed to speak in class. In fact, they respond with "the most basic mechanism of embodied agency" (Bucholtz & Hall, 2016, p. 184) such as eye gaze, gesture, and bodily movements without talk to perform a particular social action, that is, elicit assistance from an instructor. All types of yoga work on a physical and discursive level since the body is considered both discursive and material; however, as Hauser (2013) has argued with the style and practice of Bikram in particular, it challenges socially learned cultural attitudes towards personal limits and pain, which she found in her study of speech patterns. The linguistic, embodied, and thus also performative style of this dialogue and social practice unsettles embodied discourse and social and cultural ideologies of this activity as well as sensory relations and affective domains. The performative act of engaging in this kind of yoga may also unsettle social and cultural ideologies of Bikram practitioners since this style of yoga is often described as 'military' and 'stringent,' consisting of quick directives primarily by means of orders and commands requiring practitioners' undivided attention, focus, and concentration. In her study of speech patterns, Hauser (2013) found that the style and practice of Bikram in particular challenge socially learned cultural attitudes toward personal limits and pain. My findings support Hauser's results in that individuals engaged in a regular Bikram practice often discussed the feelings of pleasure and pain simultaneously which emerged as a type of register (Gonçalves, 2024). Individuals' ability to endure and voice pain on both a physical and mental level indexed ambivalent feelings of exhaustion, happiness, and cleansing, processes that appeared to be highly valued among practitioners and therefore also enregistered by them.

In my interviews with participants, the distinct forms of speech that came to be socially recognized were those of both pleasure and pain that were often talked about simultaneously, as in the following example of Martin, a yoga instructor, who described his first experience of a Bikram class in 2011.

Extract (1)[2]

1. Martin: and erm first time I did Bikram yoga erm was there in Thailand and I more or less I think
2. already in the first class I decided that, **it was horrible actually it was horrible** erm but, but, I
3. same time erm there was something I thought that this, this, I have to do this and I think I already
4. then decided to erm, not decided but it was a thought going to teacher training I think alr-already,
5. already then, I don't know what it was, no, but yeah, same time it gave me, **it's horrible wh-wh-**
6. **what was the also a good feeling after but the you know?** it was so sweaty and it was erm
7. yeah, it was I don't know what, yeah. It was **a combination of horrible but same time gave me**
8. **a, a good feeling**

The contradictory embodied feelings of both pleasure and pain (lines 2, 5–8) that Martin experienced during his first class eventually led him to complete the teacher training, which he later describes "like a boot camp yeah it's it's, it's taken to the taking you to the limit." Speaking of Bikram teacher training as a "boot camp" denotes stringent military-like experiences of immense suffering while at the same time being a sign of social class distinction and exclusivity, since not all teachers complete the training, nor is this training available to everyone due to its high costs, approximately US$12,000 for a two-month course located in Los Angeles and other parts of the world.

Martin was not the only practitioner who discussed the mixed embodied sensation of this practice, but it appeared to be part of the register of local Bikram yoga practitioners and an example of what has been referred to in sociolinguistic studies as indexical iconization, influenced by the work of Eckert (1990) in her seminal study of jocks and burnouts. According to Bucholtz and Hall (2016), indexical iconization means that in order for individuals "to make semiotic sense of themselves and others, individuals link specific ways of being in the world to ideological expectations regarding specific ways of speaking" (p. 180). As such, the ways in which Martin as well as other practitioners spoke about their Bikram experiences always seemed to entail the discussion of both very negative and simultaneously very positive bodily and mental sensations of their practices. Students rarely stated either/or, and thus the combination of mixed sensations is what became indexically iconized among practitioners.

In some instances, the actual Bikram dialogue and ways of speaking in class did not align with students' expectations of yoga. This was the case with Jane, a Bikram yoga practitioner and employee of BYO (receptionist), who discusses her experiences with different kinds of students at the studio who tried Bikram and also alluded to the mixed bodily sensations of both challenging and good. In extract 2, we see how individuals are categorized based on those who make it through the strenuous practice and continue and those who leave because it does not match their ideological expectations of what yoga is or should be.

Extract (2)

1. Jane: But some people there were like "Wow this was **challenging**" but they kind of **feel good**
2. because **they made it through class** and, but then you have others that don't, **they just leave**
3. **after half an hour or hour and they are kind of upset** . . . I had a couple of those lately.
4. Kellie: People that had left?
5. Julie: Yeah.
6. Kellie: And they come and talk with you?
7. Julie: Yeah. I kind of try to talk to them to figure out what made them leave, to get them into a
8. better mood, so they might come back and try Yin or something like that . . .
9. Kellie: What do they usually say?
10. Julie: Well, I had two ladies the other day and **they complained about the constant talking** of
11. the teacher. **This is not what they associated with yoga. They didn't think that this was yoga. It just**
12. **didn't match.**

Similar to Martin, Jane describes students who also explain the mixed sensations of this challenging form of yoga, feeling good (line 1) and surviving a class (line 2). This is juxtaposited to the students who do not make it, leave a class (lines 2, 3, and 7), complain (line 10), and are subsequently upset (line 3). Within the context of Bikram, first-time students are given explicit instructions from both receptionists and teachers when they sign in not to leave the class in any circumstances but to lie down on their mats if they are uncomfortable, feeling nauseous, or dizzy. The reasons for this are threefold and have to do with students' safety as well as a main philosophy about Bikram yoga in general, namely inclusivity: first, by keeping students in the room, teachers are able to monitor their state. If students leave the room and faint, teachers run the risk of students getting seriously injured and not being able to attend to them. Second, by keeping students in the room, students remain part of the class despite not being able to complete all postures, indexing their inclusion and commitment to a difficult practice that taps into diverse sensory relations, including sight, smell, hearing, the vestibular system, and proprioception. Third, being mentally and physically uncomfortable is a driving ideology behind Bikram that taps into diverse affective domains, which, when done successfully, offers individuals physical, mental, and societal rewards in the form of acknowledgement and distinction (Bourdieu, 1984). For example, upon completing a class, first-time students are acknowledged by instructors by first name and by fellow students with a round of applause. This ritual indexes social and sensorial relations and serves as a kind of initiation and informal welcome into the Bikram community on a local level, signaling newcomers' strength and willingness to challenge themselves despite the numerous emotional and physical discomforts the practice entails that experienced practitioners have also overcome.

This also resonates with the neoliberal project, where the refinement and enhancement of the self is key and largely determined through self-discipline (Bailey et al., 2022; Gonçalves, 2024; Rosen, 2019). Within the context of Bikram, commitment to self enhancement through self-discipline includes doing the 90-minute class in a heated room, where individuals are drenched with sweat and where olfactory and vestibular senses are heightened and classes have been described as "very uncomfortable." This also points to the iterative activity and process of Bikram that is time consuming and entails commitment and self-discipline from newcomers, experienced practitioners, and instructors in order for mental and physical results to be made, seen, and felt by individuals. The iterative activity of Bikram on the part of teachers is done primarily through the 'dialogue' and thus spoken language. In extract 2, we see how two ladies "complained" about "the constant talking of the teacher" (line 10) in class, which did not resonate with their ideologies of yoga in general (lines 11 and 12) that tend to be stereotypically described as relaxing and healing, where less noise or even silence is highly valued. As such, their auditory senses may have been overloaded, pointing to individuals' sensory and social relations.

6. Language ideologies as embodied practice: a question of time and temporality

We see the different and entangled language ideologies emerge in the next three extracts between a more experienced practitioner and instructor, Martin; a fairly new teacher, Harry; and a self-proclaimed "intermediate" practitioner, Inez. In my interview with Martin, he discusses his teaching philosophy before making the claim that language does not matter for him.

Extract (3)

1. Martin: some people some, some erm teachers are more doing good, I'm more like I think if you get
2. good feedback you, you'll do even better, that's my philosophy but maybe it works different for
3. other people, it's just I like it, I like to hear positive things but erm
4. Kellie: and does it make a difference for example in what language the class is being taught?
5. Martin: no, I don't think so, la-**language does not erm matter so much for me**, it's more about how
6. they are motivating you, motivating, the, the students

For Martin, one's teaching style, which taps into social relations between students and instructors, emotion, and affect on the part of instructors appear to supersede his multilingual practices within the interaction of Bikram classes. For him, "good feedback" (line 2) and hearing "positive things" (line 3) again index affective domains and sensory relations that influence his own practice, which he carries into his teaching and also incorporates into his individualized Bikram script. Interestingly, Martin is one of the few teachers who can teach in both Norwegian and English despite his Danish background, indexing his array of language repertoires within this particular context and the symbolic capital attached to it (Bourdieu, 1991). For Woolard (2021), "even when representations are cast as strictly linguistic, for example, in formal grammars or classifications of language families, they implicate social relations" (p. 2). In this example, ideologies of language are very much entangled with specific social relations, which in this case may function to signal and legitimize Martin's superior status as a long-time and experienced Bikram practitioner whose social identity is indexed by his occupational expertise and whose ability to easily switch between languages serves as a process of differentiation (Bakhtin, 1986).

Another teacher, Harry, a Norwegian national, feels more comfortable and also more confident in English since he taught in Australia for several months before returning to Oslo. In extract 4, he discusses the differences between teaching in English versus Norwegian.

Extract (4)

1. Harry: and I still do it because I feel my grasp of the dialogue in English, and teaching in English
2. is . . . and just communicating yoga in English is stronger than Norwegian.
3. Kellie: okay.
4. Harry: and **I haven't set aside the time to learn the Norwegian dialogue**.
5. Kellie: right, okay.
6. Harry: because I have fifty other projects I do and right now, **I don't feel the need to do it**. I know
7. that goes around the teachers a lot. But **you change your knowledge, based on the language** you
8. use, Norwegian indicated this.
9. Kellie: mhm.
10. Harry: and I know **I taught in Norwegian, and I become a completely different teacher, I come off a**
11. **lot softer when I teach in Norwegian**.

In this extract, entangled ideologies of language and embodied practices emerge. Here, English is equated with confidence and strength (lines 1 and 2) and therefore is also valued very differently than Norwegian. Such ideologies tap into the indexical theorizations of language in terms of social relations, emotion, and affect as well as multilingual practices and iterative activities. It also highlights the semiotic process of iconization (Irvine & Gal, 2000), where participants "treat linguistic forms as if they were depictions of the character of speakers associated with them; social indexes become indexical icons. Speakers are taken to be the way that they supposedly sound" (Woolard, 2021, p. 10).

For Harry, teaching in English may be equated with a more authentic yogic identity given Bikram's establishment in the US as its original geographic location. By using English only in this context, Harry's position as a Bikram yoga teacher becomes iconic in that the language he teaches in resonates with the original conceptualization of the practice as well as his previous experience of teaching in Australia. In order for Harry to be able to teach Bikram in Norwegian, he's aware that he'd have to commit to learning it (line 4), indexing this verbal instruction and social practice as an iterative activity, which takes time to acquire and master. Due to his full mastery of the English dialogue, the popularity of English classes at BYO, and other teachers responsible for teaching primarily in Norwegian, he does not feel the need to learn the Norwegian dialogue (line 6). His reasons are not only due to the time factor but also based on his ideologies of himself when using Norwegian versus English for pedagogical purposes (line 10). For Harry, different languages are equated with different types of knowledge accumulation, value, power, sensory relations, and indexical iconization. For Harry, teaching in Norwegian is associated with softness, tapping into emotion and affect as well as sensory relations. Affective domains and social and semiotic roles of the senses emerge in any Bikram class due to the consistent verbal dialogue that is compounded and entangled by the heat and humidity, where the embodied practice emerges as a challenging semiotic assemblage. In this context, using English appears to be the only option for Harry to make semiotic sense of himself and others in terms of how he links ways of being to specific ways of speaking. Here, English is equated with authenticity, powerful instruction, and the language used to disseminate a challenging and stringent practice, while Norwegian is connoted with 'softness' and perhaps leniency, the latter of which is not tolerated in Bikram, well-known to be military-like, uncomfortable, and difficult. In other words, the practice of Bikram in English only is iconized, resembling its original object of embodied practice.

Interestingly, entangled ideologies around language choice also emerged in my interviews with yoga students and practitioners. In extract 5, Inez discusses her preference for monolingual rather than multilingual instruction.

Extract (5)

1. Inez: no, **I don't have a preference in language as long as they stay in the same language** the whole
2. class, or **more or less**, I mean if you do some things in the different language but if you switch like
3. every other, then **I get confused**, yeah, then, I then, **I don't get into the zone**

Although Inez has been practicing Bikram for eight years and considers herself an "intermediary" practitioner, the language instruction of Bikram matters to her. Inez's language ideologies and preferences resonate with discourses of linguistic purism, despite the fact that language ideologies are "morally and politically loaded because implicitly or explicitly they represent not only how language is, but how it ought to be" (Woolard, 2021, p. 2). For Inez, language choice with regard to instruction is very much entangled and oscillates between consistency and purism to leniency and mixing, which could be interpreted as indexing one's linguistic and embodied flexibility. Inez initially claims that language use should be consistent, with no variation during the entire class (line 1). Her claim is then progressively softened through her use of the informal approximation "more or less," indexing a tolerance of linguistic variation to a certain degree with "some things" (line 2). However, switching too often is not tolerated and leads to confusion (line 3).

For me and for several of the practitioners I spoke with, one of the main advantages of Bikram is its set routine and sequence that does not allow for variation. As such, it is monotonous and mundane, which was also regarded by some students as 'boring.' According to intermediate and advanced practitioners, the factors that do change are teacher's teaching style and their language and the time one practices, and what emerged as very relevant for many, were individuals' physical, mental, and emotional state, tapping into affective domains and sensory relations at a specific moment in time. For Inez, a Norwegian national, who speaks both English and Norwegian fluently, switching languages allows her to tap into her own multilingual practices and linguistic repertoires as well as the instructors and the spatial repertoires that are connected to interactivity, emotion, and effect, which are negatively depicted when instructors mix and entangle languages. For Inez, engaging in an already physically strenuous practice compounded by a teacher's multilingual practices through dialogue instruction emerges as a further challenging entanglement, leading to confusion (line 3) and prohibiting her from entering "the zone" (line 3) of moving meditation and her embodied practice. This interpretation points to both the interactive and interactivity of Bikram while simultaneously alluding to Inez's habitus (Bourdieu, 1991) and the "implicit knowledge and ingrained sensibilities that are inscribed in the body through repeated social experience" (Woolard, 2021, p. 2).

7. Concluding remarks

In this chapter I explored the discourses of work and leisure by taking account of the embodied and linguistic ideological entanglements of Bikram yoga practitioners in Oslo, Norway. I have attempted to account for the semiotic assemblages present in my analysis, including the relevance of things, the consequence of bodies, and the significance of place pointing to a broader understanding of the total semiotic fact. This required analyzing a lot more than language (i.e. scripts and interviews) but delving into the significance of things like heat, sweat, discomfort, and its consequences on individuals' bodies and practice while seriously considering the relevance of one's place locally, which inevitably indexes one's social class status in terms of the political economy on a national and global level given yoga's current international reach. Overall, this meant trying to capture the linguistic, embodied, performative, and thus semiotic practices of Bikram in its entirety as best we can in order to understand the subtle metasigns that emerge within a particular time and place. Doing Bikram already indexes a number of semiotic ideologies and systems of signification with regard to the self and others, one's body, ideas about health, physical fitness, self-discipline, and the neoliberal project and the sociocultural values we attach to them, which are reinforced on different socio-cultural scales and a variety of material means. Future studies aiming to analyze embodied practice and language ideologies should account for the intertwinement of numerous factors that may take the form of explicit linguistic signs that are indexical and even iconic of individuals' social practices, while not losing sight of the subtle metasigns that emerge in social interaction and their inherent meaning potential.

Notes

1. Lululemon is a yoga apparel brand based in Canada with over 600 stores worldwide. BYO sold Lululemon yoga paraphernalia at the studio. Many of the company's online events and programs were emulated offline at BYO (see Gonçalves, 2024 for a thorough discussion).
2. . . . indicates pause in transcription.

References

Angouri, J., Marra, M., & Holmes, J. (Eds.). (2017). *Negotiating boundaries at work: Talking and transitions*. Edinburgh University Press. https://doi.org/10.1017/s0047404518000428

Bailey, A. K., Rice, C., Gualtieri, M., & Gillet, J. (2022). Is #YogaForEveryone? The idealized flexible bodymind in Instagram yoga posts. *Qualitative Research in Sport, Exercise and Health*, *14*(5), 827–842. https://doi.org/10.1080/2159676X.2021.2002394

Bakhtin, M. M. (1986). *Speech genres & other late essays* (V. W. McGee, Trans. & Ed.). University of Texas Press. https://doi.org/10.7560/720466

Beilharz, K. (2011). Tele-touch embodied controllers: Posthuman gestural interaction in music performance. *Social Semiotics*, *21*(4), 547–568. https://doi.org/10.1080/10350330.2011.591997

Blackledge, A., & Creese, A. (2017). Translanguaging and the body. *International Journal of Multilingualism*, *14*(3), 250–268. https://doi.org/10.1080/14790718.2017.1315809

Blommaert, J. (2017). Chronotopes, scales and complexity in the study of language in society. In K. Arnaut, M. S. Karrebaek, M. Spotti & J. Blommaert (Eds.), *Engaging superdiversity: Recombining spaces, times and language practices* (pp. 47–62). Multilingual Matters. https://doi.org/10.21832/9781783096800-005

Bourdieu, P. (1984). *Distinction: A social critique of the judgement of taste* (R. Nice, Trans. & Ed.). Polity.

Bourdieu, P. (1991). *Language and symbolic power*. Harvard University Press.

Bucholtz, M., & Hall, K. (2016). Embodied sociolinguistics. In N. Coupland (Ed.), *Sociolinguistics: Theoretical debates* (pp. 173–200). Cambridge University Press. https://doi.org/10.1017/cbo9781107449787.009

Canagarajah, S., & Minakova, V. (2022). Objects in embodied sociolinguistics: Mind the door in research group meetings. *Language in Society*, *52*(2), 183–214. https://doi.org/10.1017/s0047404522000082

Cavanaugh, J., & Shankar, S. (Eds.). (2017). *Language and materiality: Ethnographic and theoretical explorations*. Cambridge University Press. https://doi.org/10.1017/9781316848418

Coupland, N. (Ed.). (2016). *Sociolinguistics: Theoretical debates*. Cambridge University Press. https://doi.org/10.1017/cbo9781107449787

Eckert, P. (1990). *Jocks and burnouts: Social categories and identity in the high school*. Teachers College Press.

Geertz, C. (1977). *The interpretation of cultures*. Basic Books.

Gonçalves, K. (2020). *Labour policies, language use and the 'new' economy*. Palgrave Macmillan. https://doi.org/10.1007/978-3-030-48705-8

Gonçalves, K. (2024). From the side, you should look like a Japanese ham sandwich, no gap anywhere: Exploring embodied, linguistic, and nonlinguistic signs in enregisterment processes of Bikram Yoga in online and offline spaces. *Signs and Society*, *12*(1), 83–108. https://doi.org/10.1086/728148

Gonçalves, K., & Kelly-Holmes, H. (Eds.). (2021). *Language, global mobilities, blue-collar workers and blue-collar workplaces*. Routledge. https://doi.org/10.4324/9780429298622

Gonçalves, K., & Lanza, E. (2024). Familyscapes. In R. Blackwood, S. Tufi & W. Amos (Eds.), *The Bloomsbury handbook of linguistic landscapes* (422–440). Bloomsbury Publishing.

Gonçalves, K., & Schluter, A. (2024). *Domestic workers talk: Language use and social practices in a multilingual workplace*. Multilingual Matters. https://doi.org/10.21832/9781800416765

Gullberg, M. (1998). *Gesture as a communication strategy in second language discourse: A study of learners of French and Swedish*. Lund University Press. https://doi.org/10.1075/ttwia.55.06gul

Gullberg, M. (2011). Multilingual multimodality: Communicative difficulties and their solutions in second language use. In J. Streeck, C. Goodwin & C. LaBaron (Eds.), *Embodied interaction: Language and body in the material world* (pp. 137–151). Cambridge University Press.

Hauser, B. (2013). *Yoga traveling: Bodily practice in transcultural perspective*. Springer. https://doi.org/10.1007/978-3-319-00315-3

Irvine, J. T., & Gal, S. (2000). Language ideology and linguistic differentiation. In P. Kroskrity (Ed.), *Regimes of language: Ideologies, polities, and identities* (pp. 35–84). School for American Research.

Keevallik, L. (2010). Bodily quoting in dance correction. *Research on Language and Social Interaction*, *43*(4), 401–426. https://doi.org/10.1080/08351813.2010.518065

Keevallik, L. (2013). The interdependence of bodily demonstrations and clausal syntax. *Research on Language and Social Interaction*, *46*(1), 1–21. https://doi.org/10.1080/08351813.2013.753710

Kendon, A. (1990). *Conducting interaction: Patterns of behavior in focused encounters*. Cambridge University Press. https://doi.org/10.1017/S0272263100011700

Kendon, A. (2004). *Gesture: Visible action as utterance*. Cambridge University Press. https://doi.org/10.1017/cbo9780511807572

Kusters, A., De Meulder, M., & Napier, J. (2021). Family language policy on holiday: Four multilingual signing and speaking families travelling together. *Journal of Multilingual and Multicultural Development*, *42*(8), 698–715. https://doi.org/10.1080/01434632.2021.1890752

Kusters, A., Spotti, M., Swanwick, R., & Tapio, E. (2017). Beyond languages, beyond modalities: Transforming the study of semiotic repertoires. *International Journal of Multilingualism*, *14*(3), 219–232. https://doi.org/10.1080/14790718.2017.1321651

Madsen, L. M. (2015). *Fighters, girls and other identities: Sociolinguistics in a martial arts club*. Multilingual Matters. https://doi.org/10.21832/9781783093991

Marra, M., Holmes, J., & Vine, B. (2022). What we share: The impact of norms on successful interaction. In J. Mortensen & K. Kraft (Eds.), *Norms and the study of language in social life* (pp. 185–210). De Gruyter. https://doi.org/10.1515/9781501511882-008

McDonald, E. (2013). Embodiment and meaning: Moving beyond linguistic imperialism and social semiotics. *Social Semiotics*, *23*(3), 318–334. https://doi.org/10.1080/10350330.2012.719730

McNeill, D. (1981). Action, thought, and language. *Cognition*, *10*(1–3), 201–208. https://doi.org/10.1016/0010-0277(81)90047-0

McNeill, D. (2005). *Gesture and thought*. University of Chicago Press. https://doi.org/10.7208/chicago/9780226514642.001.0001

Mondada, L. (2014). Bodies in action: Multimodal analysis of walking and talking. *Language and Dialogue*, *4*, 357–403. https://doi.org/10.1075/ld.4.3.02mon

Mondada, L. (2016). Challenges of multimodality: Language and the body in social interaction. *Journal of Sociolinguistics*, *20*(3), 336–366. https://doi.org/10.1111/josl.1_12177

Mondada, L. (2019). Contemporary issues in conversation analysis: Embodiment and materiality, multimodality and multisensoriality in social interaction. *Journal of Pragmatics*, *145*, 47–62. https://doi.org/10.1016/j.pragma.2019.01.016

Murray, S. (2005). Introduction to "thinking fat" special issue of social semiotics. *Social Semiotics*, *15*(2), 111–112. https://doi.org/10.1080/10350330500154592

Nevile, M. (2015). The embodied turn in research on language and social interaction. *Research on Language and Social Interaction*, *48*(2), 12–51. https://doi.org/10.1080/08351813.2015.1025499

Pennycook, A. (2010). *Language as a local practice*. Routledge. https://doi.org/10.4324/9780203846223

Pennycook, A. (2017). Translanguaging and semiotic assemblages. *International Journal of Multilingualism*, *14*(3), 269–282. https://doi.org/10.1080/14790718.2017.1315810

Pennycook, A. (2020). Translingual entanglements of English. *World Englishes*, *39*, 222–235. https://doi.org/10.1111/weng.12456

Pennycook, A. (2023). Toward the total semiotic fact. *Chinese Semiotic Studies*, *19*(4), 595–613. https://doi.org/10.1515/css-2023-2023

Pennycook, A., & Otsuji, E. (2015). *Metrolingualism: Language in the city*. Routledge. https://doi.org/10.4324/9781315724225

Pietikäinen, S. (2021). Assemblage of art, discourse and ice hockey: Designing knowledge about work. *Journal of Sociolinguistics*, *26*(5), 1–15. https://doi.org/10.1111/josl.12470

Rosen, A. (2019). Balance, yoga, neoliberalism. *Signs and Society*, *7*(3), 289–313. https://doi.org/10.1086/703088

Schneider, B., & Heyd, T. (2024). Introduction: Unthinking language from a posthumanist perspective. *Signs and Society*, *12*(1), 1–13. https://doi.org/10.1086/728243

Scollon, R., & Scollon, S. W. (2003). *Discourses in place: Language in the material world*. Routledge. http://doi.org/10.4324/9780203422724

Shankar, S., & Cavanaugh, J. (2012). Language and materiality in global capitalism. *Annual Review of Anthropology*, *41*(1), 355–369. https://doi.org/10.1146/annurev-anthro-092611-145811

Streeck, J., Goodwin, C., & LeBaron, C. (2011). Embodied interaction in the material world: An introduction. In J. Streeck, C. Goodwin & C. LeBaron (Eds.), *Embodied interaction: Language and the body in the material world* (pp. 1–28). Cambridge University Press.

Williams, R. (1977). *Marxism and literature*. Oxford University Press. https://doi.org/10.1017/s0047404500005698

Woolard, K. A. (2021). Language ideology. In J. Stanlaw (Ed.), *The international encyclopedia of linguistic anthropology* (pp. 1–21). John Wiley & Sons. https://doi.org/10.1002/9781118786093.iela0217

9
DIGITAL ASSEMBLAGES AND THEIR ENGLISH ENTANGLEMENTS

Digital design, voice assistant use and smartphone setting choices of translingual speakers in Berlin

Didem Leblebici and Britta Schneider

1. Introduction

Digital technologies have become ubiquitous in everyday life, and many people spend at least as much time interacting via messengers, artificial language tools or on social media platforms as they do in face-to-face settings. Since the 1990s, linguistic research has studied language practices in the context of digital technologies (e.g. Androutsopoulos, 2007; Herring et al., 2013). More recently, there is increased interest in the fact that the workings of media technologies – that is, writing, printing, digital transmission and algorithmic intervention – impact how humans interact and how we conceive of it (Jones, 2015; Varis & Hou, 2020: 236). Posthumanist approaches and the study of entanglements of language have brought to the fore that material environments, among them human-produced technologies, shape language practices and linguistic epistemology (Pennycook, 2018; Schneider & Heyd, 2024). Interaction and media technologies are thus in a dialectical relationship to each other: bringing across messages depends on the media we have at our disposal, while the design of media technologies is entangled with language practices and language ideologies. For example, the printing press has allowed for the distribution of written text in relatively large territories and is intertwined with concepts of standard language and the establishment of national publics (McLuhan, 1964). Media technologies can therefore be understood as semiotic-material assemblages (Bennett, 2010), which co-construct the wider, societally distributed assemblages that impact how we engage with and relate to each other.

In this chapter, we explore the entanglement of digital technologies with Anglophone social and material histories by studying the design of voice assistants and smartphones and the role of English in translingual speakers' use of such devices. This serves as an illustrative case of how translingual practices interact with

DOI: 10.4324/9781003441304-13

Anglophone hegemonic digital materialities and the entanglements of US-based language technology design. Both discussions show the urgency of considering semiotic–material entanglements if we want to understand and critically question sociolinguistic realities beyond methodologically nationalist and cognitivist approaches to language (Schneider, 2019).

Investigating which language ideologies shape media technologies and how translingual speakers engage with digital devices is well suited to follow the call to study social semiotic trajectories and the interconnectedness of material and language practices – and to thus understand language as materially intertwined assemblage (Pennycook, 2020, 2024). Language technologies come into being in relation to specific discourses, desires, computational requirements and political–economic conditions. Using digital devices to communicate with each other means to become involved with many different kinds of materiality – from electric circuits and cables to computer chips and servers, screens, keyboards, microphones and loudspeakers. Besides, the functioning of digital technologies relies on phenomena that we are probably more hesitant to call 'material': the software that makes websites run, the numbers and letters used for coding or the sounds that come out of a loudspeaker. And yet, letters and numbers, computer code as well as sounds are not immaterial but can themselves be understood as assemblages of form-meaning elements. We come to realize that any interaction "requires some sort of expressive form – signs" (Gal & Irvine, 2019, p. 89). While brains, vocal folds, ears, face muscles, hands, arms and the air flowing out of our lungs allow us to create the signs we traditionally call 'language', digital media technologies depend on more widely spatially distributed materialities and form assemblages that have specific socio-technical histories.

The signs that are understood to make up English hold a particularly prominent place in digital assemblages. This is entangled with various factors: the history of computing (Ceruzzi, 2003), discourses and practices of economic deregulation in the 1990s that have allowed for a global economic market on which a handful of US American companies became dominant (on English and neoliberal policies, see Pennycook, 2020, p. 228), the invention and distribution of the internet and discourses of efficiency in technology, all of which have influenced language ideologies in technology contexts (Gramling, 2020; Schneider, 2022). The dominance of English in language technology design is in an uneasy relationship with their extremely popular use by speakers of very diverse language backgrounds worldwide. In addition, technology design typically reproduces language ideological histories of Western modernity. Most devices reproduce territorial monolingualism and anticipate monolingual speakers of the standard language of the country in which a device is physically located. So far, language technologies rarely accommodate translingual practices or mobile lifestyles.

The study we present in the following develops critical perspectives on the entanglements of English and language technology design and studies narratives of translingual users with a migration trajectory, reporting on their experiences, choices and practices with digital voice assistants and smartphone settings. We study young, urban, educated, translingual users with a recent history of migrating from Turkey to Berlin, Germany, and ask how they deal with and react to Anglophone hegemonies in technology design. Which creative practices do they develop to appropriate the technologies to their own needs and desires? As data of users is collected by companies, their doings, in turn, may eventually impact the functioning and design of the devices. This shows that, despite a continuing English dominance, users of digital technologies are not passive recipients but contribute to an ever more complex socio-technical-linguistic assemblage that will influence how we communicate and what we understand to be prestigious forms of interaction in the future.

We first present theoretical backgrounds, based on the notion of posthumanist entanglements. We relate this to the concepts of superdiversity and translanguaging to grasp the specific sociolinguistic realities of the speakers our study engages with. The methodological approach is introduced in the section thereafter, which is followed by an analytical discussion of language technology design and interview passages in which users of voice assistants and smartphones report on their experiences and practices with these tools. The chapter ends with a discussion and conclusion.

2. Socio-technological entanglements in a superdiverse world

In humanist European histories, languages have been conceived as immaterial cognitive systems that are proof of the rational capacities of humans (see e.g. Bauman & Briggs, 2003). Saussurean structuralist linguistics and Chomskyan understandings of language as based on universal grammar have continued this legacy throughout the 20th century (Heller & McElhinny, 2017). It is only relatively recently that a consideration of language as material and bodily practice has come to the fore, which is linked to an overall greater interest in the interaction between humans and their material environments in the humanities and social sciences in fields such as posthumanism (Braidotti, 2013), science technology studies (Sismondo, 2010) or actor-network-theory (Latour, 1987). An understanding of language as material phenomenon can be found in approaches that study the role of the body in sign-making (Bucholtz & Hall, 2016) but also in the fields of distributed language (Cowley, 2011) or in posthumanist applied linguistics (Pennycook, 2018). All these approaches emphasize that linguistic sign-making cannot be explained without a consideration of non-human and material environments. In this context, the notion of *entanglement*, which is highlighted in the present volume, aims to "shift the sociolinguistic focus towards a more profound sense of interconnectedness . . . , by questioning assumed divisions between humans and non-humans (Pennycook, 2018), between living and non-living existents" (Pennycook, 2020, p. 225). Similar to Foucauldian traditions (Foucault, 1979, 1991), in which, for example, the architecture of schools or prisons is discussed as interrelated with discourses about social order, hierarchy and control, the notion of entanglement entails the idea that material environments are dialectically intertwined with forms of power. As another example, Pennycook discusses electric wires in the Philippines' urban cityscapes as indexical of economic development and power structures (2020, p. 225).

Clearly, the existence, distribution and use of digital devices like computers, smartphones or AI tools are also embedded in and entangled with social power and with social discourses, for example, on economic development and competition, technological progress, participation in global public space and practices of digital surveillance. When it comes to language practices in digital contexts, we see, therefore, that digital interaction cannot be understood as analogue to face-to-face interaction. Language in online or digitized settings is based on the affordances of the tools (Jones et al., 2015), which are, again, entangled with economic, political and social discourses that impact the design of tools and the functions of devices, programmes or platforms. Social media platforms, for example, encourage specific types of storytelling and performance of self (Georgakopoulou, 2016) in an overall context that displays ideologies of quantification (the more 'likes', the better) and aims to collect data in the age of surveillance capitalism (Zuboff, 2019). Yet, the impact of technological affordances on language practice is nothing new – traditional notions of *languages* as standardized systemic entities are not conceivable without the technologies of writing and nationally ordered print industries (Linell, 2005; Ong, 1982). We can infer from this that "[l]anguages have long been subject to economic and material forces, be they capitalist, communist, neoliberal, feudal, or otherwise" (Pennycook, 2020, p. 226). The notion of *language assemblage* (Pennycook, 2024) intends to grasp this notion of language as constantly under construction, an outcome of social action that involves bodies and things (ibid.). It understands language as socially and materially constructed phenomenon that is entangled with its living and non-living environment.

While monolingual standard language culture is based on the technologies of national print capitalism, multilingual and diverse language practices have attracted a lot of attention in the last decades, which is not least due to the increase of transnational digital interaction. A stronger interest in and higher status of multilingual diversity is related to patterns of economic globalization and practices of migration that are enabled by cheaper travel and the prestige of mobile lifestyles. The notion of *superdiversity* describes advanced conditions of diversity that are characterized by complex intersections of ethnicity, nationality, gender, language, religion, economic and immigration status (Vertovec, 2007). Whereas older approaches to diversity oftentimes approached cultural and linguistic difference as appearing in stable categories (*ethnicities/nationalities/languages*), the concept of superdiversity emphasizes that we have to do with much more intricate social realities in which individuals cannot be defined on grounds of their citizenship status or territorial location only. In superdiverse settings, the study of language has to consider that we are confronted with increasingly disentangled relations of language use and national territory – for the study of English, this implies that we have to go beyond an understanding of national Englishes and have to include phenomena like English in Korean pop (Rüdiger, 2021), the role of English in sales encounters of African speakers on Chinese markets (Che & Bodomo, 2021) or the impact of English in social media practices worldwide (Dailey-O'Cain, 2021).

In superdiverse contexts, we expect speakers who engage in language practices that have been referred to as *translanguaging*, that is, "the deployment of a speaker's full linguistic repertoire without regard for the watchful adherence to the socially and politically defined boundaries of named (and usually national and state) languages" (Otheguy et al., 2015, p. 281). The notion of translanguaging recognizes the fluid and dynamic nature of language use and regards linguistic entities like *Spanish*, *German* or *English* as socio-political constructs (Makoni & Pennycook, 2007). It has been applied in educational contexts to support the recognition of the complex and rich linguistic repertoires of pupils in superdiverse environments (García & Li, 2014). While the linguistic phenomena studied are often the same as those previously referred to as *codeswitching*, the analytical framing is different as languages are not taken as given systemic entities but are treated as the result of performative sedimentation in specific cultural contexts (Pennycook, 2004). Translingual speakers are described as basing their language choices on communicative goals, which not always necessitates the adherence to traditional language norms and often includes forms of blending resources of what has been understood as different 'languages'. In recent work, the notion of translanguaging has been expanded to include transmodal languaging, for example, in deaf communities, who use signs, gestures, material environments and technologies to interact (De Meulder et al., 2019; Kusters, 2024).

When we study the entanglements of digital devices with English and their impact on translingual speakers, we cannot approach speakers as defined by nationality or location but must take into account their specific verbal and multimodal repertoires as well as their mobility trajectories and local living conditions. Research on digital discourses and digital language practices has very often been conducted in English-speaking contexts and has not necessarily focused on the role of superdiverse language repertoires and the sociolinguistic hierarchies that technologies entail. And yet, when we have a closer look at technology design, we quickly see that speakers of dominant European standard languages, and above all, speakers of English, are strongly advantaged, which is entangled with social and political histories, the history of digital computing and the logics of data-based applications (Leblebici, 2021). In our study, we encourage a reflection on the technological design of digital devices and provide insight into how translanguaging speakers use them.

3. Methodological approach

In the first part of our analysis, we focus on the role of English in the programming of voice assistants and smartphones. We base this on previous academic work on the discourses that impact tech culture from the realms of science technology studies and critical computational linguistics. Our insights are furthermore informed by an ongoing qualitative study of social discourses and language ideologies in language technology design, based on a meta-theoretical discourse analysis of academic publications from computational and computational linguistic disciplines and on expert interviews with technology specialists (see Schneider, 2022, to appear).

To analyze the discourses associated with English among translingual speakers and to understand their entangled practices with digital tools and AI technologies, we draw on ethnographically informed research that combines offline and online participant observation, voice history data of Alexa interactions and qualitative interviews (see Leblebici, 2021, 2024). The participants of this study, four women and six men, have migrated from Turkey to Germany, within the last 10–15 years and actively engage with voice assistant technologies, such as smart speakers (e.g. Alexa) or integrated digital assistants in smartphones (e.g. Siri). Leblebici's Turkish background facilitated the establishment of connections, enabling a comprehensive exploration of interviewees' use of voice assistants through participant observation, the collection of Alexa's automatic transcription of voice data and qualitative interviews conducted between 2021 and 2023. The participants under consideration in this paper live in Berlin, which has a long history of migration from Turkey, particularly in the context of so-called 'guest worker' schemes (Terkessidis, 2000). The users we study here, however, have few connections to this population and typically orient towards educated urban lifestyles in a rather 'cosmopolitan', culturally diverse and consumer-oriented environment (Maly & Varis, 2016; Richard, 2000). Their ages range from 23 to 44 at the time of the last interview. The group is evenly split between university graduates actively employed in fields such as engineering, marketing and architecture, and university students specializing in economics, engineering and law. The high educational level is anticipated given the context of individuals self-identifying as 'New Wave' migrants, explicitly distinguishing themselves from the previously mentioned Turkish 'guest worker' diaspora (Oldac & Fancourt, 2021).

During the initial semi-structured interviews conducted in Turkish, participants were queried about their utilization of voice assistants, covering aspects such as purpose, motivation and duration of use. Their language preferences and rationales, the selection of gendered voices and the influence of other individuals on their device usage were also explored. During participant observations, the entanglement of voice assistants with various other digital technologies became apparent. Notably, smartphones played a pivotal role, facilitating activities ranging from configuring and navigating smart speakers to utilizing voice-based GPS in cars and engaging with integrated voice assistants. Consequently, in subsequent interviews, this topic was introduced to inquire about participants' language choices on their mobile devices. The interview data is transcribed predominantly in Standard Turkish and coded using the grounded theory method, seeking to formulate theoretical perspectives based on empirical data (cf. Glaser & Strauss, 2017/1967). An inductive coding approach was applied, wherein codes were not pre-defined. These codes closely align with the participants' articulated statements, forming the foundation for constructing higher-level categories and theoretical concepts. One such overarching category has been formulated on the basis of statements that pertain to the role of English when interacting with digital devices. Before we discuss some examples, we first elaborate on the entanglement of technology design and the English language.

4. English in technology design and use

4.1. Language technology design and its entanglement with English

Today's digital language technologies are based on a long cultural history that includes traditions of visual sign making, such as the use of phonetic symbols and the writing of numbers, mathematical discoveries and computational practices. While this is not the place to delve deeper into these fascinating developments (see Ceruzzi, 2003; Pasquinelli, 2023), it is safe to say that computers and other digital devices are strongly interwoven with practices of power. Digital technologies are found in almost all spheres of life and are crucial in contexts of military and defense, social control and administration, global business, research and education (Crawford, 2021). Current critical discussions on technological development and, in particular, on the practices of machine learning and the application of big data technologies (also often referred to as *artificial intelligence* – not least due to marketing reasons; for a critical discussion of the term, see Katz, 2020), highlight some of the social problems that technological practices generate and enforce. Above all, massive data collection allows for the surveillance of human interaction in an unprecedented scale, which is a crucial asset in global business and advertising but has also been used in political contexts, for example to (illegitimately) influence elections in democratic states (Jones, 2015; Rushkoff, 2019; Zuboff, 2019). As computational technologies play a fundamental role in securing global power positions in capitalist society and are associated with discourses of mastery, efficiency and control, it does not come as a surprise that technology and gendered desire are linked so that technological competences are intertwined with the performance of masculinity (see Pennycook, 2020, p. 228; Wajcman, 2010). The historical development of computing and machine learning is furthermore entangled with the reproduction of social orders that have ties to colonial racism (e.g. Katz, 2020) and sexist exclusion (Ensmenger, 2015).

In terms of language ideological entanglements, the close link between global power hierarchies and technology, and the fact that the undisputed global technology providers are a handful of US American companies (Microsoft, Google, Meta, Amazon, Apple), which are backed by the US government (Crawford, 2021), has led to a strong hegemony of English in technology development, at least in the Western world. The absolute majority of programming languages is based on English keywords and syntax and all new software and hardware of the previously mentioned companies are first developed for an English-speaking audience. English grammatical peculiarities, for example, the highly analytical nature of English morphosyntax, form the basis of most language technologies, and it is not always easy to make systems work for languages with different grammatical structures. In the following quote, a German-based language technology designer (interviewed in the study on language ideologies in technology design; see Section 3) reports on the structural-linguistic challenges associated with this practice once the tools are adapted to other languages.

Excerpt 1: English in software implementation

The problem is that many systems are designed and initially implemented in English
And then in other languages, due to linguistic complexity, additional levels occur, which can partly be retrofitted in the implementation, but partly not
And you have to make a great effort to conceal these shortcomings somehow
And in this respect, I think there are indeed limitations in some places, due to the fact that systems are developed by native speakers of English who do not know any other languages
[translated from German; see end of chapter for transcription conventions]

The computational linguist reports on the fact that grammatical structures that were not part of the original software design are difficult to implement retrospectively. He additionally assumes that many developers are monolingual English speakers. The latter argument is difficult to prove, and perhaps not even likely. And yet a monolingual English framework is common in technology design.

The status of English is enforced in the computational sciences in academia as English is also the language to talk *about* technology (on English in academia, see Piller & Cho, 2013). Furthermore, and this is today maybe even more crucial, English is the most widely used language in online settings. As most of today's machine learning technologies require large amounts of data to enable algorithmic pattern recognition, and as those data are usually taken from the web, this implies that machine translation or generative language devices (e.g. ChatGPT or voice assistants) are always first designed for English. The status of English in computational contexts, therefore, is so dominant that critical computational linguist Emily Bender suggested that it should be mandatory at computational conferences to "name the language you are working on," given the common practice of understanding English language data as representative of 'language' in general (Bender, 2019, n.p.). The dominance of English obviously privileges those competent in English; in addition, it has been shown that the grammar of English has started to influence the grammar of languages for which less data is available (Lauscher et al., 2020). The latter has to do with computational practices in which English is used as reference corpus in almost all attempts to create technologies for other languages (Costa-jussà et al., 2022; Bapna et al., 2022; van Esch et al., 2019). These tendencies are further reinforced by practices of artificial data creation, used to enable machine learning techniques for languages for which little machine-readable data exists, where English data is translated into other languages to produce larger datasets (Lauscher et al., 2020; Costa-jussà et al., 2022; Virtanen et al., 2019). The entire socio-technical context of big data machine learning thus demonstrates "the unequal distribution of linguistic resources in relation to other resources" (Dovchin et al., 2016).

Besides the hegemony of English in online contexts, in programming languages, in technology development and in data practices, we can observe that Western language ideologies – referential, monolingual and standard language ideologies – strongly prevail in the design of digital tools and devices. Thus, contemporary chatbots mostly lack the capacity to decode or produce non-referential functions of speech (e.g. politeness markers, intonation or social indexicality, see Höhn et al., 2023). Monolingual and territorial language ideologies also prevail: Smartphones have monolingual settings suggested to the user on the basis of country location (which users can change); and search engines suggest websites and language choices based on the territorial location of the device from which a search is performed (see also Kelly-Holmes, 2019, p. 34).

With voice assistants, the limitations of language ideologies that frame language as a referential communication code based on hegemonic varieties of standard languages that are associated with specific locations, become even more apparent. Voice assistants mostly only process the standard variant of a language. Speakers of non-standard varieties often struggle in using the gadgets. This has been shown for speakers of African American English (Koenecke et al., 2020), for regional varieties of British English (Markl, 2022) and for L2 speakers of English (Beneteau et al., 2019; Wu et al., 2020). Also, as voice recognition tools were originally trained with voices of male speakers, female users tend to be less well recognized (Tatman, 2016).

At the time of writing this text, companies are trying to counteract these discriminatory functions, also referred to as 'biases'. In December 2023, Amazon's Alexa worked for several varieties of English (US, UK, Canada, Australia, India), two varieties of French (France, Canada) and three varieties of Spanish (Spain, US, Mexico). All other languages were only offered in one standard variety. Since these technologies are, after all, designed for profit, it is not surprising that the linguistic communities to be targeted first are those that are expected to be large, to be wealthy enough to buy the tools and to have constant access to electricity and the internet (which is necessary for the device to work). There is the possibility to use some voice assistants (Alexa and Google Assistant) bilingually; that is, the device notices whether the one or the other language is spoken. It is not, however, possible to code-mix or switch languages within sentences.

There is today a huge body of work that problematizes gendered, racial and linguistic discrimination, above all, from the computational sciences (e.g. Blodgett et al., 2020; Crawford, 2017; Höhn et al., 2023; Markl, 2022; Martin & Wright, 2023; Savoldi et al., 2021; Zhao et al., 2017), and it is surprising how little interdisciplinary interaction there is between computational and sociolinguistic work. Returning to the question of the entanglement of English and digital technologies, the previous observations explain the strong dominance of English in language practices that are entangled with technological devices. The design of digital technologies reproduces "the linguistic ideologies that maintain the language myth in the first place" (Pennycook, 2020, p. 223); that is, they construct language as materializing in stable monolithic and monolingual codes that transmit information and as bound to national territories. We can also observe that dominant and hegemonic forms of speech – the standard languages of some of the world's richest states, most of which were colonizers in earlier times – are, at least today, those that are most strongly supported in technology design. This makes "some types of knowledges, practices, repertoires, and bodies more legitimate, and therefore more visible" (Kerfoot & Hyltenstam, 2017, p. 5). Thus, smartphones and voice assistants make language practices which are already hegemonic even more visible, while marginalizing minority languages and those languages that are rarely displayed in machine-readable datasets. Overall, colonial hierarchies, neoliberal practices and the entangled dominance of English are very visible in digital technology. In the next section, we give some examples of how translingual users react to this.

4.2. Translingual speakers' entangled Englishes in digital devices

In this section, we analyze reports of translingual speakers in superdiverse environments about their experiences with digital devices. Our focus lies particularly on the language choices individuals make and how they metalinguistically contemplate these preferences in relation to their mobility trajectories, local living conditions, language ideologies and multimodal repertoires.

Despite a shared sense of belonging to a community of 'new wave' migrants from Turkey in Germany, assumed to share similar experiences of mobility trajectories and higher educational backgrounds, participants exhibit diverse language preferences for their digital devices. While acknowledging that English versions of digital technologies seem to be the best-supported option, some participants, based on their specific needs or desires, opt for using their gadgets in Turkish, German or another language. Interestingly, when residing in Berlin, similar practices emerge among some informants, particularly regarding the adoption of English smartphone settings. When questioned about the use of voice assistants, one interviewee initiates a broader reflection on his language choices, starting with his decisions regarding smartphone configurations after his migration to Berlin.

Excerpt 2: Entanglements of imagined local living conditions and language choices in Berlin

Böyle Berlin'e taşındığımda sonradan şey yaptım [dil ayarlarını İngilizceye çevirdim]
Onun da sebebi hani (.)
Bir şey olur acil bir şey olur telefonum kaybolur biri bulur başıma bir şey gelir
O zaman en azından hani kimin ne olduğunu bilmeseler bile
Mother father çok basic bir şey hani
Öyle daha rahat olur diye düşündüm onu öyle yaptım [. . .]
Anne falan desem hani ismi Anne olan bir tanıdık olabilir

After I moved to Berlin I did that [changed the language settings to English]
The reason is actually (.)
If something like an emergency happens my phone gets lost and someone finds it [or]
if something happens to me then even if they don't know anyone really
They can at least understand mother father
It is very basic I mean
I thought it would be easier that's why I did it [. . .]
If I said anne [Turkish for mother] it could get mistaken for some acquaintance named Anne

Similar to the experiences of two other participants, he emphasizes the importance of using his phone in English, noting the wish for potential emergency responders to understand the language of his device and effectively communicate with the right contacts. Migration to another country prompts him to reconsider, reconceptualize and adapt his phone settings. These translingual smartphone users envision scenarios in which a person who does not know them may gain access to their phone to get in touch with their close relatives. Given the Berlin context, the participant argues that this hypothetical individual might not comprehend that anne signifies 'mother' in Turkish but would associate it with the name of an acquaintance (as 'Anne' is a common German female name). In his reappropriation of national language ideologies, the potential interlocutor in this scenario is not imagined as someone who speaks German in Germany but rather English in Berlin. There is an interesting link to the notion of the 'imagined audiences' in social media research (Marwick & boyd, 2011; Androutsopoulos, 2014). While the situation depicted is not a social media space, a comparison can be drawn. The interviewee imagines a particular English-speaking audience of Berlin citizens. As a matter of fact, due to the previously Soviet-oriented education system from GDR times, we observe that, in East Berlin, many people do not actually speak English. And yet, the user finds it suitable to opt for the English term *mother* rather than *Mutter* in German. This adjustment reflects a strategic maneuver aligning language settings with his superdiverse linguistic environment, in which English plays a central role (on the role of English in Berlin, see also Schneider, 2012).

The perception that English is the prevailing language for local communication transcends the confines of the Berlin context, extending its relevance to other urban areas. Practices of travel mobility significantly contribute to the entanglements of English with smartphone settings. The study participants who routinely travel to Turkey to visit their families and friends are compelled to consider how they will be utilizing their smartphones both in Germany and Turkey. This underscores their communication needs across different locations. In Excerpt 3, a participant reflects on his English language preferences, which are entangled with his mobility trajectories.

Excerpt 3: Entanglements of language choices and mobility trajectories

Hani telefon İngilizce benim için
Bir de şimdi söyle bir (.)
Biraz anneanne görüşü olacak ama
Acil bir durum olur bir şey olur
Herkes Almanca bilmiyor
Türkiye'de bu telefon elinde bayıldın kaldın hiçbir şey yapamaz kimse

I mean the phone is in English for me
There is also this thing now (.)
It will be like a grandmother's view but
If an emergency happens or something happens
Not everyone can speak German
If you pass out with this phone in your hand in Turkey no one can do anything

Similar to the participant in Excerpt 2, he elucidates a parallel emergency scenario which he calls "a grandmother's view," which could be interpreted as a perspective of a cautious caretaker, thereby extending the discussion to an alternative context. This participant not only reflects on the scenario within the Berlin context but also envisions its potential unfolding in Turkey. The speaker assumes that individuals in Turkey are more inclined to comprehend English rather than German, further emphasizing the anticipation that English is spoken by most people transnationally.

Besides imagined audiences in case of an emergency, technological constraints play another pivotal role in shaping language preferences. Particularly those with stationary smart speakers encounter limitations, as Turkish is not provided as a language option in any of them,[1] demonstrating the discrimination of non-European languages by the industries (see also Markl, 2022; Leblebici, 2021, 2024). Consequently, the users of this study have to opt for English or German settings to operate smart speaker devices. The following excerpt underscores this technological constraint through the lens of a participant who employs Siri in Turkish but (has to) resort to using Alexa and Google Home in English. In discussing the optimal language choice for his voice assistants, he engages in metalinguistic reflections about Turkish and English synthetic voices.

Excerpt 4: Entanglements of synthetic sound design and English

Didem:	Hani böyle farklı dillerde denedin mi? Hangisi sana kulağına daha iyi geliyor o şeylerde?
Interviewee:	İngilizce
Didem:	A öyle mi? Hepsinde mi?
Interviewee:	Hepsinde en iyi İngilizce geliyor bana
	Çünkü aslında Türkçe de fena değil
	Ama robot olarak konuştuğu için böyle (.) hani (.)
	Kelimeleri böyle sırayla konuştuğu için
	Böyle biraz tutuyormuş gibi falan geliyor ondan çok da sarmıyor
	Hani böyle bi robotla konuşuyormuşum hissi
	Ama İngilizcede konuşunca öyle bi his gelmiyor
Didem:	*Did you try out other languages? Which one sounds like the better option for you?*
Interviewee:	*English*
Didem:	*Oh really? In all of them?*
Interviewee:	*English seems to be the best of all of them to me*
	Because actually Turkish is not bad
	But it's like that because it speaks as a robot (.) you know (.)
	Since it speaks the words separately it seems like it is holding a little bit
	so I don't really enjoy it
	It feels like I'm talking to a robot
	But when I speak in English it doesn't feel like that

A recurring theme in the interviews revolves around the perception that the English synthetic voice sounds the best in terms of auditory quality when compared to Turkish or German, regardless of the individual's language preferences. As displayed in Excerpt 4, the participant characterizes the English synthetic voice of Alexa and Siri as the "best" choice, while deeming the Turkish voice sounds "robotic" due to issues in intonation and pronunciation. He characterizes these difficulties as a consequence of the tendency to pronounce ("hold") each word separately rather than integrating intonation into the overall sentence structure.

It has to be acknowledged that the notion of a voice sounding 'robotic' is context dependent and could be desirable or expected in some synthetic voice applications, in case a non-humanlike or 'robotic' sound might be intentionally sought after to avoid the 'uncanny valley' effect, which might otherwise evoke 'feelings of eeriness' with a synthetic voice that closely resembles a human one (Moore, 2019; Mori, 2012/1970). However, in commercial voice assistants like Siri or Alexa, the overarching design goal is geared towards achieving 'humanness' and 'believability' through a voice that closely mimics human qualities, which is particularly emphasized in their marketing (Sweeney, 2016). Consequently, a 'humanlike' voice is an expected attribute in these machines, and the user in this context expresses a preference for such a quality, disapproving of the perceived 'robotic' nature of the Turkish synthetic voice.

While defining the abstract quality of 'humanness' in synthetic sound poses challenges, the perception of the Turkish synthetic voice as inferior to its English counterpart can be attributed to the hegemony of English in the development of these language technologies (see above). This influence is particularly evident in text-to-speech conversion methods (those used in voice assistants), where the reliance on large spoken data corpora becomes a limiting factor for Turkish, classified as a 'low resource' language in technology development (Gokay & Yalcin, 2019). Also, working with Turkish introduces considerable complexities to language technology development due to the language's morphosyntactic structure, which significantly differs from English (Budur et al., 2020).

In addition to technological constraints, there seems to be an association of voice assistants' English synthetic voices with popular Anglophone media cultures and science fiction narratives. Interviewees draw parallels between their practices and well-known science fiction films like *Her*, where a man develops a romantic relationship with a synthetic female voice, and popular cartoons like *The Jetsons*, portraying a futuristic family whose lives are entirely automated and optimized by various digital technologies. These associations are entangled with a particular cultural image of voice assistants expected to generate synthetic speech in English. As one participant expressed, using digital devices in other languages feels akin to "watching those original movies in dubbed versions." A Siri user in the study demonstrated unfamiliarity with the Turkish voice option until prompted by Leblebici to specify language preferences for his voice assistant. During the interview, this participant started exploring alternative options for the first time and assessed various available synthetic voices in different languages and tried out Turkish and English.

Excerpt 5: Entanglements of science fiction discourses, synthetic voices and English

Siri: Ben Siri, senin sanal asistanın (erkek sesi)
Siri: Ben Siri, senin sanal asistanın (kadın sesi)
Interviewee: Çok çok çok (.)
Sapkınca geliyor gerçekten Türkçe @
Hiç doğal gelmiyor ses tonu
Ya bir de belki de benim ana dilim olduğu için öyle o yüzden daha böyle kritize edebiliyorum bunu ama

Siri:	I am Siri your virtual assistant (İngiliz İngilizcesi, erkek sesi)
Interviewee:	Bu bana çok daha şey geliyor hani tamam
	Bambaşka bir dünyadayız hani o Star Trek'teyiz ben bununla konuşabiliyorum
	Ama Türkçe konuştuğum zaman şey diyorum
	Sen Apple'sın benimle niye Türkçe konuşuyorsun?
	Bir de böyle çok değişik bir tonlamayla
Siri:	*I am Siri your virtual assistant (Turkish male voice)*
Siri:	*I am Siri your virtual assistant (Turkish female voice)*
Interviewee:	*It sounds very very very (.) perverted.*
	I mean really Turkish @
	It doesn't sound natural at all
	Maybe because it is my mother tongue, so I can criticize it like this
Siri:	*I am Siri your virtual assistant (British English, male voice)*
Interviewee:	*This sounds to me like okay,*
	We are in a completely different world like Star Trek I can talk with this
	But when I speak Turkish I say
	You are Apple why are you speaking to me in Turkish?
	And with such a different intonation

The user associates the synthetic voice in British English with Star Trek, a series renowned for depicting human–machine interactions, which the user considers fitting to the cultural context of using voice assistants. This representation intertwines English with broader Anglophone popular media cultures, envisioned as the origin of these devices. Additionally, there is a correlation made between Siri and Apple, the company producing and marketing the product. The participant considers it as more appropriate for a US-based company to "speak with" him, operationalized through a voice assistant, in English. The Turkish synthetic voice is viewed as inappropriate, "perverted" or "robotic" within this cultural context. This particular cultural image associated with voice assistants is entangled with the hegemonic variants of English, as there is an expectation of voice assistants to generate synthetic speech in (Standard) English, above all American but also British English (see also Leblebici, 2024).

While some users anticipate that voice assistants speak in English, participants also express a desire for their devices to accurately recognize and pronounce their Turkish names. Their accounts highlight a prevalent technological constraint wherein devices can not automatically process non-English names. Consequently, some individuals resort to creating personalized solutions, using specific functionalities to train their voice assistants in correctly articulating their names. An interviewee shares an insightful experience, recounting the realization that Siri failed to vocalize her name, prompting her to explore alternatives.

Excerpt 6: Recognizing and learning non-English names

Interviewee:	[Siri] artık adımı söylüyor @
Didem:	Aa çok iyi onu öğrettin mi yoksa?
Interviewee:	Ben sordum evet çünkü adımı okuyamıyordu
Didem:	Nasıl okuyordu ki?
Interviewee:	Okumuyordu nasıl okunuyor ki diye bi şey sordu bana
Didem:	he:: Türkçe bi de?
Interviewee:	İngilizceyken mi sordu onu hatırlayamıyorum şu an
	Galiba İngilizceyken sordu evet
	Adımı geçiyordu yazıyordu
	ama okumuyordu yani
	Ben de işte adımı söyledim
Didem:	Aa çok iyi
Interviewee:	Aynen denedi bi şeyler
	En yakın olanında karar verdi
	Is it right is it right diye
	dedim tamam okay @
Interviewee:	[Siri] can say my name now @
Didem:	Oh very good did you train it then?
Interviewee:	Yes I asked it because it couldn't read my name [out loud]
Didem:	How did it read it?
Interviewee:	It didn't read it
	It asked me how it is read or something
Didem:	Oh so in Turkish?
Interviewee:	I can't remember if it asked me in English right now
	I think it was when it was set in English
	It showed my name it wrote my name
	But I mean it didn't read it [out loud]
	I then told my name [she pronounced her name]
Didem:	Oh very good
Interviewee:	Exactly so it tried out some stuff
	It decided on the closest one
	It said [English] is it right is it right
	I said okay [English] okay @

As indicated in the excerpt, the participant notes that she initially lacked awareness that the device entails a function by which she is asked to 'teach' it the correct pronunciation of her name – in other words, the companies encourage users to provide more data, especially in 'lower-resource' languages. At the same time, through her engagement with the technology, she uncovered a feature that enabled her to take agency and influence the device's outputs. During the interview, Leblebici inquired if she had "trained" the device, echoing the terminology used by other participants.

However, this interviewee differed in her approach, emphasizing how she "asked" or requested Siri to articulate her name accurately, engaging in a dialogue simulation. In her narrative, the act of requesting rather than training emphasizes that she retains some control yet perceives the technology as having its own agency. Despite her active involvement in determining which synthetic output is "the closest one" to an accurate pronunciation, the participant's portrayal of Siri as the ultimate decision-maker contributes to the construction of the technology as an autonomous entity in the interaction.

What adds another layer of intrigue is her recognition of a design feature inherent in the technology. Voice technologies operate on text-to-speech algorithms, converting written texts into spoken outputs. In this context, she perceives Siri's inability to "read" her name as a noteworthy observation, blurring the boundaries between reading, speaking and listening within the technological entanglements of language.

Overall, the participants in this study have shown creative ways of engaging with digital devices, where language choices are influenced by how they imagine the linguistic competences of the local environment in which they live, which tools work in which language, other technological affordances and, finally, cultural associations. Thus, the linguistic choices in using smartphones or voice assistants are not, as projected by companies, based on monolingual territorial national spaces but intertwined with mobile lifestyles, superdiverse contexts, narratives of popular culture and the technological design of devices. All of these aspects are entangled with English in one way or another.

5. Conclusion: the hegemonic order of digital language assemblages

In this chapter, we have explored the entanglement of digital technologies with Anglophone social and material histories as we have studied the design of voice assistants and smartphones as well as translingual speakers' experiences with such devices. In terms of language ideological constructions, we have, first of all, seen that the design of digital language technologies strongly favors a concept of language as a fixed system. The idea that *languages* are objective entities and that these can be produced by machines is not questioned by the participants of this study. Ideas of languages as stable lexical and morphosyntactic rules, deriving from specific national contexts, are also reproduced in technology design – digital language technologies actually rely on this idea and machine learning requires masses of similar-looking and normative data to allow for pattern recognition. Despite constructivist criticism towards such practices, we should not forget, however, that language-material assemblages that contribute to constructing language as entities in and via text, books or digital language technologies can enhance the status of minority languages. It can give speakers access to public spaces, co-construct community, and it can also be practical in many contexts (Kramsch, 2000; Siegel, 2005; Street, 1995).

However, in digital materialities, English is a strongly hegemonic assemblage. It is materialized in software and in hardware, and because of this, gains in status as a global resource, entangled with political, economic and technological practices of power. As a consequence, as the previous interview passages have shown, English also plays a crucial role in how individual users customize and use digital devices. For practical reasons, due to cultural traditions and sometimes out of sheer necessity, participants of this study often rely on setting their systems to English – but by implementing non-English forms, they also open a crack to digital devices becoming translingual assemblages. Still, aims to "delink English from its origins and ownership and to shift the centre of English from the Global North" (Pennycook, 2020, p. 222) so far have not been very successful in the case of digital technologies, as the 'Big Five' (Microsoft, Apple, Amazon, Meta and Google) are all US based and globally acting companies. All support standard English as 'normal' unmarked means of communication and as ground on which technologies for all other languages are produced. This affects everyday smartphone language practices and interactions with voice assistants. The language-technological entanglements of English in digital technology make English the number one prestige language, and we, as authors, while typing these words into our Apple laptops to make letters appear on our screens in a shared Google doc, reproduce and enforce this hegemonic assemblage, which is very practical for us, as – speaking from a rather peripheral place at the German-Polish border – hardly anyone would read this text if we used other language resources or shared our thoughts verbally or written on paper.

Essentialist approaches and hegemonic practices of using ordered standard English contrast strongly with an idea that is currently prominent in sociolinguistics, namely that of moving away from "frequency and regularity oriented, pattern-seeking approaches to a focus on spontaneous, impromptu, and momentary actions and performances of the individual" (Wei, 2011, p. 1224). Digital devices and the reproduction of linguistic patterns by algorithmic tools (often referred to as *artificial intelligence*) depend on patterned logics. The linguistic order of digital interfaces strongly prefers monolingualism. It is not unlikely that attitudes towards human languages of those working in technology industries will be influenced by computer languages, where a strict word-function logic applies. Simultaneously, in machine learning, frequent word sequences found in data sets are reproduced and rarer words or constructions disappear (Shumailov et al., 2023). Given this situation, understanding how humans interact informally and spontaneously is important, but the study of hegemonic – and ordered – language materializations is equally crucial. Thus, as critical language scholars, we not only have to study how individuals interact with each other, but we also need to understand which forms of regularity and which patterns are put into machines. In other words, if we want to critically analyze socio-technological language assemblages that influence speakers' perception and use of language, we have to engage with computational practices. These define which language forms are considered worthy and commercially promising so that they are implemented in devices and software. In this sense, we support Pennycook's idea to widen "the scope of language studies from a narrow conception of language as system to a broader vision of social semiotics while also providing scope for an alternative materialist politics" (2020, p. 223). Computational practices – collecting linguistic data in digital form, programming self-learning algorithms or building devices with which even more data can be collected – should be included in future critical language research to contribute to these alternative materialist politics. Current alternative digital language data activism like the African *Masakhane* community, the *Mozilla Common Voice project* or *papa reo* are steps in that direction.

Finally, these observations question the ontology of *language*. Digital language technologies reconfigure what it actually means to 'read', to 'write', to 'speak' and to 'listen' (Jones, 2015). Can Siri 'read' a name, and does it 'speak'? Who is 'listening' when we type or speak with computers? Our traditional notion of human language as an immaterial system of signs is radically questioned once we realize that we interact with and build our material environments that mold what we conceive of as 'language'. Thus, "we may assert that language has always been more-than-human" (Demuro & Gurney, 2023, p. 97).

Transcription Conventions

(.)	short pauses
@	laughter
?	raise of voice
Line break	new idea/proposition (with capital first letter, based on topic and stress pattern)

Note

1 In the process of writing this chapter, Apple introduced HomePod in Turkish (see https://shiftdelete.net/homepod-turkce-siri-destegi-kazandi). For Google Nest and Amazon Alexa, there is no support yet.

References

Androutsopoulos, J. (2007). Bilingualism in the mass media and on the internet. In M. Heller (Ed.), *Bilingualism: A social approach* (pp. 207–230). Palgrave Macmillan.

Androutsopoulos, J. (2014). Languaging when contexts collapse: Audience design in social networking. *Discourse, Context & Media, 4–5*, 62–73. https://doi.org/10.1016/j.dcm.2014.08.006

Bapna, A., Caswell, I., Kreutzer, J., Firat, O., van Esch, D., Siddhant, A., Niu, M., Paljeka, P., Garcia, X., Macherey, W., Breiner, T., Axelrod, V., Riesa, J., Cao, Y., Chen, M. X., Macherey, K., Krikun, M., Wang, P., Gutkin, A., . . . & Hughes, M. (2022). Building machine translation systems for the next thousand languages. *arXiv*. https://arxiv.org/abs/2205.03983

Bauman, R., & Briggs, C. (2003). *Voices of modernity: Language ideologies and the politics of inequality*. Cambridge University Press.

Bender, E. M. (2019). The #BenderRule: On naming the languages we study and why it matters. *The Gradient*. https://thegradient.pub/the-benderrule-on-naming-the-languages-we-study-and-why-it-matters/

Beneteau, E., Richards, O. K., Zhang, M., Kientz, J. A., Yip, J., & Hiniker, A. (2019). Communication breakdowns between families and Alexa. *Proceedings of the 2019 CHI conference on human factors in computing systems*, 1–13. https://doi.org/10.1145/3290605.3300473

Bennett, J. (2010). *Vibrant matter: A political ecology of things*. Duke University Press.

Blodgett, S. L., Barocas, S., Daumé III, H., & Wallach, H. (2020). Language (technology) is power: A critical survey of "bias" in NLP. *Proceedings of the 58th Annual Meeting of the Association for Computational Linguistics*, 5454–5476. https://doi.org/10.18653/v1/2020.acl-main.485

Braidotti, R. (2013). *The posthuman*. Polity.

Bucholtz, M., & Hall, K. (2016). Embodied sociolinguistics. In N. Coupland (Ed.), *Sociolinguistics: Theoretical debates* (pp. 173–197). Cambridge University Press.

Budur, E., Özçelik, R., Gungor, T., & Potts, C. (2020). Data and representation for Turkish natural language inference. *Proceedings of the 2020 Conference on Empirical Methods in Natural Language Processing (EMNLP)*, 8253–8267. https://doi.org/10.18653/v1/2020.emnlp-main.662

Ceruzzi, P. E. (2003). *A history of modern computing* (2nd ed.). MIT Press.

Che, D., & Bodomo, A. (2021). When Africans meet Chinese: Is calculator communication a form of World Englishes? In B. Schneider & T. Heyd (Eds.), *Bloomsbury World Englishes: Paradigms* (pp. 274–288). Bloomsbury.

Costa-jussà, M. R., Cross, J., Çelebi, O., Elbayad, M., Heafield, K., Heffernan, K., Kalbassi, E., Lam, J., Licht, D., Maillard, J., Sun, A., Wang, S., Wenzek, G., Youngblood, A., Akula, B., Barrault, L., Gonzalez, G. M., Hansanti, P., Hoffman, J., … & Wang, J. (2022). No language left behind: Scaling human-centered machine translation. *arXiv*. https://arxiv.org/abs/2207.04672

Cowley, S. (2011). Distributed language. In S. Cowley (Ed.), *Distributed language* (pp. 1–14). John Benjamins.

Crawford, K. (2017). The trouble with bias – NIPS 2017 Keynote – Kate Crawford (Video). *The Artificial Intelligence Channel*. https://www.youtube.com/watch?v=fMym_BKWQzk&t=2592s

Crawford, K. (2021). *Atlas of AI*. Yale University Press.

Dailey-O'Cain, J. (2021). Digital Englishes and transcultural flows. In B. Schneider & T. Heyd (Eds.), *Bloomsbury World Englishes: Paradigms* (pp. 224–240). Bloomsbury.

De Meulder, M., Kusters, A., Moriarty, E., & Murray, J. J. (2019). Describe, don't prescribe: The practice and politics of translanguaging in the context of deaf signers. *Journal of Multilingual and Multicultural Development*, 40, 892–906.

Demuro, E., & Gurney, L. (2023). Can nonhumans speak? Languaging and worlds in posthumanist applied linguistics. *Linguistic Frontiers*, 5, 92–105. https://doi.org/10.2478/lf-2023-0015

Dovchin, S., Sultana, S., & Pennycook, A. (2016). Unequal translingual Englishes in the Asian peripheries. *Asian Englishes*, 18(2), 92–108.

Ensmenger, N. (2015). "Beards, sandals, and other signs of rugged individualism": Masculine culture within the computing professions. *Osiris*, 30, 38–65.

Foucault, M. (1979). *The history of sexuality. Volume 1: An introduction*. Allen Lane.

Foucault, M. (1991). *Discipline and punish: The birth of prison*. Penguin.

Gal, S., & Irvine, J. T. (2019). *Signs of difference: Language and ideology in social life*. Cambridge University Press.

García, O., & Li, W. (2014). *Translanguaging: Language, bilingualism and education*. Palgrave Macmillan.

Georgakopoulou, A. (2016). From narrating the self to posting self(ies): A small stories approach to selfies. *Open Linguistics*, 2, 300–317.

Glaser, B. G., & Strauss, A. L. (2017/1967). *The discovery of grounded theory: Strategies for qualitative research*. Routledge.

Gokay, R., & Yalcin, H. (2019). Improving low resource Turkish speech recognition with data augmentation and TTS. *2019 16th international multi-conference on systems, signals & devices (SSD)*, 357–360. https://doi.org/10.1109/SSD.2019.8893184

Gramling, D. (2020). Supralingualism and the translatability industry. *Applied Linguistics*, *41*, 129–147.

Heller, M., & McElhinny, B. (2017). *Language, capitalism, colonialism*. University of Toronto Press.

Herring, S., Stein, D., & Virtanen, T. (Eds.). (2013). *Pragmatics of computer-mediated communication*. de Gruyter.

Höhn, S., Migge, B., Schneider, B., Dippold, D., & Mauw, S. (2023). Language ideology bias in conversational technology. *CONVERSATIONS 2023–7th International Workshop on Chatbot Research, Applications, and Design*. https://2023.conversations.ws/program/

Jones, R. H. (2015). Surveillance. In A. Georgakopoulou & T. Spilioti (Eds.), *The Routledge handbook of language and digital communication* (pp. 408–411). Routledge.

Jones, R. H., Chik, A., & Hafner, C. A. (2015). *Discourse and digital practices*. Routledge.

Katz, Y. (2020). *Artificial whiteness: Politics and ideology in artificial intelligence*. Columbia University Press.

Kelly-Holmes, H. (2019). Multilingualism and technology: A review of developments in digital communication from monolingualism to idiolingualism. *Annual Review of Applied Linguistics*, *39*, 24–39.

Kerfoot, C., & Hyltenstam, K. (2017). Introduction: Entanglement and orders of visibility. In C. Kerfoot & K. Hyltenstam (Eds.), *Entangled discourses: South-north orders of visibility* (pp. 1–15). Routledge.

Koenecke, A., Nam, A., Lake, E., Nudell, J., Quartey, M., Mengesha, Z., Toups, C., Rickford, J. R., Jurafsky, D., & Goel, S. (2020). Racial disparities in automated speech recognition. *Proceedings of the National Academy of Sciences*, *117*(14), 7684–7689.

Kramsch, C. (2000). Literacy, equity, access for the immigrant learner. In E. Olshtain & G. Horenczyk (Eds.), *Language, identity and immigration* (pp. 325–338). The Hebrew University Magnes Press.

Kusters, A. (2024). More than signs: International Sign as distributed practice. *Signs and Society*, *12*(1), 37–57.

Latour, B. (1987). *Science in action: How to follow scientists and engineers*. Harvard University Press.

Lauscher, A., Ravishankar, V., Vulić, I., & Glavaš, G. (2020). From zero to hero: On the limitations of zero-shot language transfer with multilingual transformers. *Proceedings of the 2020 Conference on Empirical Methods in Natural Language Processing (EMNLP)*, 4483–4499. Association for Computational Linguistics.

Leblebici, D. (2021). *Language ideologies in human-machine interaction: A qualitative study with voice assistant users* [Master's thesis, Europa-Universität Viadrina].

Leblebici, D. (2024). "You are Apple, why are you speaking to me in Turkish?": The role of English in voice assistant interactions. *Multilingua: Journal of Cross-Cultural and Interlanguage Communication*, *43*(4), 455–485.

Linell, P. (2005). *The written language bias in linguistics: Its nature, origins and transformations*. Routledge.

Makoni, S., & Pennycook, A. (2007). Disinventing and reconstituting languages. In S. Makoni & A. Pennycook (Eds.), *Disinventing and reconstituting languages* (pp. 1–41). Multilingual Matters.

Maly, I., & Varis, P. (2016). The 21st-century hipster: On micro-populations in times of superdiversity. *European Journal of Cultural Studies*, *19*(6), 637–653.

Markl, N. (2022). Language variation and algorithmic bias: Understanding algorithmic bias in British English automatic speech recognition. *ACM Conference on Fairness, Accountability, and Transparency. FAccT*, *22*, 521–534. https://doi.org/510.1145/3531146.3533117

Martin, J. L., & Wright, K. E. (2023). Bias in automatic speech recognition: The case of African American language. *Applied Linguistics*, *44*, 613–630. https://doi.org/10.1093/applin/amac066.

Marwick, A. E., & boyd, d. (2011). I tweet honestly, I tweet passionately: Twitter users, context collapse, and the imagined audience. *New Media & Society*, *13*(1), 114–133.

McLuhan, M. (1964). *Understanding media: The extension of man*. Mentor.

Moore, R. K. (2019). Talking with robots: Opportunities and challenges. *arXiv:1912.00369 [Cs]*. http://arxiv.org/abs/1912.00369

Mori, M. (2012/1970). The uncanny valley [from the field] (K. MacDorman & N. Kageki, Trans.). *IEEE Robotics & Automation Magazine*, *19*(2), 98–100. https://doi.org/10.1109/MRA.2012.2192811

Oldac, Y. I., & Fancourt, N. (2021). "New wave Turks": Turkish graduates of German universities and the Turkish diaspora in Germany. *British Journal of Educational Studies*, *69*(5), 621–640.

Ong, W. J. (1982). *Orality and literacy: The technologizing of the word*. Routledge.

Otheguy, R., García, O., & Reid, W. (2015). Clarifying translanguaging and deconstructing named languages: A perspective from linguistics. *Applied Linguistics Review*, *6*, 281–307.

Pasquinelli, M. (2023). *The eye of the master: A social history of artificial intelligence*. Verso.

Pennycook, A. (2004). Performativity and language studies. *Critical Inquiry in Language Studies*, *1*, 1–19.

Pennycook, A. (2018). *Posthumanist applied linguistics*. Routledge.

Pennycook, A. (2020). Translingual entanglements of English. *World Englishes*, *39*, 222–235.

Pennycook, A. (2024). *Language assemblages*. Cambridge University Press.

Piller, I., & Cho, J. (2013). Neoliberalism as language policy. *Language in Society*, *42*, 23–44.

Richard, F. (2000). *The rise of the creative class: And how it's transforming work, leisure, community, and everyday life*. Basic Books.

Rüdiger, S. (2021). Non-postcolonial Englishes in East Asia: Focus on Korean popular music. In B. Schneider & T. Heyd (Eds.), *Bloomsbury World Englishes: Paradigms* (pp. 207–223). Bloomsbury.

Rushkoff, D. (2019). *Team human*. W.W. Norton & Company.

Savoldi, B., Gaido, M., Bentivogli, L., Negri, M., & Turchi, M. (2021). Gender bias in machine translation. *Transactions of the Association for Computational Linguistics*, *9*, 845–874.

Schneider, B. (2012). Is English a local language in Berlin? *Language on the Move*. https://www.languageonthemove.com/is-english-a-local-language-in-berlin/

Schneider, B. (2019). Methodological nationalism in linguistics. *Language Sciences*, *76*, 101169. https://doi.org/10.1016/j.langsci.2018.05.006

Schneider, B. (2022). Multilingualism and AI: The regimentation of language in the age of digital capitalism. *Signs and Society*, *10*(3), 362–387.

Schneider, B., & Heyd, T. (2024). Special issue: Post-humanist sociolinguistics. *Signs and Society*, *12*.

Schneider, B. (to appear). Transnational voices from nowhere leave no one behind: Hierarchical chronotopes in AI language culture. In S.-Y. Park & B. Bolander (Eds.), *Language and Transnationalism*.

Shumailov, I., Shumaylov, Z., Zhao, Y., Gal, Y., Papernot, N., & Anderson, R. (2023). The curse of recursion: Training on generated data makes models forget. *arXiv*. https://arxiv.org/pdf/2305.17493.pdf

Siegel, J. (2005). Literacy in Pidgin and Creole languages. *Current Issues in Language Planning*, *6*, 143–163.

Sismondo, S. (2010). *An introduction to science and technology studies*. Wiley-Blackwell.

Street, B. V. (1995). *Social literacies: Critical approaches to literacy in development, ethnography and education*. Longman.

Sweeney, M. (2016). The intersectional interface. In S. U. Noble & B. M. Tynes (Eds.), *The intersectional internet: Race, sex, class and culture online* (pp. 215–228). Peter Lang.

Tatman, R. (2016). Google's speech recognition has a gender bias. *Making Noise and Hearing Things*. https://makingnoiseandhearingthings.com/2016/2007/2012/googles-speech-recognition-has-a-gender-bias/

Terkessidis, M. (2000). *Migranten*. Rotbuch Verlag.

van Esch, D., Sarbar, E., Lucassen, T., O'Brien, J., Breiner, T., Prasad, M., Crew, E., Nguyen, C., & Beaufays, F. (2019). Writing across the world's languages: Deep internationalization for Gboard, the Google Keyboard. *arXiv*. https://arxiv.org/pdf/1912.01218.pdf

Varis, P., & Hou, M. (2020). Digital approaches in linguistic ethnography. In K. Tusting (Ed.), *The Routledge handbook of linguistic ethnography* (pp. 229–240). Routledge.

Vertovec, S. (2007). Super-diversity and its implications. *Ethnic and Racial Studies, 30*(6), 1024–1054.

Virtanen, A., Kanerva, J., Ilo, R., Luoma, J., Luotolahti, J., Salakoski, T., Ginter, F., & Pyysalo, S. (2019). Multilingual is not enough: BERT for Finnish. *arXiv preprint*, arXiv:1912.07076

Wajcman, J. (2010). Feminist theories of technology. *Cambridge Journal of Economics, 34*, 143–152.

Wei, L. (2011). Moment analysis and translanguaging space: Discursive construction of identities by multilingual Chinese youth in Britain. *Journal of Pragmatics, 43*, 1222–1235.

Wu, Y., Rough, D., Bleakley, A., Edwards, J., Cooney, O., Doyle, P. R., Clark, L., & Cowan, B. R. (2020). See what I'm saying? Comparing intelligent personal assistant use for native and non-native language speakers. *22nd International Conference on Human-Computer Interaction with Mobile Devices and Services*, 1–9. https://doi.org/10.1145/3379503.3403563

Zhao, J., Wang, T., Yatskar, M., Ordonez, V., & Chang, K.-W. (2017). Men also like shopping: Reducing gender bias amplification using corpus-level constraints. *Proceedings of the 2017 Conference on Empirical Methods in Natural Language Processing*, 2979–2989. Association for Computational Linguistics.

Zuboff, S. (2019). *The age of surveillance capitalism: The fight for a human future at the new frontier of power*. Public Affairs.

10
ENGLISH ONLINE/OFFLINE

Disentangling material and materialist perspectives of language

Ron Darvin

1. Introduction

Drawing on Pennycook's (2020) conception of the entanglements of English, this chapter argues that distinguishing material and materialist perspectives of language is a productive way to analyze such entanglements, and that examining online discourses as indexical of ideological formations, relations and modes of distribution can be useful for demonstrating this analytical process. It recognizes that particularly within online spaces, where contexts collapse (boyd, 2010), English is almost always entangled with other languages as speakers negotiate multiple identities and engage with diverse audiences. To demonstrate this point, this chapter draws on a study of the social media practices of Karina, a Filipino domestic worker in Hong Kong (Darvin, 2022), and argues that as this transnational performs identities on TikTok and Facebook, moving across languages and assembling her semiotic resources, her online interactions are entangled with offline realities. How she negotiates the material design of a platform like TikTok cannot be separated from the material conditions of her lived experiences as a worker from the Global South. Her online relationships and social networks in Hong Kong and the Philippines index particular histories and inequalities of globalization. What I would like to assert here is that one way to make sense of these complex entanglements is to disentangle the visible, embodied objects of the material world from the ideologies they index and the social effects they produce.

When users like Karina enact a translingual orientation (Canagarajah, 2013) online, they negotiate their intentions with the tools that mediate their translingual practices. While translingualism evokes metaphors of convergence and flow, to speak of the entanglements of English however is to challenge these metaphors and to make visible the materiality (Barad, 2003) through which online interactions

DOI: 10.4324/9781003441304-14

are configured by human and nonhuman actors. The materiality of a device such as a mobile phone, for instance, has the power to shape interaction, providing affordances and constraints in the way users achieve specific communicative intentions online. The materiality of platform designs and the sociotechnical structures (Darvin, 2023) that constitute their architecture shape the way users perform their identities and negotiate their linguistic and semiotic resources. In this case, space is that which interlocutors not just enter but actively construct through the linguistic and semiotic choices they make. As speakers move across spaces, they draw on their diverse repertoires constituted by the material objects and resources available in specific spaces. Translingual practices are thus semiotically mediated and entangled in different materialities as they are instantiated by different social intentions and enacted in diverse spaces.

Translingual practices are also a matter of circumstance, that is, constituted by the shifting conditions that surround the speaker and shaped by the position from which one stands, whether spatially or symbolically. Speakers have the agency to adopt a stance, to take up "a position with respect to the form or the content of one's utterance" (Jaffe, 2009, p. 3), but online, form and content are always mediated by the material space they occupy: the fields made available in a social media profile, the character limits of each field, the orthographies that a platform can read. Examining the linguistic and semiotic choices of speakers, the affordances and constraints of devices and the arrangement of material objects in a platform reveals historical layers of meaning and orders of indexicality. Examining these material components does not just enable a level of particularization but also resists reductive understandings of context that depend on simplified micro vs. macro distinctions. By dissecting the situated and often fleeting choices that speakers make online, we are able to understand how these choices are ideologically loaded and how they contribute to the materialization of particular social effects.

2. Material and materialist perspectives of entanglements

To understand these online/offline entanglements as both material and materializing, as possessing physical forms and constituting social effects, this chapter draws on a materialist theory of semiotics that recognizes how linguistic and semiotic forms index local and global scales, and their concomitant inequalities. Blommaert (2013) defines *materialist semiotics* as

> a study of signs that sees signs not as primarily mental and abstract phenomena reflected in "real" moments of enactment, but as material forces subject to and reflective of conditions of production and patterns of distribution, and as constructive of social reality, as real social agents having real effects in social life.
>
> *(p. 33)*

Recognizing signs as *material forces* is not to imbue them with determinism but to draw attention to how they can shape interactions in concrete ways. For Appadurai (2015), this mediation is not just association or translation of meanings but an embodied practice that functions as "a mode of materialization" (p. 233) where matter becomes agentive and has the power to engender effects in the world. Public signs, for instance, can organize and regulate space, imposing restrictions and directing norms of conduct. This demarcation constructs normative expectations of what to find in specific places, producing habitual interpretations of what is in place or out of place. How we perceive and interpret these signs is dependent on our visual repertoire, the culturally and socially constructed competences of decoding the explicit and implicit codes embedded in these signs (Blommaert, 2013). At the same time, these signs index (or are 'reflective of') conditions of production and patterns of distribution, affiliations with certain groups (e.g. race, ethnicity, gender, class, etc.), histories, norms and identities. This *materialist* view recognizes how language conveys meaning beyond its denotative signification and reflects the influence of economic, political and cultural forces in the social world.

The entanglements of English can thus be understood in terms of material and materialist considerations. The recognition of signs as social agents that produce material effects aligns with Kress' (2010) conception of social semiotics that underlines the centrality of design and rhetoric. As the assemblage of semiotic resources, design is the means through which a rhetor's intentions is materialized. In a social media platform, layout orients viewers and interactants to information and produces specific forms of interaction. By arranging elements from left to right, centre or margin, vertical or horizontal, layout communicates the structures and processes through which some information is valued over others. As a rhetor, the user of different platforms assembles semiotic resources to achieve particular intentions. Software engineers, the architects of different platforms, also assemble semiotic forms to achieve both technical and social intentions. In this case, the design of online spaces indexes the intentions of its designers (Darvin, 2022; Scollon & Scollon, 2003), and the interaction between users and the material structures of a platform involves a negotiation of platform design and user design.

3. The entanglement of English online/offline: Filipino domestic workers and TikTok

The Philippines, one of the world's largest sources of English-speaking migrant labour (Tupas, 2019), continues to produce 'servants of globalization' (Parreñas, 2001) who migrate from the Global South to work in the private households of the Global North. Language is central to this transnational labour migration, as domestic workers constantly negotiate their linguistic resources, acquire new ones and internalize 'scripts of servitude' (Lorente, 2017). In Hong Kong, foreign domestic workers are employed by 12.4% of households (HK SAR Census and Statistics, 2021), and 55% of the 374,000 workers are Filipino (HK Govt, 2021).

A third of these households have children aged 12 and below, and more than a tenth have elderly persons aged 60 and over. A survey of these households revealed that the common job requirements, besides "taking care of children" and "taking care of the elderly," were "knowing good Cantonese" (38.4%) and "knowing good English" (34.7%), indicating the significance of the linguistic resources of these workers for their perceived competence (HK SAR Census and Statistics, 2021, n.p.). Many households hire Filipino domestic workers for their English language proficiency and high level of education and expect them to tutor their children in English or at least facilitate their language socialization (Ladegaard, 2020; Leung, 2012; Wolfaardt, 2022). These workers would have learned this second language at school in the Philippines, where English is an official language used in education, business and government, but their first language would be one of the over 120 languages spoken in this nation-state.

After its global launch in 2017, TikTok became immensely popular among the over 200,000 Filipino domestic workers in Hong Kong as 'a stress reliever' (De Guzman, 2020). The platform's user-friendly video creation tools enable users to remix audio tracks and create 15- to 60-second videos, which include sound memes (Darvin, 2022), lip-synch videos and dance challenges. In 2019, TikTok reached 13% of the city's 5.8 million social media users (We Are Social, 2020), until ByteDance, the owner of TikTok, withdrew from the city to avoid data privacy conflicts with the local government after the National Security Law was enacted in June 2020. Despite these constraints, many Filipino domestic workers access TikTok via a VPN and continue to produce videos of dance routines, lip-synch memes and humorous portrayals of household work. In these TikTok videos and captions, Filipino workers often switch between their different languages as they communicate with both local and global audiences.

The case study presented here (Darvin, 2023) is from a qualitative study investigating the language and literacy practices of five Filipino domestic workers in Hong Kong. Data collection involved three semi-structured interviews with each of the five participants. The interviews, conducted in Filipino, English or a mix of both depending on the participant's preference, lasted between 45 and 60 minutes and took place in public locations in Hong Kong. These interviews focused on eliciting narratives about the participants' migration experiences, language learning and daily life in Hong Kong. Participants were also encouraged to share literacy artifacts such as social media posts, which served as both elicitation devices during interviews and additional data sources. Participants chose which posts they wanted to share, and in some cases, during the interview, they were asked to share posts that would illustrate the ideas they were talking about. With their consent, TikTok videos they shared were downloaded, and screenshots were taken, ensuring all shared materials were anonymized. The Filipino segments in the transcribed interview recordings were translated into English. The researcher synchronized observation notes and digital artifacts with relevant transcript sections. Initial coding involved identifying repetitions, metaphors and other patterns, which were then developed into first- and second-order codes using NVivo software. These codes were categorized into specific themes that captured the main ideas from the participants' narratives.

Thematic analysis was complemented by multimodal discourse analysis to examine how participants constructed their identities through specific lexical and syntactic choices, code-switching and stylistic variations. Multimodal transcription of TikTok videos involved capturing screenshots of every composition shift or lower-level action change. Since downloading videos from TikTok can result in the loss of metadata, additional screenshots were taken during video playback to capture captions and buttons. The transcription process included four columns: screenshots, static semiotic forms, modes and semiotic forms in lower-level actions and the researcher's notes and thematic coding. Participant assistance was enlisted to transcribe and translate utterances in Philippine languages. To analyze participants' semiotic productions on TikTok, a multimodal discourse analysis was conducted to consider how various modes of communication – such as language, image, music and layout – contributed to meaning-making (Jewitt, 2017). The unit of analysis was the mediated action, encompassing both higher-level actions (e.g., performing a dance) and the lower-level actions that constituted them (e.g., gestures, gaze shifts). Modal density, which refers to the intensity and complexity of modes within an action, was assessed to understand the significance of different semiotic resources in conveying meaning (Norris, 2004).

This chapter focuses on Karina, a 32-year old domestic worker from Davao City in the southern region of the Philippines, who has been working in Hong Kong for four years, while her two children live with their grandparents in her hometown. This long-term family separation is a consequence of the mechanisms of temporary migrant worker arrangements. Karina lives in the north but belongs to the Global South, an ethnic minority in a wealthy city, from a nation-state in Southeast Asia, where "conditions of suffering and inequality brought about by capitalism and colonialism" (Pennycook & Makoni, 2020, p. 2) persist. Karina's first language is Bisaya (also known as Cebuano), which is the lingua franca of most of the Visayas and Mindanao regions of the Philippines and which, until the 1980s, had the largest native speaker population in the country. She also speaks the national language, Filipino, fluently and English. Working in Hong Kong for a family from Mainland China and having a Pakistani boyfriend, she has learned some Cantonese, Mandarin and Urdu. Karina is very active on TikTok and speaks confidently about how TikTok works and what purpose it serves.

While the findings from this study presented here focus on Karina, they are consistent with what could be observed with the other participants in the study: that for these domestic workers from a multilingual nation-state, moving across languages is a practice that indexes colonial histories and modes of exclusion while enabling them to transgress norms and conventions online and to assert their own identities. Moving across social media platforms, recognizing audiences and performing multiple identities are part of the everyday reality of a transnational. Not only are these translingual practices in social media naturally occurring and authentically performed, but routine communicative acts of constructing a TikTok profile, creating a derivative video or engaging with others constitute 'small things' (Blommaert, 2019) expected as users construct contexts for themselves online. As part of the everyday, these social media interactions reflect not only group alignment and conviviality but also ways of positioning and distancing others. Recognizing how movement across languages, semiotic forms and social media platforms is shaped by the entanglement of social, cultural, political and economic forces: the material conditions of their lived experiences, the materiality of platform and user designs, is what enables a critical awareness of inequalities and modes of exclusion made visible through such interactions.

3.1. *Entangled with the material conditions of lived experiences*

During the interviews with Karina, it became evident that to understand her translingual practices on social media is to recognize her perceptions of different platforms and their corresponding audiences. Her contrasting modes of participation in Facebook and TikTok appear to be largely based on practical and material considerations that index certain inequalities. Karina estimates that 70% of her 600 Facebook friends are family and friends in the Philippines, while the rest are friends that she has met in Hong Kong. Her TikTok, on the other hand, is mostly about engaging with friends from Hong Kong. That her Facebook involves a mostly Philippine-based network is unsurprising, as the penetration rate of Facebook in the country is more than twice that of TikTok (We Are Social, 2022). This penetration rate can be partly explained by the fact that in the country, lower-income users can access Facebook content (except pictures and videos) without consuming data. As a video production app, TikTok cannot provide such an offer, and the differences in reach of the two platforms can be attributed to these material constraints.

Karina says that lately she has been more active on TikTok than Facebook, and the reason for this preference largely has to do with how she curates her identity as a Filipino transnational on social media. She talks about what it means to be an Overseas Filipino Worker (OFW), a term coined by the Philippine government to refer to migrant workers who are hailed as *Bagong Bayani* ('New Heroes') as they provide remittances that contribute to the GDP of the country. In the larger study, all participants talk about what it means to earn money in Hong Kong, only to send most of it to the family in the Philippines. This practice, Karina says, shapes false perceptions of what it means to work abroad.

> *Overexpecting sila sa buhay dito sa abroad. Iniisip nila is ok ka dito. Hindi ka nagpoproblema ng pera kasi nga hindi nila alam kung gaano kahirap ang buhay ng OFW. Pag wala kang family. Pag nagiisa ka lang.*

> They expect too much about what life abroad is like. They think it's okay here. That you don't have to worry about money. That's because they don't know how hard the life of an OFW is. When you don't have family. When you're alone.

Because of these perceptions, Karina has avoided posting things on Facebook. She narrates how sometimes a single post of her enjoying a buffet with friends on Facebook can lead to comments by family and friends in the Philippines about how fun and luxurious her life is in Hong Kong, even though this is far from the case. By highlighting specific moments in her life, Facebook, she believes, has the power to erase the challenges and feelings of loneliness that accompany the experience of long-term family separation.

> *Every time nagpopost sa social media, ni-le-less ko sya para hindi silang mag over think na ganito yung life dito na ay ok pala sa abroad mamuhay kasi nga malaki sahod. Lahat ng pwede mong gawin, magagawa mo, which is hindi tutuo.*

> Every time I post something on social media, I try to tone it down so that they don't think that this is what life is like, that it's ok to live abroad because you get a high salary, that there's a lot of possibility and that you can do all that you want, which isn't true at all.

Because Facebook is designed to share highlights from one's life, whether through 'Live video,' 'Photo/video' or 'Life event' or status updates that respond to the prompt, 'What's on your mind?,' the posts are designed to be current and personal and therefore ripe for scrutiny. In contrast, TikTok, as a platform that encourages the production of memes and dubbed or dance videos, provides opportunities to perform for a wider audience without having to provide more intimate details about what her life is like in Hong Kong. According to her, it has also enabled her to show a side of her that most people don't see, her dancing skills, and through TikTok she is able to receive praise for her talent. She also talks about how choosing TikTok over Facebook is a practical choice because uploading a video on Facebook consumes a lot of data, whereas TikTok compresses videos so that uploading a video does not end up using much data. This difference is particularly important because domestic workers get to gather together, produce and upload these videos only on Sundays, their day off, when they would have no access to Wi-Fi.

This material consideration is also reflected in how domestic workers have developed a preference for TikTok as a social media platform not just for creating and sharing videos but also for consuming videos.

> *Ang TikTok is, gaya naming OFW, siempre hirap kami sa buhay dito na puro trabaho, trabaho, kasi pag pinanuod mo ang TikTok nandun lahat. May kumakanta, may sumasayaw tapos may gumagawa ng funny movie parang napapanuod namin sya kahit kaunti kahit limit lang yung oras.*

> TikTok is, like for us OFWs, of course it's a hard life for us here where it's all work and work, and when you watch TikTok it's all there. You have people singing, dancing, and making funny movies, and we get to watch them, even just a few of them and even if our time is limited.

188 Entangled Englishes

Because of the nature of their work, domestic workers have very limited time for recreational activities during the week itself, so TikTok videos, being only 15 or 60 seconds long, make it ideal for the short periods of time they have for entertainment. Social media practices and preferences are entangled with material constraints, indexing the realities of a migrant worker from the Global South negotiating her place in the Global North while maintaining transnational ties.

3.2. Entangled with platform designs

On Facebook and TikTok, Karina strategically orchestrates her online presence and curates her posts in order to perform different identities for diverse audiences. These intentions shape the way she assembles her linguistic and semiotic resources online, and such curation is not unlike the way one dresses or behaves differently in diverse contexts. In her Facebook profile (Figure 10.1), she uses her real name and showcases her identity as a mother, with pictures of her three children as her cover photo. To avoid speculation from family and friends in the Philippines, she identifies as 'Single' even though she has a boyfriend in Hong Kong. By requiring users to input specific information in given fields, the design or architecture of a Facebook profile structures not only the modal density of the semiotic resources

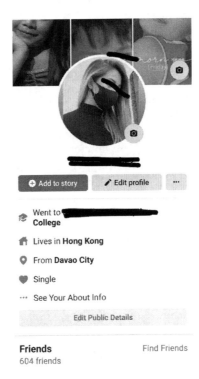

FIGURE 10.1 Karina's profile on Facebook

English online/offline 189

Karina chooses but also arranges which aspects of her identity can be foregrounded (i.e. education, place of residence, hometown, relationship status, etc.).

In contrast, the design of a TikTok profile enables Karina to choose a pseudonym, to create her own description and to move across languages, and given these affordances, Karina is able to perform a TikTok identity different from the mother she presents herself as on Facebook (see Figure 10.2). Recognizing these differences is key to understanding how Karina's performance of her identity on TikTok identity is entangled with the material design of this platform. On TikTok, she assembles her linguistic and semiotic resources not only to gain followers and expand her social network but also to assert her legitimate place in Hong Kong. Until 2021, Karina had a TikTok account where she identified herself as @karinalicious01 (revised here to maintain privacy but structured similarly to reflect the original i.e. @[real name]licious01). As @karinalicious01, she had almost 10,000 followers and

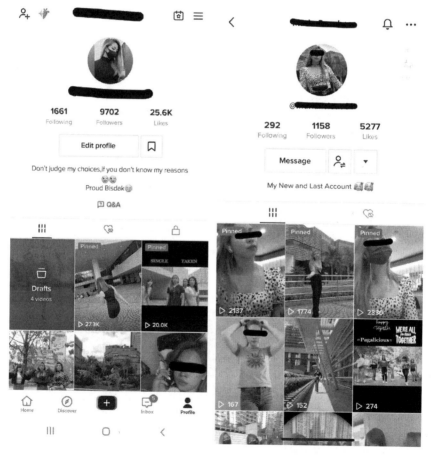

FIGURE 10.2 Karina's old TikTok account profile (left) and Karina's new TikTok account profile (right)

would post videos of her dancing or lip-synching in skimpy outfits, a past which she describes as "magulo" ('a mess') and which her conservative boyfriend did not approve of. The brief description in her old profile (see Figure 10.1) alludes to the bold and daring self that she projected: "Don't judge my choices if you don't know my reasons (wink emoji x2)," and she talks about how a significant portion of her followers were Filipino domestic workers and Pakistani men in Hong Kong. To engage with this audience, she activated a Q&A feature that enables her followers to ask questions on her profile or video comments that she in turn can then answer in her own videos.

Following her boyfriend's discontent with her former account, Karina deactivated it and established a "New and Last Account," consciously curating a more reserved online image. In this account, she says she tries to project a more conservative self, and to enact this intention, she pinned videos with thumbnails of her in long sleeves and pants, assigning these images higher modal density. In this case, her new TikTok account is similarly curated as her Facebook account, where she positions herself as a dutiful mother to her three children. Because the design of TikTok enables users to input their own words in their profiles and encourages the production of sound memes (Darvin, 2022), where utterances in different languages can serve as tracks, we can see how moving across different languages is entangled with the design of the platform. While Karina's profiles are both written in English, she moves from words to emojis and also includes in her old profile the phrase, "Proud Bisdak (face with hand over mouth emoji)." *Bisdak* is a contraction of the Bisaya phrase *Bisayang dako* ('Bisaya born and raised') which foregrounds her linguistic identity as a Bisaya speaker and which she says she added in order to connect with fellow Bisaya.

In her TikTok videos, Karina often moves across different languages: Bisaya, Filipino and English, and by doing so she is able to provide different layers of meaning in her videos. This is particularly true in meme videos where she takes a meme track, lip-synchs to it and then provides a text overlay (see Figure 10.3). In this derivative video of the meme "Palangga Girl," Karina lip-synchs to a track in Bisaya: "Oi girls ayaw mo sige pa gwapa. Kay igat gihapon pilion nila. Di ba boys?" (followed by a laugh track). She translates this into a mix of Filipino and English for me as "Girls, wag kayo always magpaganda, malalandi pa rin pipillin nila. Di ba boys?" ('Hey girls, don't always make yourself beautiful, they'll still always choose the flirty ones. Right, boys?').

In this derivative video, the intention is to lip-synch to the original track, and to do so she performs a chain of series of actions where she gazes at the camera and enacts different facial expressions. While her face occupies the entire screen and is thus granted high modal density, she provides a text overlay in English on her forehead to address a non-Bisaya speaking audience but alters some meanings to fit her own purposes: "Hey! Girls don't make yourself beautiful (pouting emoji)/Flirty Girls still they choose! (face with stuck-out tongue emoji)/Right PAKSH!T? (face with tears of joy emoji x2)." In this case, she replaces "boys" with "PAKSH!T,"

FIGURE 10.3 Karin's derivative video of the meme "Palangga Girl"

a Filipino swear word that combines *fuck* ('pak') and *shit*, to express her disapproval of men who prefer flirty women. This choice changes the tone of her derivative video to something that communicates anger or annoyance, especially as she pouts and knots her eyebrows while lip-synching "Di ba boys?," a contrast with the original video, where the creator is seen laughing at the end together with a laugh track. Karina tempers this annoyance, however, with emojis that suggest that she is making light of the swear word that she placed in the text overlay. The caption for this video is "Winner permi ang igat (hand on mouth emoji)(tears of joy emoji x2)" ('The flirty ones always win'). By moving across languages, from lip-synched speech to text overlay, and from words to emojis, Karina is able to address a wider audience while asserting her own meanings in a derivative video.

3.3. Entangled with transnational relations and class formations

Karina's translingual practices online are entangled not only with the material conditions of her lived experiences and the material designs of platforms but also with the relations and social networks she maintains in Hong Kong, which themselves index particular histories and processes of globalization. In the case of Karina, her translingual productions on TikTok enable her to connect with fellow 'Bisdak' and other Filipino domestic workers in Hong Kong. Moving across languages is entangled with the intention to perform different identities and to establish and maintain social networks. Because her TikTok videos often foreground her face, Karina says some Filipinos would recognize her in public spaces and say "Uu, ikaw si Karina sa TikTok ano?" ('Hey, you're Karina from TikTok, right?'), while some would message her on TikTok and say "Uy, mag meet up tayo. Collab tayo sa sayaw" ('Hey, let's meet up and collab on a dance.').

On Instagram, 'collab' refers to a content creator inviting another to collaborate on a Feed post or an Instagram Reel, while for TikTok, 'collab' could refer to creators doing a Duet using a split screen. For Karina, to collab with someone would be to meet face to face with another TikToker and dance together. In this case, unlike just doing a Duet online, Filipino domestic workers get to meet in public spaces in Hong Kong on a Sunday, rehearse and then film a dance together. Through these collabs, not only do they get to expand their social networks, but through public performance, these domestic workers, often hidden in the private spaces of home, are able to form communities, make themselves visible and assert their legitimate place in Hong Kong. In this case, the production of the online video is entangled with material offline conditions: the physical spaces that these 'servants of globalization' are able to claim and occupy, if only briefly on a Sunday, when almost all domestic workers are given a day off and allowed to occupy public spaces like park squares and overpasses.

On one occasion, Karina was invited by a group of Filipino TikTokers to collab and do a video for the Kilometro Dance Challenge made popular by Filipino actor and dancer Vhong Navarro and where content creators create derivative videos dancing to the song Kilometro with set choreography (see Figure 10.4). Because the intention is to perform a choreographed dance, the video is filmed in landscape orientation where what is foregrounded is not their faces (unlike Karina's earlier derivative video in Figure 10.3) but the lower-level actions of synchronized body movement and the music that links this production to the Philippines, where the track became viral. Karina describes the three TikTokers she collabs with as Ilonggo, speakers of another popular language in the south of the Philippines, also known as Hiligaynon.

Identifying her collaborators as speakers of another language is quite common in the Philippines, where these linguistic categories also signal which part of the country they are from (cf. Karina's identification as a 'Proud Bisdak'). This regionalism is a legacy of Spanish colonial rule that encouraged such "regionalistic pride and prejudice" (Agoncillo & Guerrero, 1970, p. 13) to divide and to suppress any collective desire for a nationalist revolt (Espiritu, 2005). In the study, all participants consistently positioned themselves in terms of their regional/linguistic identity, for example, Bisaya, Ilonggo, and so on. In the case of Karina's collab with the Ilonggos, they perform a dance together in Tamar Park in Admiralty district, and the caption is "Kilometro by ilongga × Bisaya

FIGURE 10.4   Collab TikTok performing the Kilometro Dance Challenge

with love." The use of 'x' here is patterned after the collab between two P-pop (Philippine pop) groups BINI and BGYO, labelled in the original meme video as BINIxBGYO. By dancing together to a song in Filipino, the representatives of two linguistic groups create a convivial space, made visible through social media.

One of the hashtags that Karina often uses in her TikTok posts, including the Kilometro collab, is #hkpagal_____ (the English suffix that follows is stricken out to maintain anonymity). According to Karina, "pagal" is 'crazy' in Urdu, and the reason she has such a translingual hashtag is that her group of female Filipino friends is connected with a group of male Pakistani friends, and they have appeared on each other's TikToks and use the hashtag to connect with each other on the platform. This phenomenon of social tagging (Lee, 2018) contributes to Karina's increased Pakistani following on TikTok; engaging with a hashtag associated with one user can navigate followers to the content of others. In Hong Kong, Pakistanis represent the ethnic minority with the highest poverty rate, with many employed as security personnel, cleaners and clerical staff (HK Govt, 2018). This demographic, however, does not include foreign domestic workers, who are classified differently because of their temporary status. While these translingual practices do broaden

Karina's transnational network in Hong Kong, such networks are delineated by boundaries of social class.

3.4. Entangled with the inequalities of globalization and migrant labour

As the Philippines positions itself in the global economy as a source of a "cheap, female labour force that has a working knowledge of English" (Tinio, 2013, p. 221), Filipino domestic workers not only internalize 'scripts of servitude' (Lorente, 2017) but are also languagized (Pennycook, 2020), entangled with the forces of a linguistic market where their English competence is traded as a commodity. For Karina, it is this particular competence that distinguishes her from other Global South domestic workers. While TikTok enables Karina to expand her social network in Hong Kong by moving across languages online, this translingual orientation also provides her with ways to position and exclude others. In Hong Kong, Indonesians make up the second biggest group of domestic workers after Filipinos, and according to Karina, it is their differences in linguistic competence that determine who employs them. Filipinos who speak English are typically employed by local families with young children because they want the Filipino worker to teach their kids English. Indonesians, on the other hand, are in demand when it comes to families where there are elderly people to take care of. The reason for this is that the Indonesian government actively trains outbound Indonesian domestic workers to learn Cantonese before they fly to Hong Kong, and for this reason, they would be able to communicate with an elderly family member, who usually speaks only Cantonese.

When Karina talks about the differences between the TikTok videos of Filipino workers and Indonesian workers, she mentions how sometimes when she watches dance or lip-synch videos on TikTok where the creators do not have to speak, she cannot tell if the creator is Filipino or Indonesian. She continues by saying that one way to distinguish them is to turn to the captions of the video.

> *Marecognize mo dun sa caption nila na mali ang English nila. Minsan nagkukulang, minsang nagsosobra. Talagang yung spelling nila mali*

> You'll recognize how in their caption that their English is ungrammatical. Sometimes, something's missing; sometimes there's something that shouldn't be there. And their spelling is all wrong.

She proceeds to show me a post of a woman she believes is Indonesian (see Figure 10.5) and points out how the caption "Done Makes Nails Guy's" is wrong and should be "Done my nails, guys."

While she is later able to confirm that the creator was indeed Indonesian, what is striking is how she uses linguistic competence as a way to determine ethnicity. She

FIGURE 10.5   Post by a female TikToker in Hong Kong

is quite convinced that because of the ungrammaticality of the English caption that the creator was Indonesian.

This way of positioning others based on their 'poor English' harks back to notions of language and power in the Philippines, where 'poor English' indexes lower-class status or a lack of education. Inscribed in this colonial legacy is the expectation that one must sound like the American colonizer and speak with 'native speaker' competence. That Karina identifies this fellow domestic worker as her ethnolinguistic Other also indexes divisions among these servants of globalization (Parreñas, 2001) and the dynamics of power that circumscribes transnational domestication (Silvey, 2004). While labour migration from the Philippines and Indonesia both involve a high level of state involvement, Filipino domestic workers often have a higher level of education than their Indonesian counterparts (Liao & Gan, 2020), and in a neoliberal market, these differences in linguistic and cultural capital shape the way transnational workers from the Global South position and compete with each other. In this particular study, the material representations of domestic workers on TikTok not only enable a materialist understanding of the inequalities of globalization and migrant labour but also amplify existing inequalities and biases that exist offline.

4. Conclusion

By examining semiotic productions on social media as shaped by material conditions and producing material effects, the case of Karina demonstrates how translingual online practices cannot be disentangled from offline realities. The online is "an extension of offline interactions" (Bolander & Locher, 2020, p. 2), and it transforms social realities (Al Zidjaly, 2019). In a study of tourist placemaking, Thurlow and Jaworski (2014) shed light on these online/offline entanglements by demonstrating how tourists recycle mediatized representations of a place and perform mediated actions in physical contexts, which are then remediated when they post videos of their actions. These resemiotizations are assembled with intentionality, and in this chapter, we see how Karina's movement across languages in TikTok is a way to negotiate her transnational identity, maintaining ties with family and friends back in the Philippines while engaging with diverse others in Hong Kong. Recognizing the affordances and constraints of social media platforms, Karina performs different selves on TikTok and Facebook in ways that are not dissimilar to how people conduct themselves differently in various offline contexts. Shifting from Bisaya to Filipino and English in her captions and videos is a natural occurrence for someone with a broad linguistic and semiotic repertoire. Through these choices, she is able to position herself as a Proud Bisaya, a Filipino in touch with viral trends in the Philippines and a transnational living in Hong Kong who develops a multicultural network and learns new languages. In contrast to offline social interactions, however, where utterances are fleeting, online interactions and productions make themselves more visible and durable through text overlays, images, captions, hashtags and posts that can be reread and replayed. This materiality enables a particular way of seeing the entanglements of English with other languages, with platform designs and offline spaces.

The entanglements of English are multiple, convoluted and messy, especially as they involve "the interconnectedness between language, place, power, objects, class, race, gender, and more" (Pennycook, 2020, p. 232). To navigate this complexity, this chapter highlights how social media makes visible these entanglements and proposes a bifocal lens that distinguishes material and materialist perspectives of these entanglements. By examining how linguistic and semiotic choices index identifications and social, cultural, political and economic relations, it demonstrates how these indexicalities can serve as nodes: the points of connection between the material and the ideological. Making these connections is not intended to establish levels or scales that value the global over the local but to help us navigate the simultaneity and complexity of the forces that have historically shaped people's lives and contingencies. Disentangling the material from the materialist enables a critical awareness of how the things we can see constitute and are constituted by those that we cannot.

References

Agoncillo, T., & Guerrero, M. (1970). *History of the Filipino people*. RP Garcia Publishing.
Al Zidjaly, N. (2019). Society in digital contexts: New modes of identity and community construction. *Multilingua, 38*(4), 357–375.
Appadurai, A. (2015). Mediants, materiality, normativity. *Public Culture, 27*(2), 221–237.
Barad, K. (2003). Posthumanist performativity: Toward an understanding of how matter comes to matter. *Signs: Journal of Women in Culture and Society, 28*(3), 801–831.
Blommaert, J. (2013). Semiotic and spatial scope: Towards a materialist semiotics. In M. Böck & N. Pachler (Eds.), *Multimodality and social semiosis* (pp. 47–56). Routledge.
Blommaert, J. (2019). From groups to actions and back in online-offline sociolinguistics. *Multilingua, 38*(4), 485–493.
Bolander, B., & Locher, M. A. (2020). Beyond the online offline distinction: Entry points to digital discourse. *Discourse, Context & Media, 35*, 100383.
boyd, d. (2010). Social network sites as networked publics: Affordances, dynamics, and implications. In Z. Papacharissi (Ed.), *A networked self* (pp. 47–66). Routledge.
Canagarajah, S. (2013). *Translingual practice: Global Englishes and cosmopolitan relations*. Routledge.
Darvin, R. (2022). Design, resistance and the performance of identity on TikTok. *Discourse, Context & Media, 46*, 100591.
Darvin, R. (2023). Sociotechnical structures, materialist semiotics, and online language learning. *Language Learning & Technology, 27*(2), 28–45.
De Guzman, C. (2020, June). TikTok connected Hong Kong's domestic workers to family and friends. Now it's gone. *Vice*. https://www.vice.com/en/article/qj4xe5/tiktok-leaves-hong-kong-filipino-domestic-worker-experience
Espiritu, Y. L. (2005). Colonial oppression, labour importation, and group formation: Filipinos in the United States. In K. Ono (Ed.), *A companion to Asian American studies* (pp. 332–349). Blackwell.
HK Govt. (2018). *Hong Kong poverty situation report on ethnic minorities 2016*. https://www.povertyrelief.gov.hk/pdf/Hong%20Kong%20Poverty%20Situation%20Report%20on%20Ethnic%20Minorities%202016.pdf
HK Govt. (2021). *Statistics on the number of foreign domestic helpers in Hong Kong*. https://data.gov.hk/en-data/dataset/hk-immdset4-statistics-fdh/resource/063e1929-107b-47ae-a6ac-b4b1ed460ac3
HK SAR Census and Statistics. (2021). *Thematic household survey report No. 72. Employment of domestic helpers*. Census and Statistics Department. Hong Kong SAR.
Jaffe, A. (2009). Introduction: The sociolinguistics of stance. In A. Jaffe (Ed.), *Stance: Sociolinguistic perspectives* (pp. 1–28). Oxford University Press.
Jewitt, C. (2017). Multimodal analysis. In A. Georgakopoulou & T. Spilioti (Eds.), *The Routledge handbook of language and digital communication* (pp. 69–84). Routledge.
Kress, G. (2010). *Multimodality: A social semiotic approach to contemporary communication*. Routledge.
Ladegaard, H. J. (2020). Language competence, identity construction and discursive boundary-making: Distancing and alignment in domestic migrant worker narratives. *International Journal of the Sociology of Language, 262*, 97–122.
Lee, C. (2018). Introduction: Discourse of social tagging. *Discourse, Context & Media, 22*, 1–3.
Leung, A. (2012). Bad influence? – An investigation into the purported negative influence of foreign domestic helpers on children's second language English acquisition. *Journal of Multilingual and Multicultural Development, 33*(2), 133–148.

Liao, T., & Gan, R. Y. (2020). Filipino and Indonesian migrant domestic workers in Hong Kong: Their life courses in migration. *American Behavioral Scientist*, *64*(6), 740–764.

Lorente, B. P. (2017). *Scripts of servitude*. Multilingual Matters.

Norris, S. (2004). *Analyzing multimodal interaction: A methodological framework*. Routledge.

Parreñas, R. S. (2001). *Servants of globalization: Women, migration and domestic work*. Stanford University Press.

Pennycook, A. (2020). Translingual entanglements of English. *World Englishes*, *39*(2), 222–235.

Pennycook, A., & Makoni, S. (2020). *Innovations and challenges in applied linguistics from the Global South*. Routledge.

Scollon, R., & Scollon, S. W. (2003). *Discourses in place: Language in the material world*. Routledge.

Silvey, R. (2004). Transnational domestication: Indonesian domestic workers in Saudi Arabia. *Political Geography*, *23*(3), 245–264.

Thurlow, C., & Jaworski, A. (2014). "Two hundred ninety-four": Remediation and multimodal performance in tourist placemaking. *Journal of Sociolinguistics*, *18*(4), 459–494.

Tinio, M. T. (2013). Nimble tongues: Philippine English and the feminization of labour. In L. Wee, R. B. H. Goh & L. Lim (Eds.), *Politics of English: South Asia, Southeast Asia and the Pacific* (pp. 205–224). John Benjamins.

Tupas, R. (2019). Entanglements of colonialism, social class, and *Unequal Englishes*. *Journal of Sociolinguistics*, *23*, 529–542.

We are Social. (2020). Digital 2020: Hong Kong. *DataReportal*. https://datareportal.com/reports/digital-2020-hong-kong

We are Social. (2022). Digital 2022: The Philippines. *DataReportal*. https://datareportal.com/reports/digital-2022-philippines

Wolfaardt, J. F. (2022). Bilingual Hong Kong primary school children's vocabulary: The impact of Filipina domestic workers. *International Journal of Bilingualism*, *26*(6), 767–783.

PART IV
Entanglements of education

11
ENTANGLING ENGLISH TEACHING WITH CONTENT TEACHING

Reflections of an English language educator in a content and language integrated learning context

Keith S. T. Tong, Fay Chen, and Angel M. Y. Lin

1. Introduction: entanglement, assemblage, and context

'Entanglement' refers to a phenomenon in quantum physics in which particles such as electrons, photons, or atoms can become 'entangled' in such a way that the state of one particle cannot be described independently of the state of another particle, regardless of the distance between them. Einstein famously called entanglement "spooky action at a distance," since the particles seemed to be communicating faster than the speed of light. If relationships exist, even if they are not visible, English language education, which relies on countless relationship dynamics, not only the conventional relationships inherent to any educational context, such as teacher–student, student–student, teacher–administrator, but also relations between 'native' and 'nonnative' Englishes (Kachru, 2011), adopting an entangled approach may prove to be fruitful in uncovering various 'invisible' contexts at play. Stressing the limitations of "decontextualized education research," Sobe and Kowalczyk (2017) distinguish between big "C" Contexts and little "c" contexts, with the former referring to "the set of historically and socially significant discourses within education research that interweave actors and objects and govern what is possible to think and to do" and the latter "the set of named elements that are seen as comprising a given setting" (p. 198). They go on to expound on how the notions of 'entanglement' and 'assemblage' could be applied to studying relationality and to understanding complex relations of co-evolving and co-patterning:

> The comparative education researcher who takes Context as a "matter of concern" is not interested in the traditional object of study contained within a context, but rather examines the relationality between objects and contexts: how they come to be intelligible and conjoined, and to what effect(s). This approach

DOI: 10.4324/9781003441304-16

raises to the surface the question of what makes it possible for us to see objects as objects – particularly as problems to be studied. . . . "entangled approaches" can be particularly useful for studying and understanding these relationships.

(Sobe & Kowalczyk, 2017, pp. 199–200)

Key to taking this approach is understanding education as an 'Assemblage,' which in Deleuze and Guattari's (1980) philosophy refers to a dynamic system that comprises heterogeneous elements, which can include objects, bodies, ideas, and social relations. These elements come together in specific configurations, forming temporary and contingent structures. Assemblages are characterized by their capacity to change and transform, always with the potential for new connections and relations to emerge.

Hence, an 'entangled approach' that embraces the idea of relations existing in assemblages allows the researcher to explore heterogeneity and ephemerality in social interactions that are, on the other hand, patterned and ordered. By studying education phenomena and practices as assemblages, researchers can understand social embeddedness and their effects, including in the realms of policy, practice, process, and outcomes. In this critical reflection chapter, drawing on the theories of entanglement and assemblages, the auto-narrative is chosen as a method to present Keith's critical reflections on different kinds of entanglements experienced. Auto-narratives involve using life stories to explore individuals' personal and professional experiences, particularly those of teachers. This approach emphasizes the significance of personal narratives in shaping professional identity and practice. By incorporating these life histories into educational research, the methodology provides a richer, more nuanced understanding of education. It captures the complexity of educators' lives, revealing how personal visions and professional commitments influence their responses to educational reforms, thus offering insights that transcend traditional, practical approaches (Goodson & Gill, 2011).

In the next section, we shall provide the context of the critical reflections, followed by Keith's reflections. The role of Fay and Angel lies in dialoguing with Keith as he was engaged in this both deeply personal but also deeply social reflective process, while all authors participate in co-shaping the textual representation, itself reflective of an entangled approach to the auto-narrative as a critical research praxis.

2. English medium instruction as a universal trend and EMI in Taiwan

In 2016, the British Council published a report on English medium instruction (EMI) education development in the world, in which the following was reported: "There appears to be a fast-moving worldwide shift, in non-anglophone countries, from English being taught as a foreign language (EFL) to English being the medium of instruction (EMI) for academic subjects such as science, mathematics, geography and medicine" (Dearden, 2016, p. 4). Using data from 55 countries, the report describes a general global trend toward a rapid expansion of EMI provision. Concerns have been expressed over the fact that EMI policies are often instated top-down, with the public harboring equivocal attitudes (Dearden, 2016). Another concern involves a lack of infrastructure to support EMI implementation, including a shortage of linguistically qualified teachers, a lack of pedagogical guidelines for effective EMI teaching and learning, and a dearth of relevant professional development programs for EMI teachers (Dearden, 2016).

One of the case studies cited in the Dearden report involves Taiwan, where there was a higher investment in EMI evident at the university level, particularly in English, commerce, engineering, MBA, and IMBA programs, implying that EMI had not made a noticeable impact on Taiwanese students at the elementary and secondary levels. One comment in the report rings true: "The majority of university professors speak English since most of them have a Ph.D. degree. However, that does not mean they are well-trained to deliver courses in English" (Dearden, 2016, p. 31). Many of us might be compelled to investigate the language ideologies shaping the problematic assumption that one who has earned a doctoral degree is likely to be a speaker of English. However, it is difficult to ignore the reality that many university teachers were not prepared and that the situation was even more unsatisfactory at secondary and elementary school levels.

Guided by the trend of internationalization of higher education, Taiwan has encouraged universities to launch EMI since the early 2000s. Initially, EMI was first implemented by elite universities to attract international students for their MBA programs (Wu, 2006). By 2005, two leading universities in Taiwan, National Taiwan University (NTU) and National Cheng Kung University (NCKU), had reported an offering of 420 and 205 EMI courses, respectively (Wu, 2006). By 2013, EMI had grown to 29 Taiwanese universities, introducing 92 full degree programs through English (Macaro et al., 2018). Studies in Taiwan have reported favorable results on college students' English learning. Yeh's (2014) study showed that approximately 75% of students claimed via self-assessment that EMI had a positive influence on their English and in particular their listening comprehension. Yang (2015) reported that college students' receptive skills, measured by the General English Proficiency Test, improved significantly after two years of English medium instruction. A study by Tai (2015) also showed progress in writing fluency of university students over one semester of instruction mediated in English.

In December 2018, the National Development Council of Taiwan, under the auspices of the Executive Yuan of Taiwan (the policy-making organ of the government) announced a bilingual policy for all educational stages (Ministry of Education, Taiwan, 2018). In the document entitled *Blueprint for Developing Taiwan into a Bilingual Nation by 2030*, the government made clear its intention to establish Taiwan as a "bilingual country," which "would enable Taiwan to become more internationally competitive" (Ministry of Education, Taiwan, 2018, p. 2). Subsequent documents were published by the Ministry of Education on how to achieve the policy through the promotion and implementation of EMI education at all levels in the education system – elementary, secondary, and tertiary. The policy sparked much debate in society and in academia, with support and misgivings expressed by academics. Taiwan's National Federation of Teachers' Unions and other groups have found issues with the policy and appealed to the Ministry of Education to terminate the policy, citing concerns over the feasibility in teaching content materials in English (Lee, 2023). Other scholars would go further to suggest the need for a critical examination of the traditional approach to English teaching and learning in Taiwan, advocating for one based on multilingualism and informed by content and language integrated learning (CLIL) and translanguaging (Tsou, 2021). Meanwhile, Gupta and Lin (2023) suggest viewing and examining the policy with a "critical lens" so as "to look beyond mere *effectiveness* and to raise more fundamental questions about the contentious adoption of the EMI policy and its potential consequences in Taiwan" and that by discussing such consequences from pedagogical, cultural, and socioeconomic points of view, we "could fill the research gap, thereby providing implications for policymakers, researchers, educators, and students and suggestions for opening up more opportunities for adopting EMI with critical awareness" (Gupta & Lin, 2023, p. 64).

It was in this context that Keith, an English language teaching professional with over forty years of EMI experience and former head of a university center for language education in Hong Kong, was appointed visiting chair professor at the National Pingtung University (NPTU) in southern Taiwan in July 2020, tasked with giving counsel to university administrators and providing support for teachers and students. This also afforded him the opportunity to gain valuable insights into the reality of EMI implementation through working closely with teachers and students at a university. This also resonates with Lin's (2015) discussion of "researcher positionality" as "a kind of critical methodological reflection that aims to bring to consciousness the different kinds of ideological assumptions and power relationships underlying their discipline's research paradigm" (p. 24).

Owing to COVID-induced travel restrictions, Keith did not make his first trip to NPTU until April 2021, when he met with the core members of the university administrative team, some faculty members, and a few students but at a moment when all teaching was still done online. Over a few subsequent visits, he was able to gradually learn much about the teaching and learning culture of the university, as well as establishing relationships with some teachers. Full engagement with the stakeholders was finally made possible in the fall semester of the 2023–2024 academic year, when Keith managed to negotiate himself into doing collaborative teaching with two content teachers in three courses based on the CLIL model. As a result, he was able to get into close contact with teachers and students, as well as the university's teaching and learning culture, that is, the shared patterns of beliefs, values, behaviors, and artifacts of NPTU. Gradually, the 'engagement' that he saw morphed into a different phenomenon, that of *entanglement*: relations which are generated via different channels and modes of interactions, effects, side-effects, and after-effects brought about by various actions and involving different and multiple stakeholders, not exactly 'spooky action at a distance' but definitely a web of actions, interactions, and intricate relationships with a substantial and long-lasting impact.

3. A conceptual framework for capturing elements of entanglement

In order to capture the various strands and elements of entanglement, Keith presents a provisional conceptual framework (see Figure 11.1), with three partially overlapping circles representing three main areas in which entanglement is likely to occur as a result of the CLIL-informed collaborative teaching intervention adopted. They are "teacher pedagogy," "student affect and self-efficacy," and "student agency."

Teacher pedagogy is key to success in EMI education. Tertiary teachers in Taiwan, like those in many other countries, have mostly not undergone pedagogic

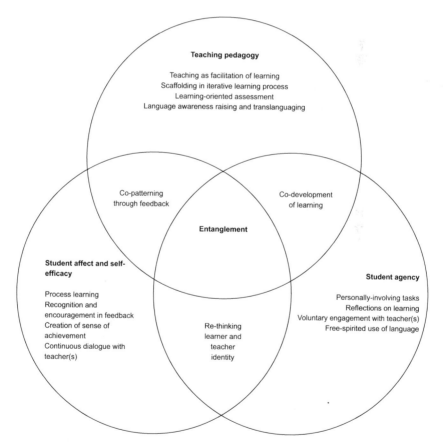

FIGURE 11.1 Entanglements among teaching pedagogy, student affect and self-efficacy, and student agency

training, and having to teach their respective subjects in English to students who may not be ready for EMI education presents extra challenges to EMI teachers. In Taiwan, Tsou (2015) and Pineda et al. (2022) have studied the training needs of CLIL teachers and proposed a glocalized approach to such training: "By implementing glocalized teaching practices, CLIL teachers are empowered to use culturally and linguistically marked strategies to better prepare learners to interact successfully in the world" (Pineda et al., 2022, p. 3).

The other two areas, 'student affect and self-efficacy' and 'student agency,' are also essential aspects directly related to success in EMI implementation. In a document published in 2021, the Taiwan Ministry of Education writes:

> The government has launched the Bilingual 2030 policy precisely to boost the competitiveness of Taiwan's young generation. Building on our national advantage as a Mandarin-speaking nation, it aims to further enhance English communication skills among young people. Equipped with better proficiency in English, they will be able to use the language as a tool for absorbing knowledge, broadening their international outlook, and bolstering their global competitiveness.
>
> *(Ministry of Education, Taiwan, 2021, p. 4)*

The term "young generation" denotes an abstract concept which is not particularly useful when it comes to universities striving to achieve success with EMI implementation. We would argue that a more effective approach would be recognizing and respecting the young people as independent-thinking and feeling individuals who have lived through over ten years of experience in learning English, or rather 'studying,' often to no avail. They are often unsure about why they should learn English and learn it well and have not felt a sense of purpose, not to mention a sense of achievement in the learning process. This is often documented in the literature which calls for a movement towards a pedagogy of multiliteracies, for example:

> Driven by high-stakes tests for high school and college admission, the curriculum design of Taiwan's English classrooms has mostly focused on testing vocabulary, grammar, reading, listening and writing skills. This type of learning inadvertently encourages memorization and repetitive practices, which favour a certain type of learner, while affording few opportunities for active learning or critical thinking. Aspects that cannot be easily tested on the paper-based examination, for example, oral communication, have not been prioritized.
>
> *(Chen & Tsou, 2021, p. 82)*

This is why it takes a different approach, like that of entanglement, to reveal how learning to use English in their subject content studies can engage them in meaningful, authentic language use or, more specifically, to shed light on how these young people of Taiwan, through tasks and activities such as reflective writing, can achieve agency and as a result feel a sense of self-efficacy.

3. Adoption of the auto-narrative for reporting evidence of entanglement

In the following, Keith attempts to capture his perceptions, observations, and insights in the form of an 'auto-narrative.' Using the first person *I*, Keith reflects and expounds on how the happenings in the co-teaching exercises constitute an entanglement of concepts, notions, strategies, relations, and outcomes. In discussing the auto-narrative as a tool for reporting research and as a means of structuring human experience, Gajek (2014) writes:

> A narrative can be recognized as a monologue, which is a communicative form of self-presentation of the narrator and representation of the world as seen by him/her. It presents a chronologically ordered sequence of events, developing over time and related to persons and events. Its content can be the life of the storyteller or other people, located in the socio-cultural context, including an account of personal experiences or supplemented by information from other sources.
>
> *(p. 27)*

Citing Horsdal (2004), Gajek (2014) distinguishes between two kinds of memory: "autobiographical episodic memory allows us to keep the memories of ourselves as participants in various past events, and the ability to store and 'playback' words or objects is ensured by semantic memory" (p. 22). The following is an attempt to play back specific scenarios, agents, objects, and words and to frame them in the semantic scope of entanglement. The aforementioned Venn diagram serves to illustrate how we see different kinds of entanglement enacted.

The creation and enhancement of the Venn diagram guided Keith in the organization of his experience, where entanglement was manifested in various contexts and events, and at the same time allowed him to relive his experience, as a teacher, learner, and researcher and generate nuanced and rich understandings of such experience and related phenomena. Second, it motivated Keith to take a deep, hermeneutic approach in exploring and making sense of the many facets of interaction, or entanglement, taking place among the stakeholders, for example, teacher–teacher interactions, teacher–student interactions, and student–student interactions and, more importantly, the double, triple, and multiple hermeneutic processes and outcomes. The elements in the intersections between the three circles are indeed informed by these considerations and interpretations.

4. Recollections of entanglement of various kinds

4.1. Entanglement of the first kind: teaching pedagogy

One of my collaborating teachers was Prof. J from the Department of Special Education. While Prof. J freely admitted to me that she had received no formal training in teaching, her training in occupational therapy would make her a very patient speaker. She would always speak at an accommodatingly slow pace in lectures, though she was not tuned in to the art of *paraphrasing* her lecture input to facilitate comprehension by her students. It was only during a discussion with me that Prof. J began to think about teaching in terms of *facilitation* of learning when I suggested to her that she did not need to give all information away as the lecturer and could have engaged students in discussing issues instead. This was, to my understanding, Prof. J's first encounter with the idea of interactive classroom and constructivist learning and teaching.

Regarding the use of language, Prof. J was serious about staying true to the EMI nature of the course but seemed to need more awareness about language use and translanguaging notions and strategies. She shared an anecdote with me in the middle of the semester after I had to miss two classes owing to my own commitments. A student asked Prof. J if she could ask a question *in Chinese*, and she immediately said "No" and told the student to ask it in English. And the student curtly replied: "I have no questions." To this I suggested that she could have tried translanguaging by allowing the student to ask her a question in Chinese and for her to repeat the question in English and then give the answer in English. There are many different ways of doing translanguaging in different contexts (Mendoza et al., 2024). This particular way, which is akin to language brokering (Baker, 2017), helps scaffold the learning and cushion the change in use of L1 and L2 in a subtle way and at the same time avoid having negative feelings generated with regard to EMI learning.

The collaboration in teaching this course perfectly illustrated the entanglement of teaching pedagogy between a content teacher and a language teacher. Two teachers with very different histories in teaching, areas of professional expertise, and pedagogical beliefs and attitudes had to overcome initial unfamiliarity and gradually develop a mutually enhancing collaborative approach in delivering the course. At my suggestion, an end-of-course questionnaire survey was conducted. A few students took the opportunity to celebrate the accomplishment of a difficult task, completing an EMI course. One student wrote that she did not like being criticized by the teacher and then added, "But it's okay. I have improved my English now~ Thanks." The student responses reflected an entanglement of feelings, fear of and aversion to taking a course via EMI, and eventual feelings of redemption and accomplishment.

4.2. Entanglement of the second kind: student agency

Another collaborator of mine was Prof. G. We were involved in teaching two music courses, "Piano Music Appreciation and Analysis" and "World Music," the former to twenty music majors and the latter to over forty students from diverse disciplinary backgrounds. "Piano Music Appreciation and Analysis" involves music majors honing their piano playing skills and provides the opportunity for them to play live to different audiences (admittedly not what the course title suggests). Given the different natures of the two music courses, I identified 'reflective journal writing' as one learning task which could serve the purpose of engaging students' intellect as well as emotions. It did not turn out to be easy to have the students grasp the rationale of writing reflective learning journals because, to many university students in Taiwan, all assignments are perceived as some kind of test of their knowledge, coming with definitive marks assigned by the teacher. In short, the personally involving tasks caught them off guard at the beginning and only began to ignite their interest much later, but towards the end of the semester, most students were 'writing their minds' instead of 'searching for the expected answers to score marks.' This also made the marking process increasingly enjoyable for me. This constituted an interesting entanglement of student agency in the learning process. Although a template was provided to guide the students in their writing of the learning journals, there was no suggestion as to the length of their writing. I was most excited to see that some students were writing with a free spirit as we entered the latter half of the semester, showing that the students indeed 'had something to say' and 'wanted to say it.'

In the "World Music" course, the final assessed task involved students forming groups of four and presenting a music genre of their choice. In previous incarnations of this course, Prof. G would deliver all her content in lecture mode, and this time, on my suggestion, students exercised *agency* in forming congenial groups and apparently enjoyed the research process. Based on my experience of teaching in Hong Kong, I also made provisions for student groups to rehearse their presentations and seek feedback. Students' reluctance to participate in the feedback sessions led to the revelation that they did not initially see the prospect of subjecting themselves to criticism from the teacher as an 'opportunity.' Dialogic learning experiences are rare in Taiwanese higher education, dominated by lecture and summative assessments (Lin & Lin, 2021). The students' eventual participation and recognition of the value of the feedback session was further evidence of entanglement in the learning experience involving empowering students and activating student agency.

4.3. Entanglement of the third kind: student affect and self-efficacy

Tertiary students in Taiwan demonstrate a tendency to lack confidence in using English, despite having learnt the language as a school subject for ten years or more prior to entering university (H. Lin, 2019). It is sad that many students could recall unpleasant experiences of English learning which result in a sense of defeat. In an examination system which focuses on accuracy in language usage, instead of language use, and with over-emphasis on scores achieved in standardized tests, instead of real-life use of English, learners find success hard to come by (Chang, 2014).

The process learning experience outlined previously may constitute a first encounter with a different approach to learning English, in which one could use the English language for one's own sake, to communicate thoughts and feelings to real-life audiences who would listen and respond and engage with one's psyche and intellect. They also encountered a 'very different' teacher in me, who would read their writing, focusing on their ideas and not their language accuracy; would let them know that he enjoyed reading it; and would reassure them that they had done good work. This personifies entanglement of the third kind: when student affect is engaged and self-efficacy is deeply felt through engagement with and assurance from the teacher.

In the penultimate lesson of a course named "Introduction to Early Intervention," I brought some 'prizes' to give to students to recognize good work, including a baseball cap from my former university in Hong Kong. While I was looking for the best speaker among the student presenters, a little voice told me that I should instead give it to Student S. This was one student who chose to write *three* drafts for her reflective report and who had made impressive efforts to speak spontaneous English instead of relying on a memorized script. Student S would, after a few days, write an email message to thank me for the baseball cap, which she said she would wear on her travels. In the email message, she reveled in the thought that she "now knows many ways to improve her English," though she did not forget to apologize for her "not so good" English. I was glad that I made the split-second decision to reward *attitude* and *perseverance* instead of 'good' performances, for here is precisely where student affect and self-efficacy are entangled.

4.4. Entanglement of the fourth kind: co-development of learning between teachers and between teachers and students

Prof. J of special education took up the option of having me as a co-teacher on the recommendation of a colleague. She could probably never have envisaged the fact that I had influenced the delivery of her course in a holistic way, namely focusing on how to engage students in self-directed learning and reflective learning. She would share her presentation slides with me, and I would make suggestions for refinement. We also co-assessed all the student performances in presentations and writing, and we would discuss the marks assigned. This also reveals 'entanglement' and 'assemblage' in the sense of how interactions and interdependencies between different components contribute to the construction, maintenance, and transformation of systems, in this case teaching and assessment.

In a discussion after the course finished, Prof. J confessed to me that she initially thought that I would only be 'coaching' her on how to use English in EMI teaching for two to three weeks. She was 'horrified' to see me staying on and persistently involved in the teaching and planning for the whole semester, confessing that she would get nervous with me in the audience. Teachers who are non-native English speakers in the Expanding Circle frequently experience 'impostor syndrome' (Bernat, 2008), characterized by a lack of confidence in their English proficiency. Prof. J admitted to this complex of feeling judged whenever English was used. In the end, she thanked me for reassuring her that all she had to do was use English naturally and spontaneously without having to worry about grammar and accuracy. I would not have comprehended the phobia Taiwanese students *and* teachers might suffer in using English, probably under the influence of native-speakerism (Holliday, 2006; Ruecker & Ives, 2015), or this amalgamation of their histories and experiences in their English learning and English use, without getting into the *context* of my work through exploring the assemblage of factors and issues in the process.

Interestingly, my most fruitful learning experiences came in the shape of two lunches with students. At one lunch I asked a student majoring in music where he would like to go if he had the opportunity to go on an international exchange, and he mentioned Vienna. I told him I had been to Vienna several times, and whenever I went there I felt regretful about not having learned music and not playing any musical instrument. I then suggested that he should learn some German on top of improving his English, and he said he was pondering it. It seemed that the teacher–student relationship was significantly strengthened over one lunch, by virtue of a bringing together of personal experiences and future aspirations, as if our lives were intertwined in a subtle, entangled way.

4.5. *Entanglement of the fifth kind: co-patterning of learning experiences through two-way feedback between students and teachers*

The three courses described previously are very different in nature, but one common practice adopted in the approach was for me to provide *constant feedback* to students and to seek continuous improvement. The aforementioned special education course required students to do outreach work and report back in speaking and writing, with teachers providing prompt feedback. Students, on the other hand, were also encouraged to give feedback via different means. When I had to take a two-week leave of absence in the first half of the semester, Prof. J took the opportunity to ask students how they were coping with EMI learning. Prof. J also asked the students why they did not perform well in a short test I gave on definitions of "Special Education" terminology. The students replied to say that they were expecting multiple-choice items and did not expect to have to do freehand writing of long phrases and sentences. This explained to me why many tertiary students in Taiwan might struggle to speak or write (Chang, 2014). The emphasis has always been on the *receptive skills* of listening and reading with their English learning (Yang & Gosling, 2013). When I asked my English-teaching colleagues why they did not ask students to do any writing assignments, the answers would be "Because they can't write."

To me, they were mixing up the cause and the consequence. When I used my influence to include two writing assignments in each English for academic purposes (EAP) course plan, the teachers would bargain for shorter lengths, claiming that "Taiwanese students cannot write so many words." The English paper in the university entrance examination, incidentally, has always required candidates to write

120 words. This practice of teachers over-accommodating for student inadequacies was very worrying to me. If not for Prof. J's intervention, I would not have learned about the mismatch in expectations between the students and me when I was setting the test. It also underlines the importance of such entanglement of actions. The reflective learning journal on the two music courses had dual purposes: engaging students and hearing their feedback. As mentioned, the students in both courses took time to warm to the writing tasks, owing to multiple reasons, one of which is a lack of understanding of and experience in reflective writing. But inertia, or lack of action, *was* feedback. I hence gave follow-up mini-sessions on how to approach reflective writing, and this eventually helped. Again, the entanglement of action, semi-action, and non-action seemed to promote and generate co-patterning of learning and change of behavior on the part of the teachers and students.

4.6. Entanglement of the sixth kind: re-thinking learner and teacher identity

The teaching and learning culture at NPTU resembles the 'traditional' Chinese method of an authoritative figure imparting knowledge in teacher-dominant lectures. Oftentimes, some professors would not even be interested in knowing the names of students. Meanwhile, the teaching and learning design of the courses in question sought to help students to find and assert their identities as tertiary students and as independent-thinking individuals. All the nuances present in the one-semester learning process would work together to achieve this through the entanglement of learning activities, tasks, student interaction with teachers, and student interactions with peers. As students on the "World Music" course grasped the idea of writing learning portfolios, the reading of such portfolios became increasingly interesting for me.

From this course, my experience with Student T was especially memorable. I was more than thrilled, indeed flabbergasted, to read Student T's full portfolio submitted at the end of the course. The playful tone and the *trendy* writing and formatting style simply astonished me. About the course, she would write: "And I really like the course, everybody is just chill and a bit shy lol!," and "I have developed a deeperrrr [sic] understanding of myself and others." She also mentioned practicing several times for her presentation, but feeling "fucking nervous" nevertheless. It was outrageous! What gave Student T the audacity to write in such a free-spirited, *unguarded* way? Many teachers might take her to task for using rude words in her writing and for her 'poor spelling.' But she was obviously being herself, fully asserting her identity and agency. I subsequently remembered an email communication with this student in Week 2 of the course, after she submitted the second installment of her portfolio. I had told her the assignment felt "cobbled together" for the sake of completing an assignment and not the student speaking her mind. She immediately wrote back to apologize and admit that she used ChatGPT to generate the writing in order to meet the deadline, and would make up for it by submitting a piece that she wrote by herself.

This illustrates how multi-faceted entanglement is at work in terms of assertion and re-formulation of learning and teaching. There was Student T asserting her identity by communicating with her professor in a relaxed and honest manner, having the strength of personality to admit to the use of generative AI, and subsequently showing even more character in writing a most enlightened reflective journal. Re-reading Student T's writing reveals an entanglement of writing styles (informal language use in an academic writing task), not to mention an interesting manifestation of identity, positionality, and agency on the part of the learner in her communication with the teacher. All this also echoes the point made earlier about co-patterning of learning experiences through two-way feedback between students and teachers.

5. Implications for EMI implementation in Taiwan

Recounting and reflecting on my experience of collaborating with two content teachers on the delivery of three courses at Pingtung University in the fall semester of the 2023–2024 academic year, I was able to gather considerable insights, bottom-up, by scrutinizing the intricate web of actions and reactions enacted by various agents through teaching and learning activities which were co-planned and co-developed over time. It was impossible to lay out the plans in procedural steps and anticipated results; it was most interesting and gratifying to witness changes as they take place and ascribe relationships to the happenings in terms of assemblage and entanglement. Viewing issues such as EMI implementation in higher education in Taiwan through the lens of entanglement, educators can achieve in-depth comprehension of both a scenario and all the elements making it up and at the same time altering it. It is pertinent that teachers and researchers wishing to understand particular issues will pay attention to both big 'C' Contexts and little 'c' contexts in their work and focus on co-happenings over time instead of merely obtaining cross-sectional views. Following are some points worth considering.

5.1. Entanglement as a non-reductionist approach

Five years have elapsed since the Ministry of Education in Taiwan issued the aforementioned 2030 *Blueprint*. There has been much debate in society, not least among academics, about the policy (Huang, 2023; Lee, 2023). On the ground level, that is, in the educational system, much work has been done at the primary, secondary, and tertiary levels to promote and implement EMI education. It is, however, most difficult to evaluate the progress and achievements (Hou et al., 2013). The Ministry of Education tends to favor reductionist quantitative data such as the number of teachers trained in EMI teaching and the English proficiency levels achieved by students in standardized tests, as well as the 'readiness' of students for EMI teaching and learning (Chen et al., 2020). This overlooks the holistic and complex nature of education and the interaction of a multitude of factors, including social, cultural, and psychological elements. While the goals and aims mentioned in the *Blueprint* are eloquently written, it takes more than rhetoric and administrative measures to ensure success in the implementation. A humanistic and holistic approach allows for an in-depth understanding of how various factors in the ecological system interact and shape the learning process and educational outcomes. By viewing the teaching and learning process as a complex set of happenings, and by seeking to understand the intricate relationships among various elements, including the most important stakeholders, we can obtain a much fuller and richer picture of the situation and as such ponder issues and ways to address them.

5.2. Entanglement as an inclusive approach

The policy documents, and subsequent measures employed by the Ministry of Education, also suggest an approach which is based on *selectivity* and *dichotomization*. For example, universities applying for funding aspire to join the privileged category of 'cultivation of major domains' universities, instead of the second-rate 'popularized enhancement' (subsequently revised to 'universal enhancement') category. There are, of course, universities that fall out of the two categories – a further distinction between the haves and have-nots. In effect, students are classified into two categories: those who can benefit from EMI education and those who cannot. University teachers are heard saying: "My English is not good enough to do EMI. I'm just a local PhD (土博士). Let the overseas PhDs (洋博士) do it." The *divisive* thinking based on geopolitical credentials is far from helpful, but an approach with *inclusive* overtones targeting *genuine* universal enhancement would have a better chance of helping Taiwan achieve its goals. In this respect, the entanglement and assemblage perspective can be a starting point in interrogating such divisive ideological positions.

5.3. Entanglement and multilingualism

In advocating for an English as a lingua franca (ELF)-informed CLIL approach for bilingual education in Taiwan, Chen et al. (2020) allude to the fact that many people in Taiwan, including teachers, have always subscribed to the English as a native language (ENL) model, which is counter-productive to the promotion of bilingualism and/or multilingualism. They identify a range of risks, including student learning outcomes being perpetually substandard "against the native benchmarks" (Chen et al., 2020, p. 178). Change of beliefs and attitudes takes time but can certainly be helped in the process by exposition of how an ELF-informed approach for teaching multiliteracies (Doyle, 2015) can work towards enhancing learners' communicative competence in the global community. Once again, the entanglement approach depicted in this report might aptly serve this purpose.

The aforementioned writing by Student T, where she notes achieving a "deep-errrr understanding of myself and others," is indeed a powerful example of how young learners can be encouraged to engage a wider range of communicative repertoires in a global world, as expounded in A. Lin (2015, 2019). Simultaneously, A. Lin (2019) leaves us with the disclaimer that diverse "pedagogical/curriculum principles alone, however, cannot solve the larger issue of domination of reified standard codes and unequal power relations that stigmatize students' communicative repertoires" (p. 14). Nevertheless, an important starting point is "changing teachers' position and understanding" (Lin, A., 2019, p. 14). Once again, this is thanks to the entanglement perspective.

6. A final note about the auto-narrative

It seems the right decision for Keith to adopt the auto-narrative as a research methodology and a vehicle for carrying and articulating the insights gained in the teaching and learning process. The event described in the chapter was never set up as research *per se*, with specific research questions and anticipated findings. Everything just happened *naturally*, in the sense that it involved no conscious or subconscious efforts to fulfill research goals. In writing his auto-narrative, Keith was able to use the first person *I* in narrating events and articulating feelings. Keith could choose words that denote subjective or even 'biased' (in a neutral sense) perspectives, instead of striving to achieve objectivity by using documented evidence. Gajek (2014) writes in her conclusion about the role of language in auto-narratives:

> It should be mentioned that we do not recreate our experiences or events faithfully, but we reconstruct them in the course of building the narrative. . . . By means of the language, we present the experienced world, although not all events are possible to be displayed and are tellable. Moreover, we are also entangled in the communication process, creating a report for a specific recipient. From all the past events, we select those that for our interpretation of reality and our own "self," and also lend credence to our story.
>
> *(p. 28)*

In writing this chapter about entanglement, Keith was able to relive his experience by telling his story. It turned out to be a most meaningful, rewarding, and, not least, *entangled* writing process.

References

Baker, C. (2017). Knowledge about bilingualism and multilingualism. In J. Cenoz, D. Gorter & S. May (Eds.), *Language awareness and multilingualism* (pp. 283–295). Springer.

Bernat, E. (2008). Towards a pedagogy of empowerment: The case of "impostor syndrome" among pre-service non-native speaker teachers in TESOL. *English Language Teacher Education and Development*, *11*(1), 1–8.

Chang, W.-C. (2014). 台灣英語教育的「變」與「不變」：面對挑戰，提升英語力 ["Changes" and "Constants" in Taiwan's English education: Facing challenges, enhancing

English proficiency]. 中等教育 *[Secondary Education]*, *5*(3), 6–17. https://doi.org/10.6249/SE.2014.65.3.01

Chen, F., Kao, S. M., & Tsou, W. (2020). Toward ELF-informed bilingual education in Taiwan: Addressing incongruity between policy and practice. *English Teaching & Learning*, *44*(2), 175–191.

Chen, F., & Tsou, W. (2021). Empowering local bilingual teachers through extending the pedagogy of multiliteracies in Taiwan's primary education. *OLBI Journal*, *11*, 79–103.

Dearden, J. (2016). *English as a medium of instruction: A growing global phenomenon*. Department of Education, University of Oxford.

Deleuze, G., & Guattari, F. (1980). *Mille Plateaux, volume 2 of Capitalisme et Schizophrenic*. Les Editions de Minuit.

Doyle, H. (2015). Multi-competence, ELF, learning and literacy: A reconsideration. *International Journal of Social Science and Humanity*, *5*(10), 887–891.

Gajek, K. (2014). Auto/narrative as a means of structuring human experience. In M. Kafar & M. Modrzejewska-Świgulska (Eds.), *Autobiography–biography–narration: Research practice for biographical perspectives* (pp. 11–32). Wydawnictwo Uniwersytetu Łódzkiego.

Goodson, I., & Gill, S. (2011). *Narrative pedagogy: Life history and learning*. Peter Lang.

Gupta, K. C. L., & Lin, A. M. Y. (2023). English-medium instruction (EMI) in higher education in Taiwan: A review and critical reflection on why, how, and for whom. In P. K. Sah & F. Fang (Eds.), *Policies, politics, and ideologies of English-medium instruction in Asian universities: Unsettling critical edges* (pp. 63–76). Routledge.

Holliday, A. (2006). Native-speakerism. *ELT Journal*, *60*(4), 385–387.

Horsdal, M. (2004). Ciało, umysł i opowieści: O ontologicznych i epistemologicznych perspektywach narracji na temat doświadczeń osobistych (A. Zembrzuska, Trans.). *Teraźniejszość—Człowiek—Edukacja*, *2*, 9–29.

Hou, A. Y. C., Morse, R., Chiang, C.-L., & Chen, H.-J. (2013). Challenges to quality of English medium instruction degree programs in Taiwanese universities and the role of local accreditors: A perspective of non-English-speaking Asian country. *Asia Pacific Education Review*, *14*, 359–370.

Huang, Y. H. I. (2023). "The majority are left behind": The promotion of bilingual education 2030 policy in Taiwan and its potential to widen horizontal inequalities. *Higher Education*, *88*, 85–100.

Kachru, Y. (2011). World Englishes: Contexts and relevance for language education. In E. Hinkel (Ed.), *Handbook of research in second language teaching and learning* (pp. 155–172). Routledge.

Lee, C. (2023, September 11). Bilingual education rollout was not trialed. Editorial & Opinion. *Liberty Times*, p. 8. https://www.taipeitimes.com/News/editorials/archives/2023/09/11/2003806045

Lin, A. M. Y. (2015). Researcher positionality. In F. M. Hult & D. C. Johnson (Eds.), *Research methods in language policy and planning: A practical guide* (pp. 21–32). Wiley-Blackwell.

Lin, A. M. Y. (2019). Theories of trans/languaging and trans-semiotizing: Implications for content-based education classrooms. *International Journal of Bilingual Education and Bilingualism*, *22*(1), 5–16.

Lin, H. W., & Lin, A. C. (2021). Conducting EMI with students of diversified backgrounds. In L. Su, H. Cheung & J. Wu (Eds.), *Rethinking EMI: Multidisciplinary perspectives from Chinese-speaking regions* (pp. 78–96). Routledge.

Lin, H. Y. (2019). Perceptions of the Englishization of higher education in Taiwan: Implementation and implications. *International Journal of Bilingual Education and Bilingualism*, *23*(5), 617–634.

Macaro, E., Curle, S., Pun, J., An, J., & Dearden, J. (2018). A systematic review of English medium instruction in higher education. *Language Teaching*, *51*(1), 36–76.

Mendoza, A., Hamman-Ortiz, L., Tian, Z., Rajendram, S., Tai, K. W., Ho, W. Y. J., & Sah, P. K. (2024). Sustaining critical approaches to translanguaging in education: A contextual framework. *Tesol Quarterly, 58*(2), 664–692.

Ministry of Education, Taiwan. (2018). *Blueprint for developing Taiwan into a bilingual nation by 2030*. https://www.ndc.gov.tw/en/Content_List.aspx?n=BF21AB4041BB5255

Ministry of Education, Taiwan. (2021). *The program on bilingual education for students in college*. https://english.moe.gov.tw/cp-117-25498-5b142-1.html

Pineda, I., Tsou, W., & Chen, F. (2022). Glocalization in CLIL: Analyzing the training needs of in-service CLIL teachers in Taiwan and Spain. *Journal of Multilingual and Multicultural Development*, 1–18.

Ruecker, T., & Ives, L. (2015). White native English speakers needed: The rhetorical construction of privilege in online teacher recruitment spaces. *TESOL Quarterly, 49*(4), 733–756.

Sobe, N. W., & Kowalczyk, J. (2017). Context, entanglement and assemblage as matters of concern in comparative education research. In J. McLeod, N. W. Sobe & T. Seddon (Eds.), *World yearbook of education 2018* (pp. 197–204). Routledge.

Tai, H.-Y. (2015). Writing development in syntactic complexity, accuracy and fluency in a content and language integrated learning class. *International Journal of Language and Linguistics, 2*(3), 149–156.

Tsou, W. (2015). From globalization to glocalization: Rethinking English Language teaching under the ELF phenomenon. *English as a Global Language Education (EaGLE) Journal, 1*(1), 47–64.

Tsou, W. (2021). Translanguaging as a glocalized strategy for EMI in Asia. In W. Tsou & W. Baker (Eds.), *English-medium instruction translanguaging practices in Asia: Theories, frameworks and implementation in higher education* (pp. 3–17). Springer.

Wu, W. (2006). Students' attitude toward EMI: Using Chung Hua University as an example. *Journal of English and Foreign Language and Literature, 4*(1), 67–84.

Yang, W. (2015). Content and language integrated learning next in Asia: Evidence of learners' achievement in CLIL education from a Taiwan tertiary degree programme. *International Journal of Bilingual Education and Bilingualism, 18*(4), 361–382.

Yang, W., & Gosling, M. (2013). What makes a Taiwan CLIL programme highly recommended or not recommended? *International Journal of Bilingual Education and Bilingualism, 17*(4), 394–409.

Yeh, C.-C. (2014). Taiwanese students' experiences and attitudes towards English-medium courses in tertiary education. *RELC Journal, 45*(3), 305–319.

12
EDUCATORS' REFLECTIONS IN AUSTRALIAN ABORIGINAL TRANSLINGUAL CLASSROOMS

Entanglement of language, culture, and emotionality

Ana Tankosić, Sender Dovchin, and Rhonda Oliver

1. Introduction

As educators and researchers, we are responsible for building safe and inclusive environments that encourage and promote diversity in the Australian education system. However, discussing topics of race, language, and culture in mainstream educational contexts often becomes challenging due to a teacher's limited access to students' diverse practices and experiences. In Australian mainstream classrooms, teachers may lack awareness of the intricacies of their students' different linguistic and cultural backgrounds and, therefore, (un)consciously promote a lack of appreciation of students' capabilities in and value of their other languages (Siegel, 2010). The translingual turn has been one of the ways aimed to rectify this; however, for it to be successful, multiple conditions need to be taken into consideration: "sufficient overlapping linguistic resources between interlocutors, teacher and community language awareness, time and space for implementation . . . [and] having educators give due recognition to the students' existing language knowledge" (Oliver et al., 2021, p. 144). In this chapter, we address teacher emotionality as another important condition that needs to be considered for the success of translingual classrooms. Due to the nature of their work, teachers are susceptible and affected by emotions on a daily basis, and they are required to constantly navigate teaching and learning together with ideologies of power and privilege (Her & De Costa, 2022; Hopkyns & Dovchin, 2024).

Building on the recent work by Her and De Costa (2022) and Nazari and Karimpour (2023), who focused on translanguaging-inflected emotional labour experienced by teachers in translingual classrooms, we discuss challenges involved in the emotional entanglement with racial, ethnic, cultural, and linguistic diversity in Australian translingual classrooms. The importance of exploring teachers'

DOI: 10.4324/9781003441304-17

emotionality in translingual classrooms lies in expanding our understanding of this space as diverse, positive, and encouraging towards also perceiving it as a space infused with strong emotions and histories, as well as stories of microaggressions, and linguicism. We weave our narrative texts with the interdisciplinary work of applied linguistics and social justice, at the same time giving countenance to psychological wellbeing to present how entanglements of language, culture, and emotionality may function in translingual classrooms. Ultimately, this chapter challenges daily experiences with language, race, culture, and power hierarchy, individually provoking us all to self-search our own racialised emotionalities in building safer translingual classrooms.

2. Translingual classrooms

The translingual turn in education focuses on how students from diverse backgrounds engage in learning while drawing on the resources available to them in their environment (Canagarajah, 2013). As a space that cultivates social cohesion in the context of increasing diversification (Heugh et al., 2017), a translingual classroom transgresses systemic boundaries of dominant cultures and languages to allow for the freedom and fluidity of practice. Translingual classrooms are a product of language reconceptualisation, which has led to a greater understanding of learners' capabilities and recognition of their cosmopolitan dispositions (De Costa, 2014). In such translingual classrooms, learners are encouraged to negotiate rich semiotic resources, expand their communicative repertoire, and bring their cultures into the learning space. These classrooms enable students from diverse backgrounds to engage in translingual practice to "convey linguistic and social information" (Grosjean, 1999, p. 286) in ways that are "both powerful and playful" (Oliver et al., 2021, p. 138). This proactive and empowering translingual space supports students of different languages and cultures to demonstrate their knowledge and what they can do with regard to the classroom content (García et al., 2017).

Translingual classrooms in Australia are a small but growing feature emanating from current migration patterns and education policy but also growing out of Australian colonial history. Pedagogically, they have the potential to improve teaching practice in contexts characterised by diversity and to make positive contributions to learning by enhancing socio-cognitive awareness in interactions (Oliver et al., 2021). While translingual practice is slowly finding its way into Australian mainstream classrooms where Standard Australian English (SAE) is still the norm, it is prevalent in community language schools and in TESOL contexts where groups of newly arrived students (e.g., refugees fleeing from the same country) share a common home language. It is also a practice that occurs in some schools in Australia where there is a high percentage of Aboriginal students who speak traditional languages or a creole (e.g., Kriol in the north of Australia), especially when students interact with each other by accessing their home languages, and/or when it is encouraged by teachers as a way to foster students' engagement in the classroom (Oliver et al., 2021). It can also occur with Aboriginal students who come to school speaking Australian Aboriginal English (AAE) rather than SAE as their first language, and in many ways, this is harder for teachers to identify.

To support the development of a translingual classroom, teachers need to be aware of translingual pedagogies, which include having an awareness of students' language and cultural backgrounds. This helps them avoid stereotyping and stigmatising non-standard practices (Siegel, 2010) and minority languages (Orellana & García, 2014). Seals et al. (2020) suggest that teachers should build their own translingual teaching resources by observing the discursive practices of their students. Instead of a traditional approach to language and culture where 'one size fits all,' there is a potential for a "universal drive" (Hopewell, 2013, p. 67) towards creating conditions and contexts for classroom practices which would address the needs of all students from different cultural and linguistic backgrounds.

The benefits of translingual classrooms are that they help address the issues of equity in education, as well as those pertaining to language, culture, race, and power hierarchies. In doing so, they help provide social justice for culturally and linguistically diverse learners in the migrant and post-colonial Australian context. However, we cannot overlook the emotional entanglements that such spaces require, and the most recent scholarship has begun to address the translanguaging-inflected emotional labour that teachers experience in translingual classrooms (Her & De Costa, 2022; Nazari & Karimpour, 2023). In the following section, we discuss the complexity behind emotional engagement with cultural and linguistic diversity in the classroom to recognise, unpack, and deconstruct emotional barriers and feelings in a translingual space infused with strong emotions, histories, and/or injustices.

3. Navigating cultural, linguistic, and emotional entanglements

Emotionality is a significant facet in teachers' perception and integration of translingual practice (Canagarajah, 2011; García, 2009; Li, 2018), as well as in navigating students' cultural and linguistic diversity in translingual classrooms. Translingual practice enables students and teachers to move beyond normative socio-political, linguistic, and cultural boundaries to engage in a free learning/teaching experience. However, students' experiences from culturally and linguistically diverse backgrounds often come with layers of politicised and racialised identities, marginalisation, and discrimination of their communities (see Tankosić et al., 2021; Oliver & Exell, 2020; Tankosić & Dovchin, 2023). Therefore, in the translingual classroom, a teacher needs to adopt different roles to develop students' diverse linguistic practices and support their translingual identities and socio-emotional growth (Li, 2018) while addressing systemic racism. In other words, teachers have to emotionally invest in managing translingual practices (De Costa et al., 2018; García, 2009; Hopkyns & Dovchin, 2024), which may be challenging to them personally.

Emotion, from a poststructuralist point of view, is "embedded in discursive and ideological practices . . . where emotions are tied to structures of power, context and emotional cultures" (Barcelos & Aragao, 2018, p. 508). Previous studies have shown that competence in local language, translingual identity, and transnational experience are important factors to consider when discussing teachers' emotionality in translingual classrooms (Alshakhi & Le Ha, 2020; Kocabaş-Gedik & Ortaçtepe Hart, 2021). However, ensuring that teachers come with translingual and transnational experiences becomes problematic, especially in post-colonial and migrant contexts such as Australia, which still operates under strong Anglo-normative educational politics. See, for example, Steele et al.'s (2022) argument for changes in teaching practices in Australia with the gauntlet to "stop measuring black kids with a white stick" (p. 400). In this regard, Her and De Costa (2022) also discuss the importance of *resisting rules* (Zembylas, 2006) in such contexts where dominant institutional culture prescribes what is deemed as appropriate or professional and explain that teachers' emotions "are not only what the teachers feel but also what they do with those feelings" (p. 2). To navigate cultural, linguistic, and emotional entanglements, teachers need to be prepared to engage in "managing, expressing, masking, and manipulating their emotions" (see Nazari & Karimpour, 2023, p. 2) to empower their students and ensure their own emotional stability. In other words, teachers need to listen, understand, and act with empathy to flatten the hierarchies of power in their translingual classrooms.

In this chapter, we share our stories of emotional engagement as teachers and researchers working with students from Aboriginal backgrounds in translingual classrooms in Australia, where navigating students' cultural and linguistic diversity becomes entangled with stories of discrimination, racism, violence, and crime.

4. Methodology

This chapter is drawn from a larger research project called "Building a safer community for migrant and Aboriginal youth in Australia." The project involves interdisciplinary cohorts, including educators and researchers from applied linguistics, public health, and psychology. The research sites include Kutja[1] school for Aboriginal students, Mongolian community language school (for migrant students), and the Ishar Multicultural Women's Health Centre. Project team members gained access to these sites through their previous research experiences and personal and professional connections in the schools and the centre. This chapter will specifically focus on Kutja school for Aboriginal students, the project cluster which was led by us – Sender, Rhonda, and Ana.

Since the overarching goal of the project was to develop and evaluate strategies for building resilience, preventing crime, and promoting community engagement among youth in Western Australia, we took a teacher role in their respective contexts and organised workshops in the form of translingual classrooms to discuss strategies that would help build youth resilience and engagement with the community. At the same time, youth were encouraged to share their stories about living as Aboriginal individuals in Australian society. We liaised with teachers and community stakeholders and engaged them in the workshops to support youth's emotional and translingual practices. We have been working closely together to explore forms of building safer communities, and the discussion was centred on their collaborative ethnographic reflections and personal experiences as educators and ethnographers in the classroom.

Researchers' positionality

Sender is a Mongolian woman living and working in Australia. Her work focuses on culturally and linguistically diverse Australians (Dovchin & Dovchin, 2023). Ana migrated from Bosnia and Herzegovina and currently lives and works in Australia. In her research, Ana investigates cultural and linguistic diversities and disparities, as well as translingual identities. Rhonda has spent her entire teaching and research career of more than 40 years, working with culturally and diverse language learners (mostly children and adolescents). In more recent times, she has worked with Aboriginal students who have Standard Australian English as their second language or dialect, including undertaking collaborative research for 15 years at Kutja. This is a boarding school for Aboriginal students from remote communities.

In the following sections, we present our narratives from Kutja school. In these narratives, we reflect on our emotional experiences and ways in which we navigate stories of racial, cultural, and linguistic diversity, but also disparity in translingual classrooms. Ultimately, these narratives help us understand how teachers' and researchers' emotionality may ultimately impact culturally and linguistically diverse children's academic and personal learning journey.

5. Kutja school: emotional, cultural, and linguistic entanglement in an Aboriginal translingual classroom

Rhonda

Relationality within Indigenous Education is key, and this also applies to research in this space. This school and my involvement there as a teacher/researcher epitomise this. A large number of the students who attend the school do so because members of their family, over many generations, have done so before them. This also reflects the longevity of this farm training school – one that was originally established in the 1940s (as a mission) to prepare young Aboriginal men to be trained in agriculture to enhance their employment opportunities. It then became a boarding school, first again only for boys, but then co-educational. It became an independent school in the 1990s.

So, whilst the school's beginning was culturally precarious (i.e., as a colonial tool for assimilation), it has become a safe place where strong relationships are formed and continue over time. These relationships between students, and also between staff and students, like many formed in schools, are ordinary – but in this situation they are also exceptional. These students come from many different, often remote communities across the state. Interaction between these groups, especially those separated by long distances and from different language nations are not usual. Boarding together, they become part of a cultural but also linguistic milieu. This can at times be fraught, but also life changing for the students. They are culturally supported by the staff but also increasingly exposed to an English environment during their time studying at the school. Their language experience reflects the translingual nature of many Aboriginal people from remote communities. They interact with those from 'home' in traditional language and/or Kriol. They will interact with others using the lingua franca used by many Aboriginal people across the nation – AAE. They often use this with their teachers, too, as it is the dialect of English with which they have greatest proficiency. As they stay at the school and especially as they undertake workplace learning and community sport, their experience with Standard Australian English also increases.

Like that of the students, my 15 years having a research relationship with this school has also been life changing – not only to me, but to all members of my immediate family. Students have visited, stayed, and even lived with us in Perth. My relationship with those who have graduated from the school is well known by many of the current students – which grants me pseudo-family status with a number of them. During this latest teacher/research visit I was granted honorary sister/mother/aunty/cousin status. For others, my use of the appropriate salutation "Where you from, whose your mob?" (Ober et al., in press), and my knowledge of their people and place grants me relational access often denied to other unfamiliar 'older white women.' In addition, because my understanding of AAE has increased and my acuity in understanding (to my ears) its heavy accent and different cadences has improved, I was provided access to deep sharing of information that might not occur with others. This opportunity to communicate beyond the surface level has been further enhanced because of my exposure (at home from a Kutja graduate who lives with our family) to Kriol and traditional language words and because I can also now understand some of the common gestures used frequently as part of these languages. Together this meant that during our interactions, students were able to engage fluidly in translingual practice when talking with me. And a number appeared to share deeply and honestly with me.

Despite my long relationship with students at the school, I was again confronted by the experiences the students shared during our time at the school. Although I have heard similar (and even worse) before, I was again saddened and alarmed by the life circumstances of these students. Some of their life experiences remain truly shocking and I particularly found the racism they have and continue to experience confronting to me as a non-Aboriginal person. However, the resilience they displayed and the humour they recounted using as part of their everyday lives (working with and through such circumstances) was once more both humbling and inspirational.

Sender

When I first entered the classroom as an ethnographer, I was deeply entrenched in various emotions, as many anthropologists call 'emotions in the field' (Beatty, 2005), in which the emotional labour of the teacher/researcher is described as the emergent, negotiated, and constantly compromised nature of the research process. However, I was burdened with the 'emotional dissonances' of the teacher/researcher (Down et al., 2006) – negative emotions such as fear, anxiety, and discomfort – as I was deeply aware how intellectually, emotionally, linguistically and culturally challenging, and politically strenuous real-world Aboriginal research could actually be (McLennan & Woods, 2018), given the high rate of transgenerational childhood trauma Aboriginal and Torres Strait Islander children have been exposed to (Atkinson et al., 2014). Atkinson et al. (2014) explained that the experiences and transfer of trauma-related behaviours and attitudes are most prevalent in Australia's Aboriginal communities due to the combined effects of colonialism and government policies and practices (e.g., child removal). As a result, young Aboriginal people have developed a low sense of safety and trust in others (Dovchin et al., 2023). Furthermore, many Aboriginal school students who were exposed to transgenerational trauma have difficulties with attention and focus, memory, language, and literacy development, as well as behavioural and emotional problems. Moreover, I also felt emotional dissonances (Down et al., 2006) due to my lack of experience in interacting and communicating with Aboriginal people. The expected language of communication in the classroom is SAE, but I was also aware that the majority of these students were AAE users (along with traditional languages and Kriol), which I was not able to comprehend.

With these two crucial assumptions in my mind, my emotional dissonances as a teacher/researcher were high, feeling mostly anxious, fearful, and uncomfortable when I set foot in the classroom. Surprisingly, after a few minutes of talking to the students, my emotional dissonances transformed into 'emotional overlap' (Feldman & Mandache, 2019) – the moments in the classroom when the emotions of both the informant and the teacher/ethnographer are mutually shared and congregate in a shared space of understanding, care, and compassion. I found myself emotionally present *with* these young Aboriginal people in a way that developed an intense, affective, and playful connection.

This emotional overlap occurred when the tape recorder was off and took place in linguistic situations when both Aboriginal students and I found ourselves in linguistic spaces that generated a sense of familiarity and intimacy. I felt at ease when the classroom interaction was not drawing on SAE but rather translingual repertoires. I was impressed to see how the majority of these students were engaging their translingual repertoires (Dovchin & Wang, 2024). They were drawing on the 'semiotic assemblages' (Pennycook, 2017) of SAE, AAE, creoles (Kriol being the common one across the north of Australia), and traditional languages (e.g. Kija, Martu) (Steele et al., 2022) to achieve their communicative meanings, express their thoughts, understandings, and feelings. They were engaging in translingual practice in often playful ways by teasing each other, while also being respectful towards us, as intruders (Steele et al., 2022).

As someone who translanguages, I immediately felt a linguistic connection. I explained to students that I could speak Mongolian, and I started to translanguage using various English and Mongolian resources. I could see the students were mesmerised, and they loved to hear that, like them, I could also translanguage. One of the students yelled, "You are like us! We speak different languages all the time!!" This made me feel emotionally safe, and I felt my emotional dissonance disappear. Perhaps, translingual practice was something mundane for these students and they felt I was one of them because I was also translanguaging just like them. As we have argued elsewhere, "rather than perceiving translanguaging as extraordinary, for Aboriginal speakers it is more likely to be considered normal, unremarkable, mundane, and as a long-existing phenomenon" (Tankosić et al., 2022, p. 1). Most importantly, we found ourselves emotionally present *with* each other as we started sharing laughs and playful translingual practice in a way that developed an intense affective connection between us (Dovchin & Canagarajah, 2019). Out of this connection, I felt an expression of intimacy that I believe was necessary for an outsider teacher/ethnographer, like myself, to remain relevant in translingual classrooms.

Ana

The school for Aboriginal youth is a space of ordinariness and precarity, translingualism and transculturalism, support and friendship, postcolonialism. Emotions become an embodiment of yarning – sharing knowledge in a safe space to build understanding and relationship. One talks, and one listens, and in that process, one tries to make sense of their positionality in the context. Navigating the space of diversity is as natural as it is demanding. Diversity of language practices, cultures, ways of being, and ways of doing brings freedom to practice, but at the same time, it requires vigilance and awareness of the indexicality of one's identity markers. As a fair-skinned European with access to neoliberal resources, I am aware of my status in the hierarchy of power, as well as the privileges that I am given just for being born in a certain body. This awareness also ties into my consciousness of social inequity. Yarning with Aboriginal youth was socially and cognitively engaging – just as every interaction is – but it was also an emotional entanglement because stories shared with me were infused with uncertainty, precarity, fear, racism, and violence.

Being born during war, and raised in post-war Bosnia and Herzegovina, I am not immune to fear, sadness, violence, and injustice. One learns how to live with these emotions by channelling them towards everyday actions of empowerment and social justice. As a researcher and a teacher, I recognised the need to differentiate between sympathy and empathy. Feeling empathy means recognising, understanding, and taking action. It is an affective response to other people's emotions, and an attempt to feel those emotions from their perspective. Temporary emotional engagement is not something teachers in translingual classrooms can afford; they need to fully engage with their students' stories to be able to address them. However, here, it is important to understand that this affective response is not about the teacher, their expectations and presumptions of what the other person may feel, but it is about students, their reality, and plethora of emotions that they experience.

Sympathy and pity do not have space in the Kutja translingual classroom. They are hurtful and subordinating, and they are colonial residue which birth a White saviour. White saviour complex represents the idea that people who are ethnically and racially different need 'saving' from a White-western person. Bosnia – the Global South in Europe – has often been the target of White saviorism, conceived as a neocolonial discursive practice rather than a phenotype-based reality. And so, it was the 'shared' distance from the White standard that brought me closer to the Aboriginal youth in Kutja school. We engaged in storytelling, while navigating our emotional entanglements. I am not surprised to have found maturity, pride, and resistance among Aboriginal youth, because these are similar to the emotions I find among ethnic communities in Australia, where the dominant structures try to place 'the other' in the place of subservience. For this reason, I emphasise the importance of empowerment as an empathetic response, because those on the social margins need 'real' support and resources to succeed.

I found this real support among Kutja teachers, whom I had the opportunity to meet through my brief involvement at the school. Their empowerment, as an empathetic response, was reflected through having real expectations of their students, all the while recognising and acknowledging their translingual practices. As a person classified as ethnic in Australia, I interpret the Kutja teachers' expectations of Aboriginal students as a sign of respect, because students' translingual identity then becomes perceived as a strength and not a weakness (see Kerrin, 2018 for IndigenousX on how the toxicity of low expectations limits Indigenous students).

6. Discussion

Our narratives reflect empathetic responses to students' life experiences, stories, and diversity in a translingual classroom, where we not only listen and feel but also respond and support Aboriginal students in navigating spaces of privilege, power, and diversity towards creating a safe environment. In reference to Her and De Costa (2022), we demonstrate the importance of emotional engagement to empower students in translingual classrooms and act with empathy to negotiate cultural, linguistic, and racial entanglements. Rhonda's growing confidence in her knowledge of Aboriginal languages, cultures, and practices grants her not only access to and respect from Aboriginal students but also the power to support them to succeed in the world of racialisation and politicisation of Aboriginal identities. Rhonda actively engages in encouraging Aboriginal students' resilience and supporting translingual practice as a freedom of expression. Likewise, Sender stresses the importance of translingual practice in the classroom as a way to build a sense of familiarity and intimacy. Ana addresses the need for understanding one's positionality in the context and emphasises empathy over sympathy in a way which urges the teacher in the translingual classroom to fully engage with their students beyond temporary interest in their needs and success.

Feshbach and Feshbach (2009) explain how the process of empathy is contingent upon *cognitive factors*, which understand the perspective and role of another person, and *affective factors*, which reflect the ability to experience emotions appropriately. In translingual classrooms, teachers need to consider both cognitive and affective factors in order to be prepared to address, teach, and support their students. This support reflects taking action to mitigate the politicisation and marginalisation of culturally and linguistically diverse students' identities, addressing their emotionality, and preparing them for life outside the classroom. Our emotional engagement with students in translingual classrooms guided us towards building safer communities where youth from diverse backgrounds are supported and perceived with the justice they deserve.

For instance, during the workshop in Kutja, students consistently expressed negative sentiments about the police – some going as far as describing their disdain, even fear, of police in general. Their perceptions that police are 'racist' and 'discriminate' against them are actually born out in other research (see Atkinson, 1993; Roberts et al., 1986). A recent study by Weatherburn and Thomas (2023) found that regardless of gender, Indigenous youth "are more likely to be prosecuted than cautioned, compared with their non-Indigenous counterparts" (p. 253). In response, and as part of our 'both-ways learning' approach (Ober, 2009) that has been used long term in our different work at this school (i.e., learning from the young Aboriginal people at the school, and providing them with information that they may in turn learn from – see Oliver et al., 2012, 2013) – we used the opportunity prompted by their responses to provide input that might serve them well in the future.

As a first step, we acknowledged that most students at the school were translingual – many of them speak a traditional language (e.g., Kija, Gooniyandi, Nyikina Mangala) and/or Kimberley Kriol (a type of creole) as their home community language, as well as AAE. We then discussed how this can lead to communication problems, especially when interacting with those in powerful positions – such as the police. We then reflected on different ways of using language – for example, we talked about how gestures are used a lot in Aboriginal society, but less so and differently amongst those who are not Aboriginal. To show students how to make communication more effective in different communicative contexts (including cross-cultural communication with authorities), we used Grice's maxims (1975) as a simple guide that they might follow. These maxims were chosen with this cohort of students because of their simplicity:

1. Quantity – say enough to be clear, but not too much
2. Quality – tell the truth and only what you know to be true
3. Relevance – only talk about things related to the topic being discussed
4. Manner – speak clearly, politely, and loud enough to be heard

Furthermore, they were chosen because of their history of usefulness as guiding principles both in the judiciary system and when interacting with the police (e.g., Ceballos & Sosas, 2018; Harris, 1995; Linfoot-Ham, 2006; Radfar et al., 2020; Siregar et al., 2021). We discussed examples of how violations of these principles can lead to misunderstandings, with incorrect assumptions being made, and in the case of dealing with the police, even determining who is or is not arrested. This information provided to the students was initially met with some of the students nodding and smiling, especially in response to the dramatisation of the examples of each, but also by a general level of silence from the majority group. However, this also signifies a language difference in translingual classrooms – silence reflecting deep listening of issues that are important (Mushin & Gardner, 2009; Walsh, 1991). This was demonstrated after the formal workshop where different students approached us and thanked us for sharing the information, saying how they thought it would be 'useful' if they interacted with the police in the future.

This example together with our narratives showcases how our emphatic engagement with students in a translingual classroom not only allowed us to understand their affect and positionality but also their needs in terms of the demands of the society that they live in.

7. Conclusion

In this chapter, we argue that translingual classrooms should always be understood in relation to the empathetic response and emotional overlap between the educators and students as there are multiple episodes of intense emotional engagements that could mediate and negotiate the boundaries between meaning and feeling, observer and observed. Experiences like the ones we presented in this chapter made the boundaries between educators and students fluid in ways that assisted in constructing a more nuanced understanding of personal experiences in the general society. Our emotional overlaps functioned at this intersection where "the sensory, imaginary, emotional, moral and intellectual dimensions of actual experience" provided knowledge (McLean & Leibing, 2007, p. xii). Emotional engagement helped us understand students' experiences and positionalities in Australian society, which in turn allowed their voices to be heard and gave them freedom to express their cultural and linguistic diversity. Our chapter re-affirms that translingualism entangled with emotions offers a unique and compelling angle into the human social and linguistic experience.

Note

1 To protect participants' identities, we used the pseudonym *Kutja* for this school (per Oliver, 2021) – a name given by the school's Elder. *Kutja* means 'learning language.'

References

Alshakhi, A., & Le Ha, P. (2020). Emotion labor and affect in transnational encounters: Insights from western-trained TESOL professionals in Saudi Arabia. *Research in Comparative and International Education*, *15*(3), 305–326. https://doi.org/10.1177/1745499920946203

Atkinson, J., Nelson, J., Brooks, R., Atkinson, C., & Ryan, K. (2014). Addressing individual and community transgenerational trauma. In *Working together: Aboriginal and Torres Strait Islander mental health and wellbeing principles and practice* (Vol. 2, pp. 289–307). Australian Government Department of the Prime Minister and Cabinet.

Atkinson, L. (1993). Aboriginal youth, police and the juvenile justice system in Western Australia. *Children Australia*, *18*(1), 14–19. https://doi:10.1017/S1035077200003278

Barcelos, A., & Aragao, R. (2018). Emotions in language teaching: A review of studies on teacher emotions in Brazil. *Chinese Journal of Applied Linguistics*, *41*(4), 506–531. https://doi.org/10.1515/cjal-2018-0036

Beatty, A. (2005). Emotions in the field: What are we talking about? *Journal of the Royal Anthropological Institute*, *11*(1), 17–37.

Canagarajah, S. (2011). Translanguaging in the classroom: Emerging issues for research and pedagogy. *Applied Linguistics Review*, *2*, 1–28. https://doi.org/10.1515/9783110239331.1

Canagarajah, S. (2013). *Translingual practice: Global Englishes and cosmopolitan relations*. Routledge.

Ceballos, C., & Sosas, R. (2018). On court proceedings: A forensic linguistic analysis on maxim violation. *Journal of Nusantara Studies (JONUS)*, *3*(2), 17–31. https://doi.org/10.24200/jonus.vol3iss2pp

De Costa, P. I. (2014). Cosmopolitanism and English as a lingua franca: Learning English in a Singapore school. *Research in the Teaching of English*, *49*, 9–30. http://www.jstor.org/stable/24398662

De Costa, P. I., Rawal, H., & Li, W. (2018). L2 teachers' emotions: A sociopolitical and ideological perspective. In J. D. M. Agudo (Ed.), *Emotions in second language teaching* (pp. 91–106). Springer.

Dovchin, S., & Canagarajah, S. (2019). The everyday politics of translingualism as transgressive practice. In J. W. Lee & S. Dovchin (Eds.), *Translinguistics: Negotiating innovation and ordinariness* (pp. 163–178). Routledge.

Dovchin, S., Dovchin, U., & Gower, G. (2023). The discourse of the Anthropocene and posthumanism: Indigenous peoples and local communities. *Ethnicities*, *24*(4), 521–535. https://doi.org/10.1177/14687968231219778

Dovchin, S., & Wang, M. (2024). The resistance to translanguaging, spontaneous translanguagers and native speaker saviorism. *Critical Inquiry in Language Studies*, *21*(4), 429–446.

Dovchin, U., & Dovchin, S. (2023). The discourse of the Anthropocene and posthumanism: Mining-induced loss of traditional land and the Mongolian nomadic herders. *Ethnicities*. https://doi.org/10.1177/14687968231219777

Down, S., Garrety, K., & Badham, R. (2006). Fear and loathing in the field: Emotional dissonance and identity work in ethnographic research. *M@n@gement*, *9*(3), 95–115.

Feldman, L. R., & Mandache, L.-A. (2019). Emotional overlap and the analytic potential of emotions in anthropology. *Ethnography*, *20*(2), 227–244. https://doi.org/10.1177/1466138118768620

Feshbach, N. D., & Feshbach, S. (2009). Empathy and education. In J. Decety & W. Ickes (Eds.), *The social neuroscience of empathy* (pp. 85–98). Massachusetts Institute of Technology.

García, O. (2009). *Bilingual education in the 21st century: A global perspective*. Wiley/Blackwell.

García, O., Johnson, S. I., & Seltzer, K. (2017). *The translanguaging classroom: Leveraging student bilingualism for learning*. Caslon.

Grice, P. (1975). Logic and conversation. In P. Cole & J. Morgan (Eds.), *Syntax and semantics, 3: Speech acts* (pp. 41–58). Academic Press.

Grosjean, F. (1999). Bilingualism, individual. In B. Spolsky (Ed.), *Concise encyclopedia of educational linguistics* (pp. 284–290). Elsevier.

Harris, S. (1995). Pragmatics and power. *Journal of Pragmatics, 23*(2), 117–135.

Her, L., & De Costa, P. (2022). When language teacher emotions and language policy intersect: A critical perspective. *System, 105*, 102745. https://doi.org/10.1016/j.system.2022.102745

Heugh, K., Li, X., & Song, Y. (2017). Multilingualism and translanguaging in the teaching of and through English: Rethinking linguistic boundaries in an Australian university. In B. Fenton-Smith, P. Humphreys & I. Walkinshaw (Eds.), *English medium instruction in higher education in Asia-Pacific* (pp. 259–279). Springer. https://doi.org/10.1007/978-3-319-51976-0_14

Hopewell, S. (2013). Strengthening biliteracy through translanguaging pedagogies. *Literacy Research Association Yearbook, 62*, 234–245.

Hopkyns, S., & Dovchin, S. (2024). Translanguaging and emotionality of English as a second language (ESL) teachers. *International Review of Applied Linguistics in Language Teaching, 62*(3), 1257–1278. https://doi.org/10.1515/iral-2024-0094.

Kerrin, M. (2018). The toxicity of low expectations limits Indigenous students. *IndigenousX*. Retrieved July 2024, from https://indigenousx.com.au/michelle-kerrin-the-toxicity-of-low-expectations-limits-indigenous-students/

Kocabaş-Gedik, P., & Ortaçtepe Hart, D. (2021). "It's not like that at all": A poststructuralist case study on language teacher identity and emotional labor. *Journal of Language, Identity & Education, 20*(2), 103–117. https://doi.org/10.1080/15348458.2020.1726756

Li, W. (2018). Translanguaging as a practical theory of language. *Applied Linguistics, 39*(1), 9–30. https://doi.org/10.1093/applin/amx039

Linfoot-Ham, K. (2006). Conversational maxims in encounters with law enforcement officers. *International Journal of Speech Language and The Law, 13*, 23–54. https://doi.org/10.1558/sll.2006.13.1.23.

McLean, A., & Leibing, A. (2007). *The shadow side of fieldwork: Exploring the blurred borders between ethnography and life*. Blackwell.

McLennan, V., & Woods, G. (2018). Learning from mistakes and moving forward in intercultural research with Aboriginal and Torres Strait Islander peoples. *Higher Education Research & Development, 37*(1), 88–100.

Mushin, I., & Gardner, R. (2009). Silence is talk: Conversational silence in Australian Aboriginal talk-in-interaction. *Journal of Pragmatics, 41*, 2033–2052

Nazari, M., & Karimpour, S. (2023). "Teacher, Man Mitoonam . . .?": Translanguaging and English language teacher emotion labor. *Journal of Language, Identity & Education*. https://doi.org/10.1080/15348458.2023.2167206

Ober, R. (2009). Learning from yesterday, celebrating today, strengthening tomorrow. *The Australian Journal of Indigenous Education, 38*, 34–39.

Oliver, R. (2021). Developing a task-based approach: A case study of Australian Aboriginal VET students. In M. J. Ahmadian & M. H. Long (Eds.), *The Cambridge handbook of task-based language teaching* (pp. 99–108). Cambridge University Press.

Oliver, R., & Exell, M. (2020). Identity, translanguaging, linguicism and racism: The experience of Australian Aboriginal people living in a remote community. *International Journal of Bilingual Education and Bilingualism, 23*(7), 819–832. https://doi.org/10.1080/13670050.2020.1713722

Oliver, R., Grote, E., Rochecouste, J., & Exell, M. (2012). Addressing the language and literacy needs of Aboriginal high school VET students who speak SAE as an additional language. *Australian Journal of Indigenous Education, 41*(2), 1–11. https://doi.org/10.1017/jie.2012.23

Oliver, R., Grote, E., Rochecouste, J., & Exell, M. (2013). A task-based needs analysis for Australian Aboriginal students: Going beyond the target situation to address cultural issues. *International Journal of Training Research, 11*(3), 246–259.

Oliver, R., Wigglesworth, G., Angelo, D., & Steele, C. (2021). Translating translanguaging into our classrooms: Possibilities and challenges. *Language Teaching Research, 25*(1), 134–150. https://doi.org/10.1177/1362168820938822

Orellana, M. F., & García, O. (2014). Language brokering and translanguaging in school. *Language Arts, 91,* 386–392.

Pennycook, A. (2017). Translanguaging and semiotic assemblages. *International Journal of Multilingualism, 14*(3), 269–282. https://doi.org/10.1080/14790718.2017.1315810

Radfar, Z. H., Sudana, D., & Gunawan, W. (2020). Gricean maxim violation(s) in the murder case of Jamal Khashoggi: A forensic linguistic perspective. *NOBEL: Journal of Literature and Language Teaching, 11*(2), 162–177. https://doi.org/10.15642/NOBEL.2020.11.2.162-177

Roberts, L., Chadbourne, R., & Murray, R. (1986). *Aboriginal/police relations in the Pilbara: A study of perceptions*. Special Cabinet Committee on Aboriginal/Police and Community Relations.

Seals, C. A., Olsen-Reeder, V., Pine, R., Ash, M., & Wallace, C. (2020). Creating translingual teaching resources based on translanguaging grammar rules and pedagogical practices. *Australian Journal of Applied Linguistics, 3*(1), 115–132. https://doi.org/10.29140/ajal.v3n1.303

Siegel, J. (2010). *Second dialect acquisition*. Cambridge University Press.

Siregar, A. F., Sumarsih, & Murni, S. M. (2021). Conversational maxims of operation targets in police investigative interviews. *Advances in Social Science, Education and Humanities Research, 591,* 165–172.

Steele, C., Dovchin, S., & Oliver, R. (2022). "Stop measuring Black kids with a White stick:" Translanguaging for classroom assessment. *RELC Journal, 53*(2), 400–415. https://doi.org/10.1177/00336882221086307

Tankosić, A., & Dovchin, S. (2023). (C)overt linguistic racism: Eastern-European background immigrant women in the Australian workplace. *Ethnicities, 23*(5), 726–757. https://doi.org/10.1177/14687968211005104

Tankosić, A., Dovchin, S., Oliver, R., & Exell, M. (2022). The mundanity of translanguaging and Aboriginal identity in Australia. *Applied Linguistics Review, 15*(4), 1277–1298. https://doi.org/10.1515/applirev-2022-0064

Tankosić, A., Dryden, S., & Dovchin, S. (2021). The link between linguistic subordination and linguistic inferiority complexes: English as a second language migrants in Australia. *International Journal of Bilingualism, 25*(6), 1782–1798.

Walsh, M. (1991). Conversational styles and intercultural communication: An example from northern Australia. *Australian Journal of Communication, 18*(1), 1–12.

Weatherburn, D., & Thomas, B. (2023). The influence of Indigenous status on the issue of police cautions. *Journal of Criminology, 56*(2–3), 253–277. https://doi.org/10.1177/26338076221146326

Zembylas, M. (2006). Challenges and possibilities in a postmodern culture of emotions in education. *Interchange, 37*(3), 251–275. https://doi.org/10.1007/s10780-006-9003-y

INDEX

Note: Page numbers in *italic* indicate a figure and page numbers in **bold** indicate a table on the corresponding page.

808Viral 21–30

Aboriginal translingual classrooms 218–220, 226–228; methodology 221–222; narratives 222–226; navigating entanglements 220–221
activism 32–33, 35–37, 47–48; Bangladesh 39–43, *41*; and enmeshed identities 33–35; multimodal discourse analysis 37; Nepal 43–47, *43*, *46*; political and social issues in South Asia 38–47
affect 209–210
Africans/Afroczechs 107, 111–114
agency 208–209
allyship 89–91, 101–102; disentangling English from colonialism 91–92; interdiscursive coherence 96–101; unease as an affective stance 92–95
assemblage 70–74, 82–83, 141–142, 158–160, 201–202; embodied 144–145; English in technology design and use 164–174; hegemonic order 174–176; methodological approach 162–164; socio-technological entanglements 160–162
Australia 218–220, 226–228; methodology 221–222; narratives 222–226; navigating entanglements 220–221

Australian Aboriginal English (AAE) 35, 40, 220, 223–224, 227
auto-narrative 207, 215
axioms of transdisciplinarity 126–127; complexity 127; logical 126–127; ontological 126

Bangladesh 39–43, *41*
Bassett, Angela 118–119, 121–122, 133–134
Berlin, digital assemblages in 158–160; English in technology design and use 164–174; hegemonic order 174–176; methodological approach 162–164; socio-technological entanglements 160–162
Bikram Yoga Oslo (BYO) 143–144, **144**, 146, 149, 152
Bikram yoga practitioners 141–142; embodied assemblages 144–145; embodied ethnography 143–144, **144**; embodied ideologies 144–154; embodied practices 142, 144–145, 151–154; pleasure and pain 145–150, **145**; time and temporality 151–154
Black, peoples racialized as 130
Black feminism 89–91, 101–102; disentangling English from colonialism 91–92; interdiscursive coherence

96–101; unease as an affective stance 92–95
Black immigrant and transnational humans 121–123
bodies 141–142; embodied assemblages 144–145; embodied ethnography 143–144, **144**; embodied ideologies 144–154; embodied practices 142, 144–145, 151–154; pleasure and pain 145–150, **145**; time and temporality 151–154

Caribbean peoples and Englishes 125–128; conceptual premises 128–133; peoples ethnicized as Caribbean 128–129
citizen sociolinguistics 17–19, 29–30; context 19–20; metapragmatics on social media 20–21; 808Viral 21–29
class formations 191–193
co-development of learning 210–211
colonialism 91–92
complexity axiom 127
content and language integrated learning (CLIL) 201–202; auto-narrative 207; co-development of learning 210–211; conceptual framework 205–206, *205*; co-patterning of learning experiences 211–212; English medium instruction as universal trend 202–205; implementation 213–215; re-thinking identity 212–213; student affect and self-efficacy 209–210; student agency 208–209; teaching pedagogy 207–208
context 201–202
co-patterning of learning experiences 211–212
cosmopolitan 55, 107, 112–114, 163
country of destination 130–131
country of origin 128–129, 130–131
COVID-19 70–73, 82–83; analyzing signs 74–82, *75*, *77–78*, *80*; context and methods 73–74
culture 218–220, 226–228; cultural entanglements 220–221, 222–226; methodology 221–222; narratives 222–226; navigating entanglements 220–221
Czechia 105–107, 114–115; *African person* frame 111–114; raciolinguistic lens 107–114

design, digital 158–160; English in technology design and use 164–174; hegemonic order 174–176; methodological approach 162–164; socio-technological entanglements 160–162
dialogue 145–150, **145**
digital assemblages 158–160; English in technology design and use 164–174; hegemonic order 174–176; methodological approach 162–164; socio-technological entanglements 160–162
digital devices 159–164, 167–174, 175
digital language assemblages 174–176
domestic workers, Filipino 183–195, *188–189, 191, 193, 195*

educators 201–202, 218–220, 226–228; auto-narrative 207; co-development of learning 210–211; conceptual framework 205–206, *205*; co-patterning of learning experiences 211–212; English medium instruction as universal trend 202–205; implementation 213–215; methodology 221–222; narratives 222–226; navigating entanglements 220–221; re-thinking identity 212–213; student affect and self-efficacy 209–210; student agency 208–209; teaching pedagogy 207–208
embodiment: embodied ethnography 143–144, **144**; embodied ideologies 144–150, **145**; embodied practice 142, 144–145, 151–154; theoretical framework 144–145
emojis 22–23, 27
emotional entanglements 220–221, 222–226
emotionality 218–220, 226–228; methodology 221–222; narratives 222–226; navigating entanglements 220–221
English/Englishes 1–2, 17–19, 29–30, 89–91, 101–102, 105–107, 114–115, 158–160, 181–182, 195–196; 808Viral 21–29; *African person* frame 111–114; and colonialism 91–92; connecting worlds and struggles 96–101; context 19–20; disentangling English from colonialism 91–92; Filipino domestic workers and TikTok 183–195, *188–189, 191, 193, 195*; globalization and migrant labour 194–195; hegemonic order 174–176; interdiscursive coherence

234 Index

96–101; material conditions of lived experiences 186–188; material and materialist interpretations 182–183; metapragmatics on social media 20–21; methodological approach 162–164; platform designs 188–191; raciolinguistic lens 107–114; socio-technological entanglements 160–162; and unease as an affective stance 92–95; in technology design and use 164–174; transnational relations and class formations 191–193; and World Englishes 2–9
English medium instruction (EMI) 202–206, 208, 210–211; implementation in Taiwan 213–215
English teaching 201–202; auto-narrative 207; co-development of learning 210–211; conceptual framework 205–206, *205*; co-patterning of learning experiences 211–212; English medium instruction as universal trend 202–205; implementation 213–215; re-thinking identity 212–213; student affect and self-efficacy 209–210; student agency 208–209; teaching pedagogy 207–208
enmeshed identities 33–35
entangled bodies 141–142; embodied assemblages 144–145; embodied ethnography 143–144, **144**; embodied ideologies 144–154; embodied practices 142, 144–145, 151–154; pleasure and pain 145–150, **145**; time and temporality 151–154
entangled Englishes *see* English/Englishes
entangled ideologies 142, 144–145; pleasure and pain 145–150; time and temporality 151–154
entangled unease 89–91, 101–102; disentangling English from colonialism 91–92; interdiscursive coherence 96–101; unease as an affective stance 92–95
ethnicization 120, 125, 128–133
ethnography, embodied 143–144, **144**
evidence of entanglement 207, 209

feedback 211–212
feminism 89–91, 101–102; disentangling English from colonialism 91–92; interdiscursive coherence 96–101; unease as an affective stance 92–95

"Fever" 56–67, *56, 62–66*; lyrical entanglements 57–62; visual entanglements 62–67
Filipino domestic workers 183–186, *188–189, 191, 193, 195*; globalization and migrant labour 194–195; material conditions of lived experiences 186–188; platform designs 188–191; transnational relations and class formations 191–193
foreign, English as 111–112

global *see* local–global interface
globalization 194–195
Global Patwa 52–54; "Fever" 56–67, *56, 62–66*; lyrical entanglements 57–62; visual entanglements 62–67; word-sound-power 54–56

heat 145–150, **145**
hegemonic order 174–176
hip-hop 32–37, 39–42, 48
humor 25–26

identities: enmeshed 33–35; local 10, 26–29, 30n1, 74, 80; re-thinking learner and teacher identity 212–213
ideologies 91–92, 142; embodied 144–150, **145**; language 151–154; pleasure and pain 145–150; time and temporality 151–154
immigrants 119–124, 128–131
implementation, EMI 213–215
inclusive approach 214
India 52–54; "Fever" 56–67, *56, 62–66*; lyrical entanglements 57–62; visual entanglements 62–67; word-sound-power 54–56
inequalities 194–195
interpretations of entanglements 181–182, 195–196; Filipino domestic workers and TikTok 183–195, *188–189, 191, 193, 195*; globalization and migrant labour 194–195; material conditions of lived experiences 186–188; material and materialist interpretations 182–183; platform designs 188–191; transnational relations and class formations 191–193
intrusive Englishes 89–91, 101–102; disentangling English from colonialism 91–92; interdiscursive coherence 96–101; unease as an affective stance 92–95; *see also* English/Englishes

Japan 70–73, 82–83; analyzing signs 74–82, *75*, *77–78*, *80*; context and methods 73–74

Kutja school 221–226
Kyoto 70–73, 82–83; analyzing signs 74–82, *75*, *77–78*, *80*; context and methods 73–74

labour *see* Filipino domestic workers
language assemblages 161; digital 174–176
language ideologies 7–9, 142–146, 151–154, 158–159, 163–168
language technology design 159–160, 163–167
languaging 119–125; spatial conceptions of 131–133
learning: co-development of 210–211; co-patterning of learning experiences 211–212
lingua franca 72–73, 107–115, 214, 223
linguistic entanglements 220–221, 222–226
linguistic landscapes 70–73, 82–83; analyzing signs 74–82, *75*, *77–78*, *80*; context and methods 73–74
listening 99–101, 174, 176; white listening subject norms 129–131
lived experiences 186–188
local–global interface 32–33, 35–37, 47–48; Bangladesh 39–43, *41*; and enmeshed identities 33–35; multimodal discourse analysis 37; Nepal 43–47, *43*, *46*; political and social issues in South Asia 38–47
local identities 10, 26–29, 30n1, 74, 80
local language: resilience over time 24–25; solidarity through 22–23
logical axiom 126–127
lyrics 52–54; "Fever" 56–67, *56*, *62–66*; lyrical entanglements 57–62; visual entanglements 62–67; word-sound-power 54–56

material/materialist interpretations 181–182, 195–196; Filipino domestic workers and TikTok 183–195, *188–189*, *191*, *193*, *195*; globalization and migrant labour 194–195; material conditions of lived experiences 186–188; material and materialist interpretations 182–183; platform designs 188–191; transnational relations and class formations 191–193

metapragmatics 20–21
methods/methodological approaches 73–74, 143–144, **144**, 162–164, 221–222
migrant labour 194–195
multilingualism 19–20, 214–215
multimodal discourse analysis 37
music 32–37, 40–44, 48

Nepal 43–47, *43*, *46*
non-reductionist approach 213–214

octopus 1–2, 7
online/offline entanglements 181–182, 195–196; Filipino domestic workers and TikTok 183–195, *188–189*, *191*, *193*, *195*; globalization and migrant labour 194–195; material conditions of lived experiences 186–188; material and materialist interpretations 182–183; platform designs 188–191; transnational relations and class formations 191–193
ontological axiom 126
Oslo 143–144, **144**

pain 145–150, **145**
Patwa 52–54; "Fever" 56–67, *56*, *62–66*; lyrical entanglements 57–62; visual entanglements 62–67; word-sound-power 54–56
pedagogy 207–208
peoples, entanglements of Englishes and 118–121; and Black immigrant and transnational humans 121–123; and racialized entanglements of Caribbean peoples 125–133; re-/imagining racialized entanglements 133–134; and transraciolinguistics 123–125
Pidgin 17–19, 29–30; 808Viral 21–29; context 19–20; metapragmatics on social media 20–21
platform designs 188–191, *188–189*, *191*
pleasure 145–150, **145**
political activism 32–33, 35–37, 47–48; Bangladesh 39–43, *41*; and enmeshed identities 33–35; multimodal discourse analysis 37; Nepal 43–47, *43*, *46*; political and social issues in South Asia 38–47
positionality, researcher 222
power 52–54; and "Fever" 56–67, *56*, *62–66*; and lyrical entanglements

57–62; and visual entanglements 62–67; word-sound-power 54–56
practices, embodied 144–145, 151–154

quantum entanglements 125–128
quantum ethos 118–121; and Black immigrant and transnational humans 121–123; and racialized entanglements of Caribbean peoples 125–133; re-/imagining racialized entanglements 133–134; and transraciolinguistics 123–125

racialized entanglements 118–121; and Black immigrant and transnational humans 121–123; of Caribbean peoples and Englishes 125–133; re-/imagining 133–134; and transraciolinguistics 123–125
raciolinguistic entanglements 105–115; *African person* frame 111–114
rap 32–33, 35–37, 47–48; Bangladesh 39–43, *41*; and enmeshed identities 33–35; multimodal discourse analysis 37; Nepal 43–47, *43*, *46*; political and social issues in South Asia 38–47
reggae 36, 52–57, 59–68
re-imagining racialized entanglements 133–134
research: linguistic landscapes and COVID-19 pandemic 72–74; positionality 222
resilience 24–25
resistance 35–37

SAE *see also* Standard Australian English (SAE) 219–220, 224
self-efficacy 209–210
semiotic practices of signs 71–72
signs: analyzing through entanglement 74–82, *75*, *77–78*, *80*; semiotic practices of 71–72
smartphone setting choices 158–160; English in technology design and use 164–174; hegemonic order 174–176; methodological approach 162–164; socio-technological entanglements 160–162
social activism 32–33, 35–37, 47–48; Bangladesh 39–43, *41*; and enmeshed identities 33–35; multimodal discourse analysis 37; Nepal 43–47, *43*, *46*; political and social issues in South Asia 38–47

social issues: South Asia 38–47, *41*, *43*, *46*
social media spaces 17–19, 29–30; 808Viral 21–29; context 19–20; metapragmatics 20–21; *see also* TikTok
socio-historical context: Pidgin 19–20
sociolinguistics, citizen 17–19, 29–30; 808Viral 21–29; context 19–20; metapragmatics on social media 20–21
socio-political activism 35–37
socio-technological entanglements 160–162
solidarity 22–23
sound *see* word-sound-power
South Asia 32–33, 35–37, 47–48; Bangladesh 39–43, *41*; and enmeshed identities 33–35; multimodal discourse analysis 37; Nepal 43–47, *43*, *46*; political and social issues in 38–47
spatial conceptions of languaging 131–133
struggles, political 95–102
students: co-development of learning 210–211; co-patterning of learning experiences 211–212; re-thinking identity 212–213; student affect 209–210; student agency 208–209
superdiversity 108, 160–162, 167–169, 174
survival 96–99

Taiwan 202–206, 209, 211, 213–215
teaching 201–202; auto-narrative 207; co-development of learning 210–211; conceptual framework 205–206, *205*; co-patterning of learning experiences 211–212; English medium instruction as universal trend 202–205; implementation 213–215; pedagogy 207–208; re-thinking identity 212–213; student affect and self-efficacy 209–210; student agency 208–209
technology design and use 164–174
temporality 151–154
theoretical framework 144–145
TikTok 183–195, *188–189*, *191*, *193*, *195*
time: and language ideologies 151–154; resilience of local language over time 24–25
tongues, listening in 99–101
transdisciplinarity, axioms of 126–127
translingual classrooms 218–220, 226–228; methodology 221–222; narratives 222–226; navigating entanglements 220–221

translingual speakers 158–160; English in technology design and use 164–174; hegemonic order 174–176; methodological approach 162–164; socio-technological entanglements 160–162
transnational humans 121–123
transnational relations 191–193
transraciolinguistics 119–121, 123–125
two-way feedback 211–212

unease 89–91, 101–102; as an affective stance 92–95; disentangling English from colonialism 91–92; interdiscursive coherence 96–101

visual entanglements 62–67
visual hierarchy *143*

voice assistant use 158–160; English in technology design and use 164–174; hegemonic order 174–176; methodological approach 162–164; socio-technological entanglements 160–162

word-sound-power 52–56; "Fever" 56–67, *56*, *62–66*; lyrical entanglements 57–62; visual entanglements 62–67
World Englishes 2–9, 12
worlds: connecting struggles and 96–101; superdiverse 160–162

yoga practitioners *see* Bikram yoga practitioners

Printed in the United States
by Baker & Taylor Publisher Services